The War of German Liberation

The War of German Liberation

The Campaign of 1813 Against Napoleon
by an Eyewitness

ILLUSTRATED

George Cathcart

LEONAUR

The War of German Liberation
The Campaign of 1813 Against Napoleon by an Eyewitness
by George Cathcart

ILLUSTRATED

FIRST EDITION

Leonaur is an imprint of Oakpast Ltd
Copyright in this form © 2022 Oakpast Ltd

ISBN: 978-1-915234-68-1 (hardcover)
ISBN: 978-1-915234-69-8 (softcover)

http://www.leonaur.com

Contents

Introduction

Colonel Cathcart's position as *aide-de-camp* in the suite of his excellent father, the late Earl Cathcart, gave him facilities for observing many most interesting transactions of the war, while it exempted him from any interest or participation in the jealousies, rivalries, and intrigues that all the while fermented around him.

His personal narrative commences with the campaign of 1813. The previous portion of the volume comprises indeed a clear and compendious summary of the operations in Russia of the preceding year; but between this and the author's own narrative there is all the difference which exists between the "this I was told" and "this I saw" of Father Herodotus.

The young *aide-de-camp*, a lieutenant of nineteen, had been preceded by his father at the Imperial headquarter of Kalisch, and joined it, at a day's journey in advance of that place, early in April. From this time till the fall of Paris he was constantly attached to it. His testimony confirms that of General Müffling in showing that the advance of the Allies into Saxony, by which they committed themselves to an immediate general action, was founded on false calculations of the French force.

He says that it was not till the 24th of April, on reaching Dresden, that they became at all aware of the extent to which Napoleon had repaired his losses; and even when they engaged at Lützen they appear to have been little prepared for the superiority of numbers which he developed before the close of the day. Both here, however, and at Bautzen they relied with justice on their great superiority in cavalry, which enabled them to break off the action almost at pleasure, and retreat with security. Lützen was not a victory, as it was the fashion with the Allies to describe it; but they lost no guns and few prisoners, and inflicted a somewhat heavier loss than they sustained. It tested also the quality of their troops, which was considered by impartial judges as better than that of Napoleon's young levies, who behaved admirably as to courage, but showed defects of inexperience.

Colonel Cathcart's volume contains some amusing incidents of the life of a staff officer on active service, but is still more fertile in lessons on the art of war, founded on observation and reminiscence. Of the former there is an instance connected with the retreat from Lützen, in which, at the expense of a cross-country ride of 30 miles and a hazardous passage of a river, Lord Cathcart anticipates the *Czar* at his quarters, and the father and son are rewarded by a *partie carrée* at dinner with His Majesty. We apprehend that these feats must have ingratiated our officers with the Cossacks, whose habits of self-direction over the plains of Germany were pretty much those of our English fox-hunters. The retreat of the Allies on Bautzen without disputing the passage of the Elbe suggests one of the many concise and pithy paragraphs for which students will thank Colonel Cathcart:—

> Sufficient examples have arisen to prove to the satisfaction of all military men, that though a large river is without doubt an important strategic feature in other respects, yet in modern warfare it is not to be relied upon as an obstacle that presents any serious feature in the way of a large advancing army; for the leader of such an army can always out-manoeuvre his opponent by concealing his movements from those on the opposite bank, while the intervention of the river is sufficient to frustrate the enemy's means of watching by patrols, and a few hours gained at a suitable point will suffice to repair an old bridge or construct a new one, even in the presence of any hostile detachment likely to be on the spot.

In the way of military sketches, we scarcely know any more striking than one in which Colonel Cathcart describes the Allied Sovereigns watching from their position at Bautzen, on the second morning, the manoeuvring of a single mass of 10,000 men drawn up under the eye of Napoleon in person. The appearance in the group of an individual dressed in "a bright yellow uniform," led to the supposition that the tasteful King of Naples, and with him his Italian levies, had joined the French Army. It was afterwards ascertained that a Saxon postilion, in his usual livery jacket, had been telling Napoleon the names of the different villages.

The sentences that ensue afford a brief but sufficient commentary on a passage of Napoleon's career which enjoys the special admiration of Mr. Alison and others as an instance of his strategic ability:—

In the following chapter it will be found that Napoleon through obstinacy—like a headstrong gambler playing a losing game—contrary to his own experience and former practice, determined to cling to Dresden and make it a centre of operations. Under existing circumstances this was a wilful departure from the principles of strategy; for by doing so he left the line of communication with his true base, the Rhine, at the mercy of his powerful enemy. The author is the more desirous of calling attention to this subject because a popular, and in most cases accurate writer of general history, has characterized this policy of Napoleon's as profoundly conceived and most ably carried into effect! He trusts that the events recorded in this book alone will suffice to justify the true principles of strategy, and prove the worthlessness of the miscalled profound conception of operations with large armies radiating from an insulated centre without reference to the true base and line of communication.

Another grand maxim—never attack without a reserve—is well illustrated by Colonel Cathcart's remarks on the cavalry affair of Liebertwolkowitz. In this action 5,000 French horse, headed by two cavalry officers of the greatest reputation as such in Europe, Murat and Latour Maubourg, had the fairest of chances for a blow, *à la Murat*, at a far inferior body of the Allies; but, as the colonel says:—

They were obliged to abandon their enterprise, and fly before a force of light cavalry which altogether could not have amounted to 2,000 men; a result manifestly to be attributed to the greatest oversight or fault a cavalry officer can commit—that of engaging his whole force without a second line or reserve.

We could wish to see Colonel Cathcart's work reprinted in a shape suited to an officer's travelling library. Lucid, concise, and pregnant, it seems to us to be equally valuable for its facts and its commentaries. Literary piracy has of late been a lion in the path of translation. We hope it may have had the compensating effect of inducing more general study of the German language. But we think our extracts will support our assertion that all the foreign books on our present list deserve translation Müffling's especially—if it were but to cheer old companions like him who to Roeder's German-French responded only with that irreverent *hee! hee!* and who, we presume, would be still less likely to understand General Müffling's German.

We must here conclude a notice which has led ourselves insensibly back to times when the "twanging horn o'er yonder bridge" was wont to awaken the thrill of mingled hope and fear in every English bosom. For our own and for all other nations of the earth we pray that the trumpet of war may long remain as silent as that postman's horn has since become;—but we are, we confess, far from confident in our anticipations on this subject. Who will not concur with the great winner of battles, that next to a great defeat a great victory is the greatest of human calamities? We cannot, however, secure peace by ignoring the lessons of war, and no time is more fit for the study of these lessons than when the danger is, or is supposed to be, remote.

Earl of Ellesmere
1858

Lord Cathcart's Introduction

A General Notice Respecting the National Character and Systems of Discipline Peculiar to the Several Nations Engaged in the Grand Contest Which Forms the Subject of These Commentaries.

To enter into tactical details in the numerous battles which are recorded in this work, would not only render it too voluminous, but would impair that perspicuity which the subject requires. When a general-in-chief gives his orders for a battle, they are communicated to his generals of corps, and by them to the commanders of divisions, and so on, in requisite detail, they are passed to brigades and battalions; but the chief does not, except in peculiar cases, prescribe the actual tactical formations to be employed, because every commander in gradation is supposed to know his duty, and, conforming to the established system of his service, is expected to carry into effect the intentions of his superior officer according to circumstances as he may find them at the moment of action; for these cannot always be anticipated with certainty.

The author, therefore, thinks it may be useful to endeavour to lay before his readers a general view of the national characters in those points which influence the practice of war, as well as the habitual system of tactics peculiar to each of the services engaged in the campaign of 1812 and 1813 in Russia and Germany; to enable the military inquirer, who may be curious in such investigation, to supply in some measure the absence of complicated details in the text by bearing in mind the peculiarities of each service in question.

The French.

There is no doubt that France in the days of Louis XIV. had attained a great degree of proficiency in all the details of the art of war; there is no doubt, also, that up to the Revolution in 1794 that art was carefully cultivated both in theory and practice. The works of Guibert and others will show to what a degree of theoretical refinement it was carried.

In the last century all the warlike nations of Europe brought their armies into the field nearly on the same system, which possibly first took a consistent form in the time of Gustavus Adolphus, and attained its highest perfection in that of Frederick the Great. This system had the formation of general lines and movements in line for its chief characteristic; and, although the primary evolutions calculated to lead to that grand object were generally in open column, and slower and more formal than those now adopted with the same view, yet they still form the basis of all modern systems of tactics.

Marlborough, the Marshals of Louis XIV., Frederick the Great, and the cotemporary generals of the imperial forces, appear to have been in their day capable of general line movements with a degree of facility and order equal, if not superior, to that now at the command of the armies of the present day, not excepting even the British and the Austrians, who have never neglected that system or entirely departed from it.

At the commencement of the French Revolution, in 1790, France possessed a regular standing army, at home and in its colonies, of about 200,000 men, in good condition, and in a high state of tactical proficiency, according to the system to which we have alluded; but the doctrines of liberty and equality are subversive of military discipline, and soon tended to demoralise the army. New levies of youths, in whom revolutionary turbulence had destroyed all moral restraint, were intermingled in the ranks, and the methodical theories previously inculcated and hitherto practised were no longer available. Some new scheme became necessary to enable superior numbers to prevail over the superior discipline of other nations.

A new system, then, was first adopted at that time, and although Napoleon availed himself of tactical proficiency whenever he could find it at his command, and was fully conscious of its value, yet his active career never gave leisure for its adequate cultivation; he was obliged therefore to follow the system which the French Revolution had first prompted, and which his great genius improved and turned to good account. It may be thus described:—

He trusted mainly to the influence of large concentrated masses of troops placed in reserve, and concealed from the enemy as much as possible. Having stationed these with judgment and deep design as to their ulterior employment, it was his custom to commence operations *"entamer l'affaire"* with numerous light troops along his whole front, whilst artillery appeared at various points, duly supported and guarded, and maintained a desultory cannonade. The object of this primary measure was often to deceive his opponents as to his real intentions, and induce them to engage and compromise their whole force along an extensive front. When this object was gained, and a sufficient knowledge was obtained of the position and circumstances of the enemy, the decisive moment was seized in which to bring an overwhelming force, *"en masse,"* preceded by a swarm of light infantry, and covered by a concentrated power of artillery, to bear on some weak or unguarded point of the enemy's position, and thereby decide the victory, which large bodies of cavalry stood in readiness to complete.

But as to any grand line movements of the whole army after the manner of Frederick the Great, nothing of that sort ever occurred, nor even, if desirable, would it have been practicable in the existing state of tactical proficiency among his soldiery. No doubt occasional deployments into line were had recourse to, for special purposes of attack or defence, by single battalions or brigades, or even larger bodies when called for by circumstances at the moment of action; but nothing like an "order of battle," as it was called in the earlier part of the last century, and which meant a preconcerted array of numerous battalions deployed and forming two or more lines, was ever thought of in the new mode of warfare. Those who may suppose that the battles in Germany in 1813 had any resemblance to those of the last century are much mistaken.

It is not just to disparage the old system, or unreservedly to approve the new one; on the contrary, the innovation may be excused as a consequence of the inability of the French commanders to act otherwise. Two advantages, however, were attained, celerity of movement in the field, and the right use of reserves.

As to celerity, on a march they appear to have been quite as active in the olden time as in modern days; but in their formations and movements to attack, they formerly observed a degree of methodical pomposity and slow dignity of motion which was not inconvenient, for it was customary on both sides; but subsequent experience has proved this to be unnecessary, and the improvements of firearms have rendered it impossible; hence, it will no longer suffice for the emergencies of war.

As to the right use of reserves, the paramount importance of this great desideratum has been amply demonstrated in the wars of the present century; and it leads to a principle of general application, whether with regard to cavalry or infantry, or whether the question be of corps or divisions, or of squadrons or battalions.

The result of a judicious combination of these systems, that is to say, celerity of movement without hurry or confusion, and the judicious use of reserves without abandoning line formation, is to be found in the histories of the campaigns of the illustrious chief to whom the command of the British Army in the Peninsula was entrusted, whose great genius enabled him to appreciate them, and render them all subservient to his purpose; and in every instance was he justified by victory.

As to the system of Napoleon, it may be characterised as a knowledge of the importance and use of masses and reserves, and the employment of increased celerity in movements of attack.

We have shown how large and concentrated bodies of troops came to be employed as reserves, and often made instrumental to the decision of a general action.

But the same rule, with respect to the necessity for reserves, was found to apply to all arms and to the smallest detachments. Even light infantry duties, though they had the appearance of irregularity, were always based on this system: every extended line of *tirailleurs* was invariably sustained by adequate small supports formed in rear, and, as far as might be, sheltered; but ready at hand to reinforce or relieve their comrades who were actually engaged. But, besides this, a sufficient and concentrated reserve was invariably stationed not far off, to sustain the whole of these advanced combatants.

Thus, when people talk of a cloud of light troops, although the appearance may have warranted that figure of speech, the duty was nevertheless conducted with method, and in accordance with these principles. The author has dwelt on this particular feature more in detail than he otherwise would have done had not the same system applied to all the other nations engaged, with this difference only, that in its application the duty of light infantry is perhaps more influenced by national character than any other tactical subject of consideration.

In that duty individual intelligence is the main requisite; and the French are, without question, by nature the most intelligent light troops in the world. The northern Germans, possibly from their extensive forests and habits as sportsmen, may be the next best: in the Austrian Army the duty is chiefly entrusted to particular corps formed of the inhabitants of wild mountainous and forest countries, as the Tyrolians, Styrians, and Croats, and they are excellent. The Russians, like the British, are better troops of position than any of the other nations; but it is difficult to excel in all things, and their steadiness in the ranks, which after all is the great object to be desired, as well as their previous domestic habits, render them naturally less apt for light infantry purposes than more volatile nations: yet in both services particular corps, duly practised in this particular branch, have proved themselves capable of being made by training equal to any men that could be opposed to them.

The observation respecting reserves applies with equal force to cavalry in all services. But the impetuous King of Naples, though aware of its importance, often neglected it; occasionally without inconvenience, but more frequently to his cost.

Whether the force engaged be 10,000 sabres or 200, it stands to reason that as the first onslaught implies a movement to the front, and in most cases in advance of the general position, even if it be crowned with success, the victors can seldom remain on the ground where their victory was gained, but must come home again to their proper place; and in doing this they must for a time unavoidably turn their horses' tails, or at least their flanks, towards the enemy. If, then, the defeated enemy have had the precaution to retain a second line or reserve, they will, of course, take advantage of this opportunity to pursue, and endeavour to retrieve the disgrace of their confederates. But if the victorious party also have not neglected the same indispensable precaution, their reserve will move out to meet the enemy's pursuers, and probably gain a second victory.

As to the French artillery, it is well known that Napoleon, having been educated as an artillery officer, always made good use of that arm, and placed great reliance upon it, often concentrating contiguous batteries, to the amount of 100 guns, to support a particular attack or strengthen a weak point in a defensive position.

Their light artillery, which accompanied movements of cavalry, was no less efficient, but there was a carelessness among them in exposing their guns in situations from whence they could not be extricated, which gave frequent occasions to the allies to take them; and in the enumeration of trophies, guns, in popular estimation, count for more than their intrinsic value, and therefore should not be sacrificed when it can be avoided.

After all, however, in a general action, when opposed to troops who have been in many battles, the fire of artillery ceases to intimidate, and its real effect, except in certain accidental circumstances, where crowded defiles or villages disputed with obstinacy place an unfortunate mass of infantry at their mercy, is in fact far less destructive than that of musketry at point blank range, or the bayonet duly brought to bear and applied with energy.

In modern warfare, therefore, artillery and cavalry, powerful as they undoubtedly are when properly applied, can only be considered as auxiliary arms: the grand movements of the infantry forces must decide the issue of a general action.

THE RUSSIANS.

Much of what has already been said has an application common to the military service of all the nations engaged in the war which forms the subject of these *Commentaries*, for all had a tendency to adopt Napoleon's system; a few remarks therefore will suffice to distinguish certain peculiarities.

The state of tactical proficiency and discipline of the Russians was in all respects superior to that which prevailed in Napoleon's armies, even before the disastrous campaign of Moscow. They were steady in the ranks and capable of line movements in their campaigns of 1806, and appear to have adopted line formations at that time, in opposition to the French system of masses and attacks in column, with good success on many occasions; but then, overwhelmed by numbers and the celerity of Napoleon's movements, in the days when the mind of that extraordinary man was in its full vigour and his military genius transcendent, the result of those campaigns was defeat and humiliation to all who opposed him.

Hence, in 1812 and 1813, the Russian generals appear to have assimilated their mode of warfare to that of their successful opponent, as if they attributed their want of success to a defect in their own system; but by adopting too constantly the use of masses and attacks in column, it may be a question whether they did not sometimes throw away the advantage they possessed in point of superior tactical proficiency.

The Russian artillery was without doubt better appointed for useful purposes, and better able to pull through or surmount obstacles than any in the field; hence they arrived comparatively sooner in position and could remain there longer than others. The almost impassable state of the roads in Russia and Poland in spring and autumn, where they had ample practice, will account for their facility in overcoming all minor difficulties, and for this their horse-power was amply sufficient.

In describing the Russian cavalry with reference to its services in 1813, it is necessary to divide it into three classes:—

1st. The Reserve Cavalry, chiefly composed of *cuirassiers*.

2nd. The lighter Regular Cavalry, of all descriptions, attached to the several corps and divisions.

3rd. The Cossacks.

Nothing could be more splendid or efficient in respect to horses, appointments, and discipline than the Russian Reserve Cavalry; but partly from the apparent reluctance of the Emperor Alexander to expose them to hazardous adventures, and partly, perhaps, from the want of an appointed leader of energy and enterprise, possessing the peculiar talent required to constitute a cavalry commander of large bodies, few opportunities were found for their employment.

With regard to the second and more numerous class of regular cavalry, those attached to the several corps of infantry, and constantly engaged with the enemy, under able and enterprising commanders, their services were of the greatest importance, whether at the outposts and in small bodies, or collectively in corps or divisions, and almost always successful though opposed to superior numbers.

On one occasion, which is recorded in these memoirs, the author was a witness to the defeat of 5,000 of Napoleon's cavalry, being the corps of General Latour Maubourg, and led on by the King of Naples; they were ultimately put to the rout by the three regiments of the light cavalry of the Russian Guard and a few squadrons of Cossacks, a force which could not have amounted to 2,000 men. This success is to be attributed mainly to superior discipline; for, though a great fault was committed by the King of Naples, it would not have been irretrievable but for the steadiness of the Russian cavalry.

3rdly. The Cossacks. Under this head, in common parlance, are often included all the mounted contingents furnished by those nomad districts of the Russian Empire, where the people are accustomed, like their Scythian ancestors, to fight on horseback, and who, according to ancient law, in which the feudal system probably had its origin, are to this day bound to come armed, mounted, and accoutred, to the standard of their sovereign when he may call for their services. Being of different nations, Asiatic as well as European, they were therefore of very various descriptions; but the fact of a warrior being able to take the field on his own horse, is at least a proof of his being a man of substance in his own nomad country.

Their corps being national, their men of rank were their officers; and though some of the most remote people sent warriors of savage appearance, and lineaments strange to European eyes, they by no means deserved the general character for cruelty or indiscipline that vulgar prejudice, and sometimes designing policy, have attached to them. They were all formed into national "*polks*," a term which is not peculiar to Cossacks, but is in fact the Russian word for a regiment. They were subject to all the stringent regulations, in respect to the police branch of discipline, which were required to be observed and strictly enforced in the Russian Army.

The Cossacks of the Don, and those from the borders of the Black Sea, were no doubt far more civilised, and superior to the others in every respect; these were generally assembled under the command of the Hettman Platof, who was frequently at the head of a corps of eight or ten thousand. When allowance is made for the roving services of a partisan corps, a duty in which Cossacks were generally employed, it is but fair to say that no greater irregularities can be charged against them than would have been committed by almost any disciplined corps placed in similar circumstances.

With respect to the wilder tribes, such as Tartars, Calmucks, Bashkirs, &c, or those who were employed in aid of commissariat arrangements, the author will not answer for discipline when detached on that essential but demoralising service, more than he would for any other troops so employed. As to their efficiency in a general action, or when opposed to regular cavalry, of force at all equal to their own, their services cannot be taken into account; imperfect training and the smallness of their horses on such occasions rendered them of little use. On outpost duty they saved much fatigue to the regular cavalry, but were never entirely trusted with that service.

As to their general utility, the author once heard the late Viceroy Beauharnois assert that the Cossacks did more good than harm to their enemies. This seeming paradox he explained by saying that on the retreat of the French from Moscow their appearance gave warning of something more formidable to be expected, and the terror they occasioned caused the columns to close up, and prevented straggling or desertion, whilst those French soldiers, who left the ranks and fell into their hands, would have been lost at any rate. Perhaps this was saying too much, yet no doubt there may have been some truth in the assertion.

The circumstances of this army were peculiar. At the time of the Battle of Jena, Prussia possessed a fine army, but not entirely a national one, for men of all German nations were incorporated in its ranks, and although most of them were old soldiers they had become veterans in times of comparative peace. The system of tactics was that of Frederick the Great; but the talents and energy of that great master of the art were wanting to put them in motion and adapt them to the new conditions of modern war. On that momentous occasion a venerable commander-in-chief had formed his army in the most orthodox manner, and in a scientifically chosen position; but Napoleon, with a celerity not hitherto considered practicable, brought the concentrated masses of a superior army to bear suddenly in rear of the left of the Prussian array.

A change of front of the whole of an old-fashioned order of battle two miles in length, by throwing back its left the quarter circle, became the only resource of the commander-in-chief of the Prussian highly disciplined army. This, of course, was too slow a proceeding for the emergency, and defeat was the consequence, followed by disasters that for a long time were irretrievable. The King of Prussia, with the feeble remnant of his armed force, struggled on, in concert with his ally the Emperor Alexander, till the Peace of Tilsit put an end to hostilities.

By the Treaty of 1812 the King of Prussia was forced to become, no doubt most reluctantly, the ally offensive and defensive of Napoleon; and a small contingent of his regular troops took part in the invasion of Russia, under the command of General de York.

At the period of the Peace of Tilsit there remained but an imperfect military organisation of a standing army in Prussia. The military ardour, however, of the Prussian nation, inherent from the memory of their glorious achievements in former days, and stimulated by a just sense of their wrongs, burst forth as soon as the predominant pressure of Napoleon's sway was removed. Not only did they arm themselves for battle, but even compelled their sovereign to overcome all his scruples as to treaties, and to place himself at their head. This national enthusiasm, however, only leads to the question of the state of discipline, for without discipline, even national enthusiasm is of very little avail in regular warfare systematically conducted, as it now is, by standing armies.

The Prussian troops, with the exception of the Guard, the Corps of De York, and a few other regiments of sufficient experience, were very deficient in regular discipline. Although General Blücher, that distinguished commander of the old school, possessed all the talent, energy, and activity necessary to adapt his measures to his means, and was almost invariably successful, yet it is but fair to remind those who are carried away by the name of the general, without considering the means at his disposal, that in all his great victories in 1813, one half of his force was composed of highly disciplined and well-tried Russians under the command of General Langeron and General Sacken. Blücher seldom had the better part of the Prussian Army under his command, but his spirit and enterprise, and his justly acquired popularity, gave him the power of gradually training the young and ardent levies, and leading them onwards to success; thus in 1813 he formed troops which proved fit for every service during the campaign of the following year in France.

It will be evident that there was not time for the new levies of the Prussian Army to arrive at tactical proficiency, and it would have been injudicious to do otherwise than to make their mode of operation assimilate to that of the enemy. Although in subsequent times of peace the Prussian Army have shown that they well know the value of the old system of line movements, when combined with the more modern one of reserves and masses and accelerated movement, and are capable of all at the present day, yet in the year 1813 this was not generally the case. The system then adopted was that of concentrated masses and the employment of light infantry, supported by columns of attack similar to what in the British service are called battalion "double columns at quarter distance in rear of the two centre subdivisions." The Prussians frequently engaged in protracted conflict for villages, and in enclosures, occasionally perhaps with unavailing pertinacity, and on those occasions the loss was always very severe.

The Prussian artillery was efficient in every respect, but certainly inferior to the Russian in cases of difficulty, and even on the line of march.

The Prussian cavalry was good and serviceable on all occasions; the master-spirit of their great commander, who was himself a cavalry officer, and was partial to the service, was infused into the subordinate commanders. Many skilful and successful achievements were accomplished by that arm during the campaign of 1813, the most remarkable of which was the affair at Hanau, entirely arranged by General Blücher himself.

THE AUSTRIAN ARMY.

The author has placed his general remarks respecting the armies engaged in this contest in the order in which they came into the field. When the forces of the Austrian Empire joined the Alliance the comparatively small armament, they had at immediate command was in a high state of systematic discipline, and their tactical doctrines were those which the author has described as line movements, and primary formations having reference thereto; in fact, a system similar to that which forms the basis of Her Majesty's Regulations at this day for the British Army.

Some new Bohemian levies were hastily brought into the field at the commencement of the campaign, and not being incorporated into other experienced corps, a measure for which there would not have been time even if the long-established system of national organisation of corps in that service had not precluded the possibility, they cannot be placed on a par with the regular army at that early period. This is mentioned here, because they had not time to be rendered capable of the system previously described, in a degree that could safely be attempted in presence of an experienced and enterprising enemy; and that of Napoleon, more applicable to new levies, not having been substituted for it to meet the emergency, they were soon brought into trouble. In consequence of this a disaster occurred at Dresden, which, when thus explained, affords a useful example, and reflects no discredit upon the state of discipline in the regular Austrian Army.

The artillery of the Austrian contingent to the Grand Alliance was old-fashioned and slow to move, but when it did arrive in position none was better or more scientifically served, and none was more efficient. Their ambulance also was comparatively cumbrous and expensive, as well as too slow for the modern rapidity of movement.

The Austrian cavalry was, perhaps, superior on the whole to that of any other power in the field. From the circumstance of there being no privileged regiments of guards, either infantry or cavalry, in the Austrian service, their few squadrons of Guards-Noble being merely appointed for purposes of state and not as belligerents, except when the emperor takes the field in person, the Austrian cavalry service generally monopolises a great proportion of the chivalry of the empire, and chivalrous commanders are never found wanting to lead them to battle: whenever an opportunity was allowed them, they never failed to do good service and to show their superiority to the enemy. Their native Hungarian hussars and Polish *hulans*, which principally constituted their light cavalry, have been imitated by all other nations since the days of Frederick the Great as closely as possible in dress, appointments, and mode of action, but are still unrivalled in practical efficiency.

In adverting to the chivalrous spirit which in a remarkable manner appeared to distinguish the officers of the Austrian Army, it may be observed that although the romantic age has long since passed away, yet the influence of the spirit which then prevailed, and which was always good in principle though sometimes carried to excess, is still to be found lingering in all those nations that were sufficiently advanced in civilisation in the time of its prevalence to have partaken fully of its advantages as well as its extravagances; and though, in subsequent times, political changes and the all-absorbing influence of commerce have modified its spirit in various ways among these nations, yet chivalry still forms an essential ingredient in the qualifications of an officer.

Soldiers led on by chivalrous officers have often proved more efficient on the day of battle than troops equal in point of physical powers and even discipline, but which had not that advantage. In illustration of this remark, we may refer to the vast superiority of the East Indian native corps when led on by British officers against people of the same national character, and not by any means deficient in knowledge of the art of war, but who do not possess that advantage.

Commerce may be considered as demoralising in respect to the principle of chivalry, inasmuch as luxury, selfishness, and the lucre of gain, have nothing in common with it; nevertheless, although Great Britain is now enslaved to the commercial Mammon, her sons have not yet degenerated, but are still pre-eminently a warlike race. Wise laws have gradually discarded what was found prejudicial in her ancient institutions, and in framing new enactments, her legislators have spared, for the most part, those established customs which have been found, after long trial, to be wholesome and good. Hence the chivalrous influence has not yet been extinguished in the British Army, for which a superabundant class of gentlemen is to be found to furnish officers.

In the days of chivalry, the term "gentleman" applied to hereditary descent, and the "*gloria majorum*" was then the stimulant to honourable conduct and valiant deeds of arms; in these days, upright dealings, good repute, and a certain income, are the more solid requirements to constitute a gentleman. Commerce and national prosperity, and, paradoxical as it may seem, even the vast debt of the country, by affording investment for moderate capitals, has enlarged the class of independent gentlemen, and their sons, with the advantage of liberal education, and inheriting the upright principles of their fathers, are, with rare exceptions, imbued with the valuable spirit which constitutes chivalry in its purest acceptation, and are ever ready to offer their services to their Sovereign as officers of Her fleets and armies.

Among the lower orders of the people of Great Britain a strong example of chivalrous influence may also be traced in this peculiar nation; for what among the gentlemen of England is called "honour," among the lower classes is called "fair play." This is evinced in their general integrity and good faith, and in their quarrels. In the latter instance, which habitually terminates in a pugilistic appeal to wager of battle, when this occurs between any two individuals after their own fashion, the mob will invariably stand by, and only interfere to prevent or chastise any foul play or infringement of this honest and really chivalrous principle. This has long and wisely been recognised, and it is to be hoped that no effeminate enactments will ever be devised that may tend to extinguish a spirit which prevents in a great measure cowardly and secret vengeance, and gives us soldiers and sailors invincible in battle.

The French nation inherit largely the spirit which has descended to them from their chivalrous ancestors, but with them *"la gloire"* is the principal manifestation of it, and constitutes their ruling motive. This is diffused through the whole community from the marshal to the recruit, and this motive is sufficient to account for the brilliancy of their achievements; but, as all violent and visionary excitement can be only transitory, the want of a more solid principle is often observable in modern days; unfortunately every solid principle has been entirely removed by the political changes which have entirely subverted their ancient institution, and rendered that nation, for the most part, regardless of all moral or religious restraint.

The Prussians, a chivalrous people of the olden time, inherit much of what was good in the true spirit of chivalry; but it may be a question whether all those territories which now constitute that monarchy are in a condition to supply the full proportion of what has been described as constituting the class of independent gentlemen requisite to furnish officers for an army of more than double the numerical strength of that now required for the protection of Great Britain and all her colonies. They are, however, essentially a military nation, and the stimulus with the generality of them is not so much the *"gloria ma-*

jorum" in its usual hereditary meaning, or even their private position in society, as the remembrance of their more proximate achievements in the Seven Years' War, when their grandfathers served with renown under their beloved and venerated sovereign Frederick the Great.

Russia cannot be included among the nations sufficiently advanced in civilisation in the age of chivalry to claim a place in this argument. The Russian soldiers, in prowess and discipline as well as vigour of constitution and animal courage, arc possibly superior to those of any of the continental nations to which these remarks have immediate reference; but in those days the greater part of the present Empire of Russia was not in a state of civilisation sufficiently advanced to derive any benefit from that institution. A reflected influence from their western neighbours, and constant intercourse with them, have, without doubt, long since established among the aristocracy of that empire a high sense of honour and every other chivalrous sentiment, but there is as yet no middle class of gentlemen sufficient to furnish officers for 600,000 men.

If the Russian Army could be rendered equally perfect both in respect to its men and its officers, which must, however, for a long time to come be impossible, no troops of the other powers on the continent of Europe could withstand them in battle in equal numbers, and otherwise on equal terms. Their subordinate officers showed themselves as brave as the men they commanded; enterprise and excitability, in short, a spirit of chivalry, alone appeared to be wanting in them. But if this may not yet have reached them, their good qualities are founded on a more solid basis—that of religion.

This principle ought to influence all Christian soldiers, and, in a greater or less degree, it does influence them, but the Russians are pre-eminently a religious people, and obedience to their emperor, and self-devotion in a good cause, form part of their religion. They are predestinarians, moreover, and in the hour of danger are content to trust the issue of events to the will of Providence.

The influence of national character is particularly observable with respect to armies in the field, under the three different circumstances of attack, of defeat, and during long and arduous marches.

The French, proverbially a brave and excitable people, are brilliant and formidable in an attack. If repulsed, a revulsion equally violent usually takes place, and would often prove fatal if it were not for the precaution of placing reserves. When these are not wanting, they are capable of being easily rallied and their lively spirit is soon restored.

The Russians are less excitable, but, nevertheless, in an attack are not to be surpassed in bravery and perseverance by the troops of any European nation, with this advantage, that they appear to be incapable of panic, and though they may be repulsed and defeated they cannot be forced to run in confusion from the field of battle.

The Prussian Armies engaged in these campaigns were for the most part very young soldiers; a spirit of enthusiasm pervaded their ranks which rendered them capable of the most brilliant achievements. In cases of defeat, the effects of momentary hurry and confusion, to which all young troops are liable, were less violent with them than with the French; but though easily rallied, and their patriotic enthusiasm soon restored, they could not rival the Russian stoicism in adversity.

The Armies of the Emperor Francis being composed of the troops of the several nations and races which constitute the Austrian Empire, not intermingled in the ranks, but formed into distinct regiments, the influence of national character and of the physical powers peculiar to each race was therefore discernible, notwithstanding the uniformity of system in respect to discipline and tactics which was common to all.

The Austrians, properly so called, were highly disciplined and brave, but the infantry of that race appeared deficient in energy when compared with the French or Prussians, and their physical powers could not be compared with those of the sturdy Russian soldiery.

The Bohemians appeared to be somewhat more healthy and robust, but did not materially differ in point of national character from their Austrian brethren in arms.

The Hungarian infantry were decidedly superior to both, in point of energy and physical power, and the select corps of grenadiers furnished by that nation were equal, if not superior, to any in the field.

If the infantry of the Emperor Francis generally appeared less vigorous than other troops in their mode of attack, it may be attributed in great measure to their somewhat antiquated system of tactics, which, though excellent in principle, requires in these days increased celerity, and adaptation to the modern practice of other nations; but in cases of failure their admirable discipline generally enabled them to retire in good order. Their formation in line in defence of positions proved on many occasions the superiority of that order of battle, in the repulse and defeat of the enemy's columns of attack.

As to all the Continental Armies engaged in the war, it is necessary to remark that the order of battalions when deployed and formed in line was invariably three deep. The only nation which places confidence in the stability of a line formed two deep, is the British, a confidence which on every occasion has been signally justified. In the days of Marlborough, the formation of the British Army was three deep.

On a March.

The French being a light-hearted nation, and being also lightly equipped, were decidedly the most expeditious marchers. The famous forced marches of upwards of thirty miles for three consecutive days, by which Napoleon brought an army to the relief of Dresden, and in a state to fight a battle, with scarcely a night's rest intervening, will establish their claim to this encomium.

If, however, we take the true test of good marching to be the time at which, after a march of a given distance, the rear of a column of 10,000 or 20,000 men comes to its ground, the Russians were decidedly the best marchers. So careful were they to ensure this most important object, that, marching perfectly at ease in columns at half-distance, an orderly-drummer was placed in rear of each battalion, who, under the direction of the adjutant, on the slightest apparent tendency to lose distance, beat a signal, which simultaneously caused every individual to correct the error without crowding or overdoing it.

The generals of brigade looked well to the intervals of battalions: it would have been a serious matter to them sometimes if they had neglected that duty, for it was the almost daily habit of the Emperor Alexander, in all the movements of the Grand Army during 1813 and 1814, to overtake the principal Russian column on its march, and canter from the rear to the front, so as to arrive at his headquarters with it; and though he was not usually harsh, and required no recognition on those occasions, he was strict, and the power of an autocrat is not to be trifled with.

This perfection of discipline in marching, long established and enforced, was the astonishment of Napoleon's army when they reached Vitepsk in 1812, following the admirable retreat of Barclay de Tolly. "*Tout y attestait la science de la guerre,—il parut plus d'ordre dans leur défaite que dans notre victoire,*" is the remark of Ségur on that occasion. The same eulogium was equally merited in every case when force of circumstances compelled the Russian Army to retire before an enemy, and was the result of their admirable discipline on the line of march.

The Prussian Army of 1813 were expeditious on a march, and their good spirit carried them forward with alacrity; but their discipline was comparatively lax, great irregularities were tolerated by way of encouragement, and, as a natural consequence, rapid diminution of strength was the invariable result.

With respect to the Army of the Austrian Empire, their system of marching generally in open column may account for the comparative tardiness of their movements.

In point of health and vigour, the Austrians and Bohemians suffered from fatigue more than the Hungarians, who appeared always healthy and robust.

In conclusion, the author wishes to remind the reader that the foregoing comparisons have reference only to the armies engaged in the particular campaigns described in these *Commentaries*.

The French Army in Spain, opposed at the same period to the British, consisted of soldiers inured to war, and in a much higher state of discipline than those whom Napoleon, in a manner which appeared almost miraculous, hurried into the field to repair the losses of his Russian disaster. It must also be observed, that what has been said respecting the French Army in Germany should only be received as general remarks, applicable to the great majority of its national components; of these the Old Guard was always kept up, both in numbers and discipline, in a most efficient state; and it is also to be remembered that a certain portion of what is commonly called the French Army consisted of Germanic contingents, many of which were far superior in their organisation to the French, Italian, and Belgian levies, which were hastily incorporated, but which constituted the greater part of Napoleon's forces.

What has been said of the Russians is strictly true, and needs no apology. There is every reason to believe that the Army of the Emperor Nicholas at this day merits the same encomium for discipline, bravery, and steadiness. The Prussian force in 1813 was gallant and enthusiastic, though young; and now that time has enabled them to cultivate the art of war more sedulously in its details, they are proficients in all that is good in the old system, and have also acquired a knowledge of the advantages to be derived from the new.

As to the Austrians, the venerable Radetsky, who was chief of the staff in the decisive campaign which is about to be described, and to whom at that time a principal share of the judicious arrangements which terminated in success may be attributed, has, by his recent glorious achievements in Italy, not only given to the world new examples of sound strategic science, but proved that the Imperial Army under his command has attained the highest state of tactical proficiency, and through practice and good guidance may at this moment be considered the most efficient army in Europe,

CHAPTER 1

Campaign of Lützen and Bautzen, 1813

In January, 1813, the wreck of the French Army in cantonments on the left bank of the Vistula, had its right at Warsaw, its centre at Thorn, and its left on the Baltic at Dantzig. Some Russian troops had already entered the Prussian territory; Wittgenstein's advanced guard was in possession of Königsberg.

The Emperor Alexander, with what remained of Koutousof's command, or, as it was called, the Grand Army, although it did not now amount to 40,000 effective men, crossed the Niemen on the 15th of January at Moritz, and marched by Suvalki, Lyck, &c. Crossing the Vistula at Plock, to avoid Warsaw, he continued his route upon Kalisch.

Murat, who was left in charge of the French Army, had established his headquarters at Posen; but soon after resigned the command to the Viceroy of Italy, Eugene Beauharnois, who appointed Rapp Governor of Dantzig, with a garrison of 20,000 men; this post Napoleon considered of the greatest importance. Four other fortresses, Thorn, Modlin, Zamosch, and Czenstochau were also garrisoned, and put in as good a state of defence as circumstances would allow. He took the same precaution with four fortresses in the second line of the Oder, *viz.*, Custrin, Stettin, Gros-Glogau, and Spandau; but all these garrisons, with the exception of Dantzig, chiefly consisted of invalids.

Schwartzenberg, after his inactive campaign, was on the right bank of the Pilica, covering Galicia; and Regnier, who had been attached to him, was at Kalisch, but upon the advance of the Russians he was forced to retire upon the Oder.

The Viceroy Beauharnois found himself unable to remain on the Oder, not only on account of the advance of the Russian Army, but of the defection of the Prussians in his rear, whom the French arms had no longer power to control. Leaving, therefore, the garrisons of inva-

RUSSIA

R. Dwina

Riga

Wilna

R. Niemen

BALTIC SEA

Dantzig

R. Vistula

Thorn

Modlin

Warsaw

POLAND

1812

Operations

GALICIA

Zamosth

Krakow

Austrian Frontier

Czenstokau

Stetin

R. Oder

Custrin

Glogau

Breslau

The Grand Line

Hamburg

R. Elbe

Spandau

Berlin

Wittenberg

Magdeburg

Torgau

Dresden

Königstein

Bohemian Frontier

Erfurt

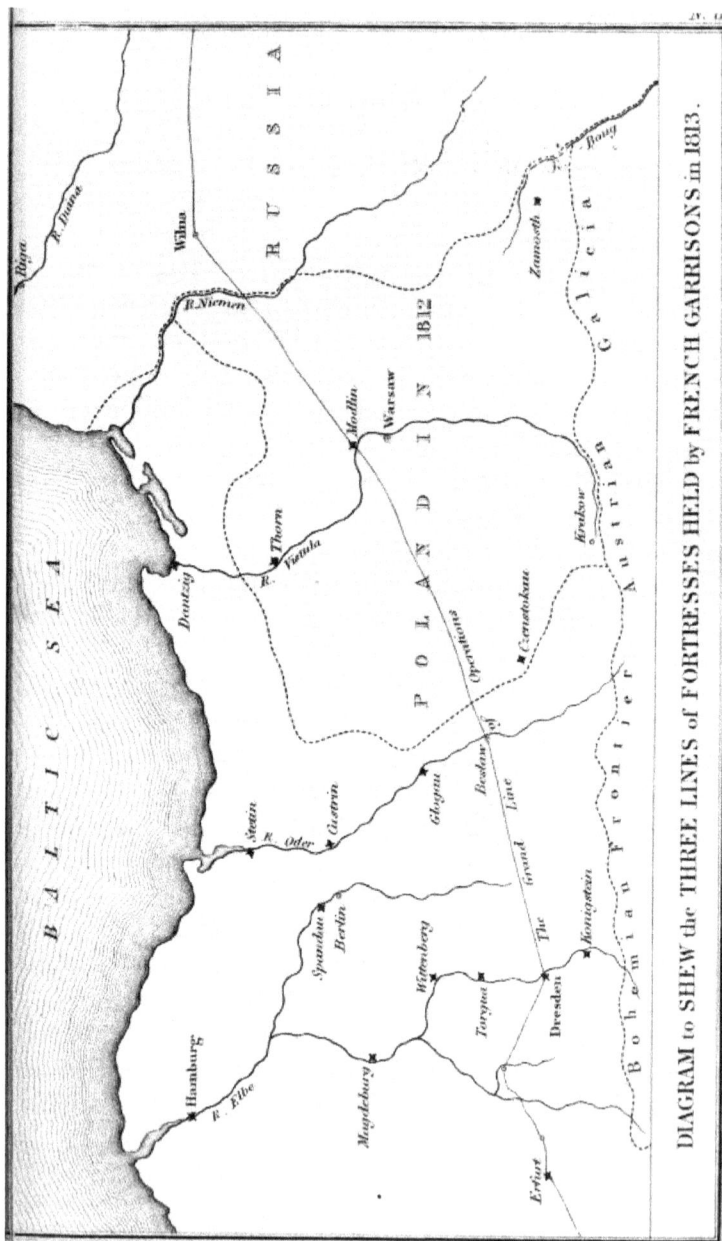

DIAGRAM to SHEW the THREE LINES of FORTRESSES HELD by FRENCH GARRISONS in 1813.

lids above-named, he retired behind the Elbe, with nearly all that was effective of the remains of the French Army of Russia, where he expected to be joined by reinforcements which Napoleon, with incredible activity and ingenuity, had already collected and set in motion.

The Emperor Alexander established his headquarters at Kalisch, as a central point from which he might bring his negotiations with Prussia to a speedy conclusion, communicate with Austria, observe and endeavour to conciliate the Poles, and prepare for the campaign of 1813. The King of Prussia, Frederick William, a man of high principle, was at this time suddenly placed in an embarrassing dilemma. On the one hand, he had but recently entered into an alliance, offensive and defensive, with Napoleon, by a solemn treaty; and "though he had promised to his cost," yet he felt himself "bound to keep that promise good." On the other hand, inclination and expediency alike pointed to a reconciliation and alliance with his ancient ally and friend the Emperor Alexander.

A less scrupulous prince might have considered at once, that at the time he acceded to the treaty of 24th of February, 1812, dictated by Napoleon, he could not be considered a free agent. Fortunately, the rising spirit of his people, and the obduracy of Napoleon, deprived him of all power to do otherwise than decide, at length, to join heart and hand in an alliance with Russia and the other powers, who had determined not to lay down their arms till the peace of Europe should be re-established on a firm basis. The middle course of a neutrality, which he is said to have contemplated at one time, was manifestly inadmissible by either party. Accordingly, on the 1st of March, the Treaty of Kalisch was signed, and he went to Breslau, where he had a most cordial and satisfactory personal interview with the Emperor of Russia, who afterwards returned to Kalisch. The King of Prussia again visited Berlin, to put his forces in motion, and organise new levies to the utmost extent of his resources.

The Austrians had agreed to accept an unlimited armistice, and were retiring to the Galician frontier.

Poniatowski, with all the Polish troops he could collect, and accompanied by some of the members of the government, had retired to Czenstochau.

Lord Cathcart, accompanied by his son, Captain Frederick Cathcart, left Petersburg on the night of the 12th of February, and reached Riga in forty-eight hours; but the thaw having commenced, they proceeded to Kalisch in *britckas*, where they arrived on the 2nd of March.

Lord Cathcart was, as usual, most cordially received by the emperor, as His Britannic Majesty's Ambassador could not fail to be at that eventful period, when victorious arms, wise counsels, and commercial wealth, had placed the balance of power in the hands of the British Government.

At Kalisch, Lord Walpole, who had returned from his secret mission to Vienna, awaited the arrival of Lord Cathcart, his mission having been discovered by the French minister, Count Otto: and the Austrian Government not being as yet prepared for any public declaration in favour of the good cause, Count Metternich had been obliged to desire Lord Walpole to quit the suburb of Vienna in which he had lodged. Soon after, when the communication with England, by Berlin and Cuxhaven, was laid open by the retreat of the enemy and the advance of Wittgenstein, Lord Cathcart despatched him to England, to acquaint the British Government with the new and promising aspect of continental affairs.

Sir Robert Wilson, who had been with the Russian headquarters during the retreat of the French Army, was also at Kalisch, and was now sent on to accompany Wittgenstein in his advance.

General Dornberg, who had hitherto been the reporting officer with Wittgenstein during the latter part of the campaign of 1812, had received the command of a small partisan corps, to serve as a nucleus upon which to form any German volunteers in the north, who might join him upon the approach of the Allies. He was particularly well adapted for this purpose, as he had distinguished himself in the retreat of the corps of the Duke of Brunswick, after the battle of Jena; and was well known in the north of Germany. With his small means he had already begun to signalise himself in the advance upon the Lower Elbe, acting in concert with the Generals Tchernicheff and Tettenborn, who held similar commands.

Lord Cathcart had quitted St. Petersburg in a light travelling sledge for the sake of expedition, leaving the author of this commentary behind in the capital, until the roads should be practicable for his father's barouche, which was intended to carry some papers of consequence: he was then in his nineteenth year, a lieutenant in the 6th Dragoon Guards, and was an *aide-de-camp* to Lord Cathcart, in his capacity of a British general on the staff. About the end of March, the author proceeded to join the imperial headquarters, and at Riga he was detained nearly three days by the breaking up of the ice on the Dwina, which, on his arrival, was in such a state, that, although he crossed it on foot, on planks laid across the rotten ice for a distance of at least half an English mile, yet it was declared to be unsafe to risk the carriage.

As soon as the ice broke, and it was possible for a boat to stem the current and avoid the blocks of floating ice, he crossed and proceeded to Memel, thence to Königsberg, and along the left bank of the Vistula. After crossing the river at Bromberg, he arrived at Kalisch the day after the Imperial Headquarters had marched; but travelling on the same night with a messenger who had been left to await his arrival, he reached the headquarters the following morning; and from that time to the Capitulation of Paris in 1814 he was constantly with the army, and had an opportunity of seeing and hearing what was going on during the following campaigns, as well as of witnessing much of their interesting and instructive details: thus he had also the good fortune to see eight general actions lost and won, in which Napoleon commanded in person, and which he will hereafter endeavour to describe.

During these campaigns the Emperor Alexander performed each day's march on horseback, and never does the author remember to have seen him use a carriage for that purpose, excepting one night's march shortly before the fall of Paris—the very night on which the advance on Paris was decided. On these occasions the emperor was always accompanied by Lord Cathcart, some of his general *aides-de-camp*, the *Grand Mareschal*, Count Tolstoi, Prince Wolkonski, chief of the staff, and a few others of his personal staff. He had for his escort a detachment of some twenty Cossacks of the guard.

It was about the first week in April that the Emperor Alexander met the King of Prussia, who had now returned from Berlin to take the field. Their interview took place on the right bank of the Oder, and they passed this river on a bridge of boats at Steinau. The Imperial and the Royal headquarters usually halted at the same town during the campaign, and at the head of the main Russian column they continued their march upon Dresden. Their reception in the towns of Silesia, through which they passed, rendered their progress more like a triumphal procession than the advance of an army so soon to be engaged with an enemy.

The King of Prussia had lost no time in pushing forward all the force that he had then ready to take the field. This consisted, first, of the corps of General Blücher, which assembled in Silesia, and which was little more than 20,000 men; this corps crossed the Elbe at Dresden, and was joined by the Russian corps under Winzingerode. Secondly, the corps of D'York, which consisted at this time of only three brigades, and was attached to General Wittgenstein. Thirdly, that of General Bülow, which remained to cover Berlin, and observe the fortresses on the Elbe; this corps was chiefly composed of new levies.

The whole combined force of the Allies, disposable, and now in motion for the purpose of carrying the war across the Elbe, amounted to very little more than 100,000 men; and the concentration of that whole force for the purpose of a general action could not, of course, be calculated upon.

The rapid movements of Wittgenstein, and the columns of the other Russian generals, in pursuit of the French corps through the Prussian territory, had not failed to arouse a spirit of hostility to the French, and a thirst for revenge in the hearts of the Prussians, who had suffered many wrongs and indignities under Napoleon's yoke; the promptness with which they took the field is sufficient evidence of this angry spirit; and it also bid fair to impel the Austrians, the Saxons and other minor German powers, even at that early period, to join the alliance against Napoleon; but as the Allies unfortunately failed to obtain complete and immediate success, through the inability of the Austrian cabinet to assume the offensive, the Emperor Alexander and the King of Prussia, in consequence of their forward movements, found themselves involved in a war beyond the Elbe to which their means were inadequate, instead of obtaining the final settlement of the great European question.

Napoleon, it is true, had been repulsed from the Moskva to the Saale; but though the distance he had fallen back was great, yet the facility with which he could re-organise his army was increased in proportion to the shortness of his communication with his base, whilst the difficulties of the Russian Army in the same respect were increased in proportion to their advance.

Napoleon left Paris on the 15th of April to join his army, which had been re-organised as follows:—

Ney had formed a corps of five divisions at Würtzburg, with which he had arrived at Erfurt.

Marmont organised the sixth corps at Frankfort on the Maine, consisting of six divisions, which he had moved forward to Gotha.

Bessières was at Eisenach, with six battalions of the Old Guard and sixteen of the young.

General Bertrand was at Coburg with the fourth corps, consisting of three divisions, one of which was composed of the Würtemberg contingent.

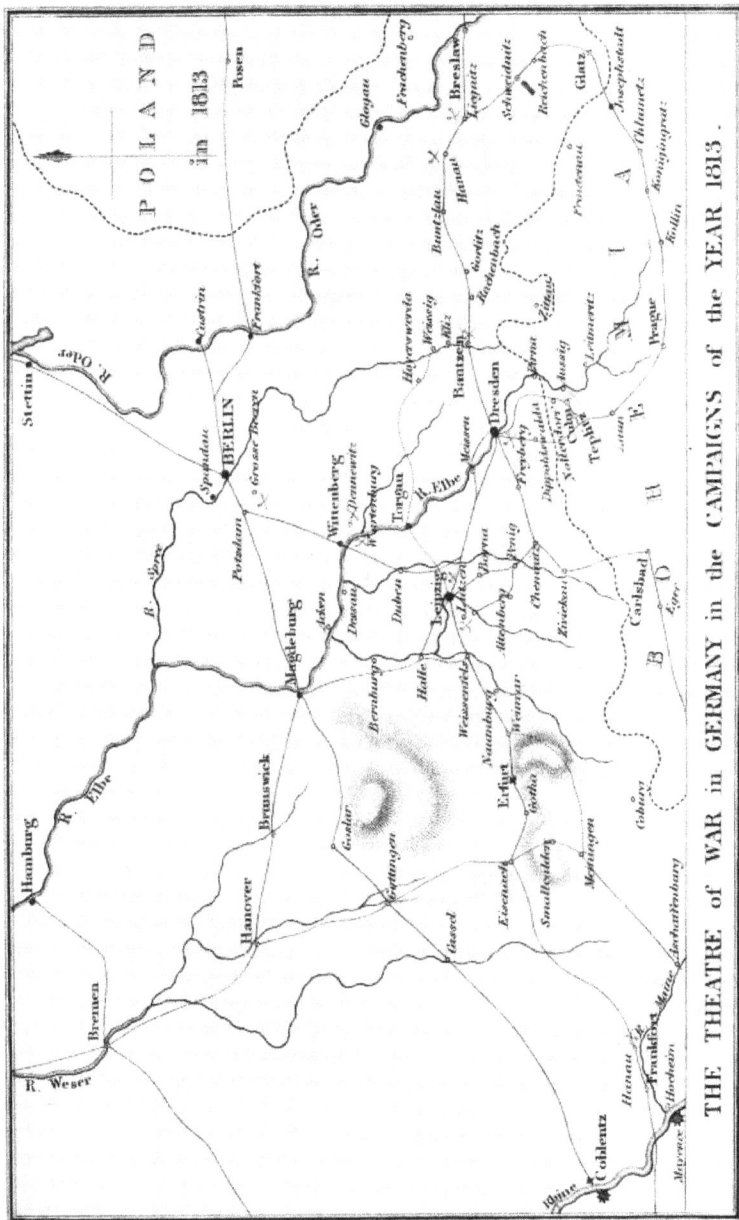

POLAND in 1813

PRUSSIA

BOHEMIA

Posen
Glogau
Freyenberg
Breslaw
Liegnitz
Schweidnitz
Reichenbach
Glatz
Josephstadt
Thunets
Konigingrat
Kolin
Prague
Leitmeritz
Brisen
Lobau
Zittau
Bautzen
Hoyerswerda
Weissig
Wurzen
Dresden
Pirna
Peterswald
Nollendorf
Culm
Teplitz
Gorlitz
Bischofwerda
Konigstein
Freyberg
Wettin
Haynau
Bunzlau
Custrin
Frankfort
R. Oder
Stettin
R. Oder
Spandau
BERLIN
Potsdam
Grosse Beeren
Jutterbuck
Wittenberg
Wartenburg
Targau
R. Elbe
Dennewitz
Dahme
Dubin
Dessau
Leipsig
Lutzen
Magdeburg
Aken
Bernburg
R. Saale
Halle
Weissenfels
Naumburg
Duben
Wachau
Maberg
Frohburg
Penig
Kriechau
Carlsbad
Eger
Coburg
Meiningen
Smallcalden
Eisenach
Gotha
Erfurt
Weimar
Gotha
Jena
Ostod
Gottingen
Goslar
Brunswick
Hanover
Bremen
R. Weser
Hamburg
R. Elbe
R. Spree
R. Havel
Hanau
Frankfort
Hochheim
Mayence
Coblentz
R. Maine
R. Rhine
Aschaffenburg

THE THEATRE of WAR in GERMANY in the CAMPAIGNS of the YEAR 1813.

Oudinot, with his corps and a Bavarian division, was at Saalfeld.

Prince Eugene Beauharnois, with the remains of the army of 1812, which had also received some recruits, and consisted of the corps of Victor, Lauriston, and Macdonald, had remained some time in cantonments, but in a defensive attitude, on the left bank of the Elbe, having his left at the junction of the Saale and Elbe, his centre at Bernberg, and his right towards the Harz mountains, with a sufficient garrison at Magdeburg; but at the end of April he marched to join the concentrating army of Napoleon with the fifth and eleventh corps, leaving Victor to occupy Magdeburg with the second.

This disposable force, though hastily gathered together, and perhaps inferior in all respects to Napoleon's former armies, amounted to 170,000 men; it was principally composed of conscripts, trained for service in the ranks on their march to join the several corps, and then distributed among the skeleton battalions prepared for their reception, with a view to mix the old and experienced soldiers as equally as possible with the new and raw recruits. The proportion of cavalry was very small, but the artillery was in full proportion, though not perfectly appointed, and of very heavy calibre; reserve artillery, and even ship-guns, having been brought into the field to replace the losses in the Russian campaign.

Napoleon's point of concentration was Leipzig.

The course of events having brought the Allied Army into the country between the Elbe and the Saale, and the sovereigns having resolved to commence hostilities in that country, Leipzig, or its immediate neighbourhood, became the *point stratégique* at which their forces must concentrate. Hence it was evident that a general action would take place at the very commencement of the campaign, unless the Allied sovereigns were prepared at once to abandon their advantage; and had they done so, considering the disparity of numbers and the fortresses held by the enemy in Poland, they had no base of operations, to trust to, short of the distant line of the Niemen.

But in resolving to open the campaign in Saxony, the inconvenience of the great distance between the Russian Army and its reinforcements was to be weighed against the probable political advantages that might result from so bold a measure. Prussia had, indeed, been enabled to join heartily in the cause, but Austria disappointed the hopes of the Allies; she appeared to doubt if their means would be adequate to maintain their advanced position, and, not being sufficiently prepared to co-operate so effectually as to turn the balance at that moment, she withheld her declaration in favour of the "good cause."

The King of Saxony had departed from Dresden before the Allied sovereigns entered the city, and had retired into the Austrian dominions, being unwilling to commit himself until Austria should set him the example, but he promised his adhesion when that of Austria should be declared. The French and Allied Armies were on the point of concentrating for a general action in the heart of his territory, and the unsatisfactory issue of the expected battle, considering the disparity of numbers, could not be doubted; in justice to bis subjects, the King of Saxony could not well have done otherwise, yet, when the Austrians did join the alliance at a later period of the war, the French being then in the actual occupation of the whole Saxon territory and Napoleon in Dresden, it was deemed an unpardonable breach of faith on the part of the Saxon king that he did not fulfil his unfortunate promise to join the alliance when Austria did so, and for this cause he has since been deprived of more than half his territory by the authority of the Congress of Vienna.

The actual state of affairs was not clearly ascertained until a few days before the 24th of April, when the Emperor of Russia entered Dresden; then the sudden and formidable renewal of Napoleon's warlike energies appeared almost miraculous, and could not have been anticipated. Sir Charles Stewart joined the army at Dresden; he was accredited to the King of Prussia, as minister plenipotentiary, to conclude a treaty of which Lord Cathcart had already opened the preliminaries. The state of the Russian Army was this:—The corps of Count Wittgenstein arrived on the 27th of April in the neighbourhood of Rötha. As the senior Russian general in the field, he had been appointed commander-in-chief of the whole Allied Army, since Field-Marshal Prince Koutousof had been taken ill on the march through Silesia, and had died during the progress of the emperor towards Dresden.

The Russian column which had passed through that city moved on to join Wittgenstein, whose headquarters were at Coldiz on the 28th; on the 30th Wittgenstein became aware of the actual movements and near approach of the French columns, from the reports of the several small advanced corps who were now retiring before the enemy. This information was immediately communicated to the sovereigns at Dresden, who left the capital that night to join the army.

Blücher with his corps was at Borna. Winzingerode, who was at

Leipzig, and whose command consisted chiefly of Russian cavalry, was ordered to make a reconnaissance on the road towards Weisenfels; and in doing so he met the French advanced corps near that place, which proved to be a part of the corps of Marshal Ney, with whom it appears that Napoleon was present. An engagement commenced, and the French Marshal pushed forward heavy columns with an evident determination to make good his ground, indicating that his supports were at hand, and that, in fact, it was the advance of a *corps d'armée*.

Winzingerode opposed the advance of the enemy with a very heavy and destructive cannonade, supported by cavalry, under cover of which he retired towards the Flossgraben, and took up a position for the night, communicating with the main army by Zwickau, in obedience to his instructions. This Flossgraben is a large muddy brook, running nearly parallel to the Elster, which crosses the high road from Weisenfels to Leipzig, and intersects this open land: the Flossgraben supplies millponds in the several villages through which it passes, and forms a military feature of some importance on a field of battle in an unenclosed country, when there is not otherwise much diversity of ground.

We afterwards learned from prisoners that Marshal Bessières had been killed by a chance cannon shot in this affair, where he had no particular occasion to have been present, as the Imperial Guards which he commanded had not as yet passed through Weisenfels.

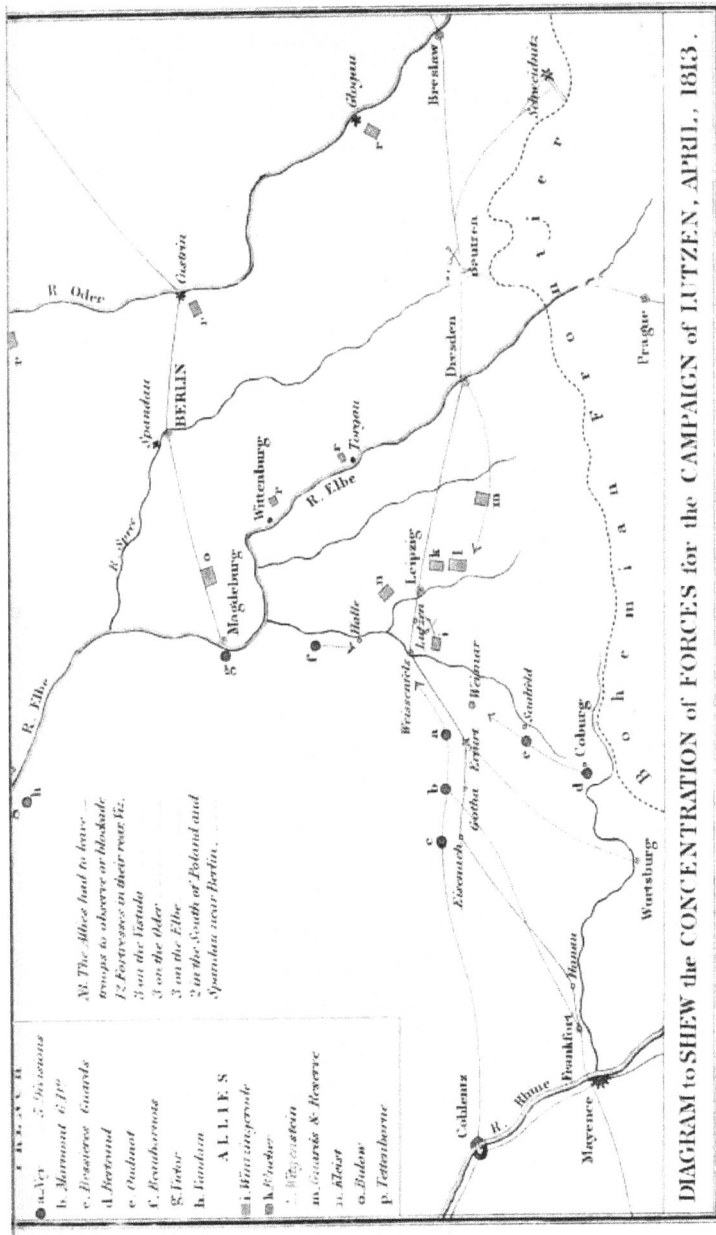

DIAGRAM to SHEW the CONCENTRATION of FORCES for the CAMPAIGN of LUTZEN, APRIL, 1813.

FRENCH
a. Ney   5. Divisions
b. Marmont 6th
c. Imperial Guards
d. Bertrand
e. Oudinot
c. Reinhartswald
g. Latour
h. Gardien

ALLIES
i. Wintzingerode
k. Blucher
l. Wittgenstein
m. Guards & Reserve
n. Kleist
o. Bulow
p. Tettenborne

N.B. The Allies had to leave troops to observe or blockade 12 Fortresses in their rear. Viz.
5 on the Vistula
3 on the Oder
3 on the Elbe
2 in the South of Poland and Spandau near Berlin.

R. Oder
Glogau
Breslaw
Schweidnitz
Custrin
Spandau
BERLIN
Bautzen
Dresden
Prague
R. Saw
Magdeburg
Wittenburg
Torgau
R. Elbe
Halle
Leipzig
Lutzen
Weissenfels
Weimar
Erfurt
Naumberg
Coburg
Eisenach
Gotha
Wartburg
Hanau
Frankfort
Mayence
Coblenz
R. Rhine
Bohemian Frontier

CHAPTER 2
Battle of Lützen

From the reports and information that had been received, it was evident that the main columns of the enemy were marching upon Leipzig, and Wittgenstein now formed a plan which was approved by the Emperor Alexander. He proposed to cross the Elster, concentrate his force on the right flank of the French line of march, and endeavour to fall upon it somewhere near Weisenfels, in the hope of engaging their columns in detail, and of gaining an advantage before they could be supported. With this view the whole army was put in motion on the night of the 1st of May. Kleist, who had been attacked at Halle, had fallen back to Leipzig, where it was intended, he should maintain himself for the present; that important post being on the direct and shortest road to Dresden, and consequently on Napoleon's line of operations.

Miloradovitch, who, with the Russian guards, grenadiers, and reserve cavalry, was at Zeitz, received orders to cross and descend the left bank of the Elster. Blücher from Borna, and Wittgenstein with his own corps and that of D'York from Rötha, marched to the town of Pegau, where they crossed; and the following day, the 2nd of May, the Allied Armies assembled in their proper order in the unenclosed country, having their right at a small village on the Flossgraben, called Werben, and the left near Dombsen, a small village on a similar brook, which runs into the Saale near Weisenfels. This position is parallel to the great line of road which passes through Weisenfels and Lützen to Leipzig, and at a distance of above four English miles from it.

This part of the country is unenclosed, but arable and under cultivation; its military features are tame, but there is a considerable undulation of surface which rises to a commanding elevation towards the centre of the Allied position, and there is a corresponding elevation opposite, sufficient to conceal the preparatory movements on both sides.

Winzingerode, who had remained during the night in the occupation of the ground to the right of the position, was moved to the left. The corps of General Blücher assembled on the right. Wittgenstein's own corps, with that of D'York, was on his left; but Miloradovitch, with the guards, &c, could not arrive till towards evening.

When Lord Cathcart, who had been present in the reconnaissance of the preceding evening, reached Pegau on the Pleisse at about five in the morning of the 2nd of May, he found the Emperor Alexander already there, anxiously watching the troops as they passed that defile. Lord Cathcart did not remain long to witness that tedious operation, but riding forward, he had time to communicate with General Blücher, and renew an old acquaintance that had been formed when they met as cavalry commanders in the north of Germany, in the year 1794. Blücher was now at the head of his corps and already on the ground; his troops were assembled *en masse*, and in high spirits. We also rode to Winzingerode, and learned from him that an enemy's bivouac was reported to be seen in the village of Gross Görschen, about an English mile and a half in our front, and immediately below the hill behind which Blücher was already posted and the rest of the Allied Army were assembling.

As soon as the passage of the Elster was effected, the Emperor Alexander came upon the ground, and upon his arrival was conducted by Wittgenstein to the top of the hill. The emperor and his suite saw the bivouac in question, about a mile below them, still occupied and the fires still smoking, but without any advanced posts. This did not appear to be any experienced or formidable body, and Wittgenstein evidently thought so, for the author then heard him promise that he would put his Imperial Majesty in possession of the enemy's corps which he saw before him within an hour's time. The King of Prussia having joined the emperor, the sovereigns and their staff dismounted, and stood on the hill near a small heap of stones, which, no doubt, indicates the spot to this day, in anxious but confident expectation of seeing this promise fulfilled by the troops, which were now advancing for the purpose, according to the following disposition:—

Battle of Lützen

General Blücher was to attack the enemy in front, and was moving forward a brigade of infantry for that purpose, supported by another in second line; their advance was covered by a Russian battery of twelve pounders and two Prussian light batteries, supported by light cavalry. As soon as the infantry should be fairly engaged in front, the cavalry and light artillery had instructions to take ground to their left, and, supported by other columns of infantry, to ascend the opposite rising ground and turn the villages: it was expected that the enemy, being engaged and entangled in them, would be easily cut off from their main columns, which were not supposed to be so near at hand as they proved to be.

The enemy's division was that of General Souham, a part of the corps of Marshal Ney, so placed as to cover the right flank of the French line of march; it lost no time in getting under arms, and occupying the outskirts of the village of Görschen. Souham had a battery of light artillery, which however could not stand against the superior fire of the Allies, who had also the advantage of the ground; three of his guns were dismounted, and the rest were withdrawn to a more sheltered post.

The Prussian infantry now attacked the first village with an impetuosity which soon made them masters of it; but Gross Görschen is only one of a cluster of nearly contiguous villages, interspersed with tanks, mill-ponds, gardens, &c, which furnished strong holding ground. The enemy driven from Gross Görschen, held Little Görschen and Ranha, and the intervening enclosures, with obstinacy. Here the progress of the attacking party was for a while arrested.

So far all promised well, fresh Prussian troops moved forward to support the attack on the villages, and the light artillery and light cavalry took ground to their left, for the purpose of turning Souham's right, according to their instructions. No sooner had the Prussian cavalry and artillery reached the foot of the opposite hill, than numerous batteries made their appearance along the ridge, unlimbered, and opened a fire that plainly showed that the division of Souham was not unsupported; but that strongly posted in itself, it formed the left of a large force already in position opposite to us: and from the prisoners we soon learned that it was in fact the whole corps of Marshal Ney, of about 45,000 men, and that Napoleon himself, with his guards, had slept at Lützen, only four English miles distant, and might therefore by this time be in the field. This force together could not amount to less than 60,000 men, who had passed the night within a few miles of the ground, and were consequently fresh and ready for action.

The three corps constituting the Allied force already in the field, might perhaps amount to 60,000 men, but certainly not more; and the corps under Miloradovitch, whose infantry could not arrive until evening, would complete their strength to about 80,000, but their whole

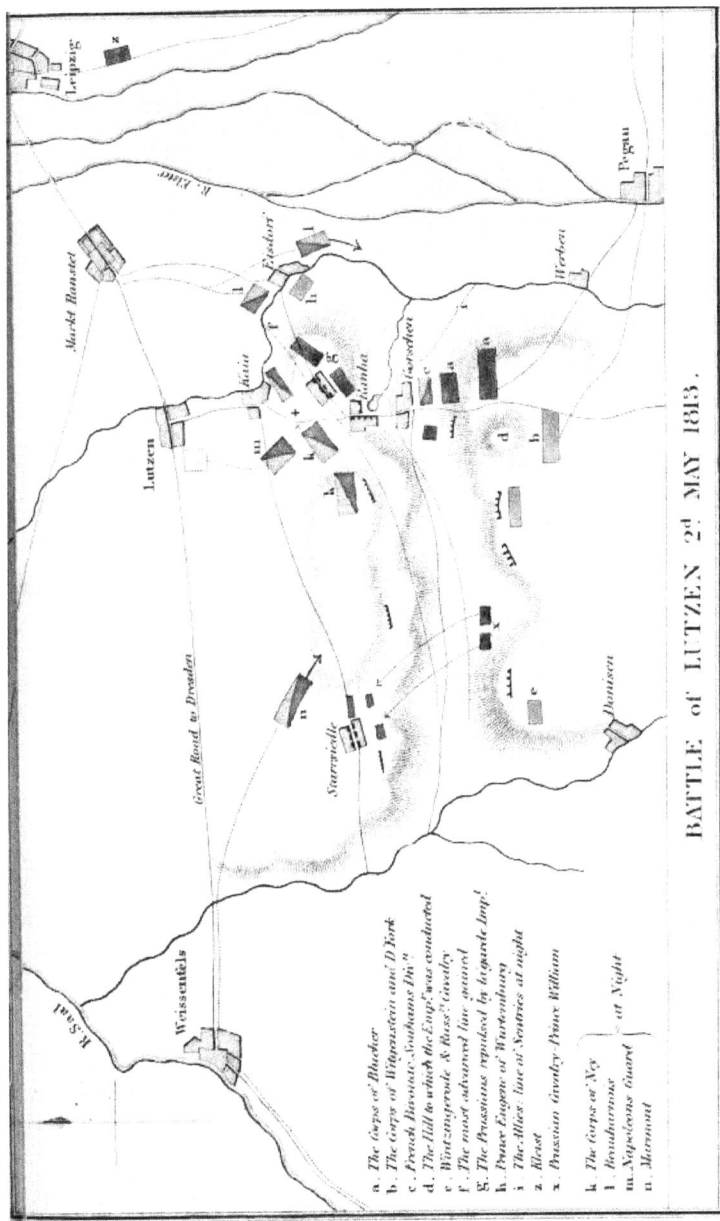

BATTLE of LUTZEN 2.d MAY 1813.

Leipzig

N

Market Ranstet

R. Elster

Lutzen

Eisdorf

Kaia

Gorschen

Pegau

Werben

Great Road to Dresden

Weissenfels

R. Saal

Starsville

Dhausen

a. The Corps of Blucher
b. The Corps of Witgenstein and D'York
c. French Bavarian Souhams Div.n
d. The Hill to which the Eng.s was conducted
e. Wintzingerode & Russ.n Cavalry
f. The most advanced line general
g. The Prussians repulsed by degarde Imp.l
h. Peuce Eugene of Wurtenburg
i. The Allies line at Sentries at night
z. Kleist
x. Prussian Cavalry Prince William

k. The Corps of Ney
l. Bondharmes } at Night
m. Napoleons Guard
n. Marmont

army, with the exception of Winzingerode's corps, which consisted entirely of cavalry and artillery, had been marching all the previous night, and were much exhausted.

A new disposition became necessary, but in the meantime nearly the whole corps of General Blücher and part of that of Wittgenstein had been committed in action, whilst endeavouring to improve the advantage gained in the village of Görschen. Napoleon took care to dispute the possession of the villages that he held in the neighbourhood with sufficient obstinacy. The remainder of the lines on either side became engaged in a cannonade along the whole front, which was upwards of two miles in extent; the artillery were supported by cavalry, under cover of which each party was bringing up troops into parallel position. Thus, the day passed, but neither could be prepared to attempt any decisive movement of attack under existing circumstances, and at that late hour.

Count Wittgenstein, however, detached a division of the corps formerly under his own immediate command, and led by Prince Eugene of Würtemberg towards the right by the village of Ersdorf, with a view to facilitate the exertions of Blücher, who now appeared to meet with considerable success in turning the enemy's left engaged in the villages; but the prince had no sooner crossed the Flossgraben with this intent, than he found himself in the presence of a superior force, which proved to be no less than the head of the Army of the Viceroy, Eugene Beauharnois, whom Napoleon had recalled from his march upon Leipzig, and who had now arrived on the French left, and was threatening the right of the Allies. The Russians were forced to retire across the Flossgraben, but Eugene of Würtemberg maintained his ground at Ersdorf till night, and did not suffer the French to *debouche* through that village.

Several affairs of cavalry of minor importance occurred on the left of the Allied Army, more of the character of reconnaissance; in one of these Prince William of Prussia, the king's brother, succeeded in breaking some squares of French infantry which he met with, unsupported, and too much in advance. On the other hand, some French cavalry surprised a Prussian regiment, which was detached, and had unbridled to feed their horses, without placing sufficient outposts.

About the time that the leading columns of the Viceroy Beauharnois came into position on the French left, Marmont, having passed through Weissenfels, brought his corps into line on their right; and to put an end to the desperate but desultory contest in the villages, in which nearly the whole corps of Ney had been engaged with that of Blücher, and in which, after great carnage on both sides, the Allies had gained much ground, Napoleon made an attack with his guards, and succeeded so far that he forced the Prussians to retire, but at nightfall they still remained in possession of Gross Görschen, and when hostilities ceased for the night, the two armies remained in parallel position; though since the arrival of the Viceroy Beauharnois, the French Army considerably outflanked that of the Allies, and stood with its left thrown forward, menacing their right and their line of retreat by Pegau; but the day was too far spent, and the night was afterwards too dark for the viceroy to press his advantage.

At about nine o'clock in the evening, General Blücher placed himself at the head of nine Prussian squadrons, and made an attack where he thought he saw a favourable opportunity; but this attack had no result of importance.

The sovereigns and their staff had quitted the field between nine and ten o'clock at night, and, with an escort of Cossacks of the guard, made their way in the dark to Pegau, where the Emperor Alexander passed the night. The King of Prussia went on to Lobestädt. There was no moonlight, and as night movements were impossible, the two armies passed the night on the ground, under arms, in full expectation of renewing the general action on the following morning.

The French Army now assembled amounted to 120,000 men at least—that of the Allies at most to 70,000. Intelligence arrived that Lauriston had forced Kleist to retire from Leipzig, and that the enemy were in possession of that city, by which Napoleon had gained command of the direct communication with Dresden. The loss of the Allies fell chiefly on the Prussians, and could not be computed at less than 10,000 "*hors de combat*;" the loss of the French was probably no less severe.

During the night, the commandant of the Allied artillery reported that the corps which had been engaged during the day had expended all their ammunition, and that the reserve was so far in the rear, that it could not be replaced by the ensuing morning. This circumstance contributed to render an immediate retreat upon Dresden indispensable.

If even an advantage could have been gained by the Allies in battle on the following day, which under existing circumstances was a contingency scarcely possible against an enemy so superior in numbers, and in possession of Wittenberg, Torgau, and Magdeburg, it is certain that the French, having the shortest and most direct road through

Battle of Lützen

Leipzig to Dresden open before them, would, if they gained the start, have possessed themselves inevitably of the Allied line of operations, intercepted their reserves and supplies, and effected the complete discomfiture of the Allied Army by a movement which, while it gave Napoleon possession of Saxony, left Prussia and Silesia at his mercy. Orders were accordingly given for a retreat before dawn in two columns; the Prussians, under General Blücher, fell back upon Borna, and the Russians, under Wittgenstein, upon Frohburg. Miloradovitch retired by Altenburg, and his corps became the rear guard of the army.

At daybreak Napoleon, finding that the Allies had retreated, and that nothing but their rear guard remained in sight, prepared to follow, leaving the corps of Marshal Ney, which had been so severely engaged on the preceding day, to repose and re-organise in the position they held. He removed his headquarters to Pegau, where we had passed the night, and the several columns of his army crossed the Elster in the following order:—Lauriston on the extreme left at Leipzig; Oudinot on the extreme right at Zeitz; the Viceroy Beauharnois at Pegau with the eleventh corps, to form an advanced guard; Marmont at Lützkewiz, and Bertrand at Prede.

It is unnecessary to give the details of the retreat of the Allies to the Elbe; suffice it to say, that as the greater part of the army had so recently advanced by forced marches along the same roads, they were unincumbered with baggage, and a country so fertile in resources furnished abundance of carts for the conveyance of the wounded. The skill displayed by Miloradovitch in covering the retreat, though he was ably followed up, and several times attacked and forced, by the Viceroy Beauharnois, enabled the remainder of the Allied Army to retire behind the Elbe, without hurry, confusion, or farther loss.

The Emperor of Russia passed the night of the battle at Pegau, whither his *britcka* containing his papers and camp-bed had been brought; and, after having been twenty hours on horseback, Lord Cathcart and his staff found the bare floor of a cottage so comfortable a couch, without even the luxury of straw, that no one seemed in any hurry to rise when we were informed, soon after daylight, that His Imperial Majesty was about to mount and depart, and that the enemy were approaching to dislodge us.

The emperor slowly rode some miles towards the rear, along the Altenburg road, conversing with Lord Cathcart about the battle; he laid great stress upon the report of the Commandant of Artillery as to the want of ammunition, which he assigned as the principal reason for not renewing the action; he spoke of the result as a victory gained on our side, and it was afterwards the fashion in the army to consider it as such, though not perhaps a victory so important in its consequences, or so decisive, as could have been wished. At length the emperor observed that he did not like to be seen riding fast to the rear, and that it was now necessary for him to go to Dresden with all expedition, and prepare for ulterior operations; he then entered his little travelling-carriage, which was drawn by relays of Cossack horses, and proceeded by Altenburg to Penig, accompanied only by General Ballocheff.

In order to frame his despatches to the British Government, Lord Cathcart was desirous of having a more satisfactory interview than was afforded by this hasty ride. He therefore sent his suite by the great road which passes through Altenburg, to ascertain with certainty whether the baggage which had halted there had received orders to return to Penig; and observing in his map the great detour which the high road makes, and hoping to overtake the emperor by pursuing a straight line across the country, he rode towards Frohburg, accompanied by the author and two Cossacks.

In the course of our ride, we came to a river; this was the Pleisse, and as it appeared fordable one of the Cossacks entered the water, but immediately sank out of his depth, and was in some danger of being drowned. A more favourable place having been discovered by the other Cossack, we crossed without much difficulty, and, after a ride of about thirty English miles on the same horses that had carried us upwards of twenty hours the preceding day, we arrived at Penig.

In a few minutes the Emperor Alexander, who had gone round by Altenberg in his carriage, drove up to the door of his quarters, and expressed no small surprise at seeing us at Penig before himself. His baggage was there, and a dinner was hastily prepared for him, which he invited us to share: this was not an offer to be declined by persons who were nearly exhausted, having tasted nothing but a cup of coffee and some bread for upwards of thirty-six hours, since we left Borna, on the night before the battle.

Accordingly, we sat down, a party of four, General Ballocheff being the fourth; and, notwithstanding his recent failure, the emperor was most agreeable and lively in his conversation. He entered more seriously into the events of the previous day, and alluded particularly to a suggestion made in the field by Lord Cathcart, who had proposed, with the Russian reserve cavalry under Winzingerode, to attempt an attack, in which he offered to act as guide against the enemy's right wing towards Weissenfels early in the day, when there was reason to think the French could not yet be in force or in position. Before making this suggestion, Lord Cathcart had gone forward to obtain a commanding view; so far as we were able to observe, the ground was favourable, and at that early period of the day, excepting ill-supported artillery, there was nothing formed in first line on the enemy's right that could have resisted so formidable an onslaught of cavalry, an arm in which the enemy were known to be much inferior.

The emperor explained that his objection had arisen from reluctance to engage that valuable body of heavy cavalry so early in the campaign; and though the attack could not have failed to produce important results at that time, he thought it might have been attended with severe losses that could not easily have been repaired. It is certain that, from the great superiority of the enemy in point of numbers, and from the manner in which their supports were gradually coming up, no decisive advantage could have been gained that day by any exertion on the part of the Allies; partial success would only have retarded their decision to effect a retreat, which must ultimately have been unavoidable; yet in arriving at that decision, a few hours lost by the Allies, and gained, as they would have been, by Napoleon, must have entailed irretrievable disasters on the combined army. After dinner the emperor proceeded to Dresden, and for that night we occupied his former quarters, where Lord Cathcart wrote his despatches to the British Government.

On the 7th the Prussians crossed the Elbe at Meissen; the Russians passed the river in two columns, one through Dresden, and one over a temporary bridge constructed about two miles higher up the river, and protected by *a tête-de-pont*.

Napoleon's headquarters were at Nossen; Marshal Ney was marching upon Torgau; Lauriston upon Meissen; and the remaining French columns were directed upon Dresden.

Sufficient examples have arisen to prove, to the satisfaction of all military men, that though a large river is, without doubt, an important strategic feature in other respects, yet in modern warfare it is not to be relied upon as an obstacle that presents any serious difficulty in the way of a large advancing army; for the leader of such an army can always out-manoeuvre his opponent by concealing his movements from those on the opposite bank, while the intervention of the river is sufficient to frustrate the enemy's means of watching by patrols, and a few hours gained, at a suitable point, will suffice to repair an old bridge or construct a new one, even in the presence of any hostile detachment likely to be on the spot.

The sovereigns, therefore, did not intend to dispute the passage of the Elbe in force; but, after destroying the bridges, and leaving light rear guards to render the passage as difficult as possible to the enemy, determined to fall back to a position suited to the strength of the Allied Army, in which to make a stand and give battle.

The neighbourhood of Bautzen is a "*point stratégique*," which appeared favourable for the purpose of covering Silesia; the surrounding country, well known in the Seven Years' War, offered a choice of good positions that rested their left upon the Bohemian frontier, which in this part is strongly marked by the Reisen Geberge, or Giants' Mountains; this is a ridge of hills covered by an impenetrable forest, and rising boldly out of a very fertile country, well cultivated and comparatively level, though by no means tame in its military features, being worn into ravines by the mountain streams, which do not lose their force till they reach the plain.

This frontier afforded a very efficient "*appui*," not from its natural strength alone, but from political circumstances that arose from the indecision of the court of Vienna, and produced a virtual neutrality which neither of the belligerent parties could venture to disregard. The position at Bautzen also covered the main communication of the Russians. It was expected that Barclay de Tolly would arrive there with some reinforcements that would repair the losses sustained by the Allies at Lützen, and he was to assume the chief command, as senior officer.

The Allies, having crossed the Elbe by the morning of the 8th of May without hurry and without receiving any molestation from their opponents, abandoned the Old Town of Dresden, which is the principal part of the city. The centre arch of the bridge had been blown up by the French on their retreat after the Russian disaster, and afterwards repaired for the passage of the Allied Army on their advance; these temporary repairs of the broken arch were now again destroyed, and the military wooden bridge above the town was burnt. The New Town and the banks of the river were occupied by some Prussian and Russian light infantry. The King of Prussia remained in the New Town, and Napoleon took up his quarters in the palace in the Old Town. The Emperor of Russia's headquarters were at Pulsnitz in the rear.

Ney's corps had marched upon Torgau, where he crossed the Elbe, and being joined by Victor and Sebastian from Magdeburg, their united forces were now on the right bank of the river.

At the distance of a few miles below Dresden, at Prossnitz, Napoleon had, it is said, in person selected a spot favourable for the construction of a bridge, where resistance was to be expected from the hostile army. It was the apex of a loop formed by the winding of the river, and a cross-fire could be established there, so that no enemy could approach to molest the workmen. He gave directions for the restoration of the pontoons above the town, and also caused the breach in the stone bridge at Dresden to be repaired; thus, the French Army effected the passage of the Elbe at three points with little difficulty on the 11th and 12th of May.

In the immediate vicinity of Dresden, on the Lusatian side, the country is very woody, and must be penetrated with caution by an advancing army. It becomes more open near Bischofswerda, and presents some good rear-guard positions which were occupied and disputed by Miloradovitch with about 10,000 Russians, while the Allied columns were concentrating at Bautzen.

CHAPTER 3

Battle of Bautzen

On the 12th of May, 1813, the Imperial and Royal Headquarters were at the town of Bautzen, and General Wittgenstein, who had been occupied in reconnoitring the available positions, then made his report to the Allied sovereigns. That night they contemplated a position with the left wing occupying Bautzen and the ridge on the right bank of the River Spree above that town; the extreme left resting upon the woody mountains which form the frontier of Bohemia; the right wing thrown a little forward, would have prolonged the line across the Hoyerswerda road, and occupied the high but open ground on the left bank of the Spree below Bautzen; thus the line would have been intersected diagonally by the river.

It is probable that this idea was the result of a determination on the part of the Allied sovereigns to avail themselves, if possible, on this occasion, of their superiority in cavalry. Whilst the left wing would have been strongly posted in a defensive position that required comparatively few troops for its occupation, the right wing might have been in full force, and would have been well posted for offensive operations; the country immediately in front being open and well adapted for the action of cavalry.

Yet the enemy's total disposable force at this time in the field amounted to at least 140,000 men, without including the corps of Victor and Davoust that were left behind on the Elbe, while the Allies, with all reinforcements, could not count more than 80,000; and from the nature of the country through which the French columns were advancing, Napoleon with the exercise of common caution could not be molested or compelled to commit a part of his army in a general action until it suited him, or until its concentration should be complete; any attempt, therefore, under the circumstances of that moment, at offensive operations on the part of the Allies, could only be attended with waste of strength, and even if successful could not have materially aided their cause.

A defensive position entirely on the right bank of the Spree, with Bautzen in the centre, was objectionable, since, from the course the river takes below the town, the right wing must have been thrown far back. Bautzen is surrounded by an old wall, and favoured by the steep bank of the Spree, yet it is a bad post, being much commanded, and it would have been a very salient point in the centre of the line, not easily supported, though it must have been the key of the position.

The sovereigns therefore resolved to occupy a parallel position about two miles farther to the rear than the line of the Spree, extending along rising grounds, having the left in the woody Bohemian mountains, the right secured by some villages, ponds, and enclosures, and the front covered by a swampy rivulet or brook, with willows on its banks, and occasional embankments, which were good holding ground for light infantry. Though the course of this brook is tortuous, yet it is more or less parallel to the Spree at a distance of about two English miles from the river, until at length it bends away near the right of the Allied position; the stream is only passable for cavalry at certain bridges or fords which were duly guarded, and all cottages and villages on its banks were occupied. From the base of the Bohemian mountains above Weissig on the left, to Preititz on the right, the whole extent might be about four English miles.

Of course, a position so extended could not be occupied fully and in force along its entire front by the Allied Army, which on paper did not count above 80,000 combatants of all arms, and probably had little more in fact than 70,000 effective men on the day of battle. The modern continental method of occupying these extended positions is sufficiently explained in the introductory notice on the system of tactics adopted in these campaigns, to render minute detail here superfluous; it will be sufficient to describe the general disposition of the corps, till we come to the day of battle.

The several Allied columns assembled and formed their bivouacs in rear of such parts of the intended position as were indicated to them by the proper staff officers, the Prussians on the right and the Russians on the left. The reserve cavalry, which assembled in rear of the centre, was to have been placed under the command of General Blücher, who was expected to make brilliant use of it, if an opportunity could be found, and it was the only arm in which the Allies were superior to the enemy. Some field-works were commenced, and an

BATTLE OF BAUTZEN

old square redoubt, on a commanding hill towards the left, which had been originally constructed in the Seven Years' War, was repaired and adapted to the new position.

On the 13th of May, the Emperor Alexander took up his quarters in a gentleman's house at Würschen, a little removed from the road to Görlitz, in rear of the centre of the position. The King of Prussia occupied the farmhouse on the road near it, and Lord Cathcart had for his quarters the small schoolhouse on the opposite side of the road.

After an obstinate affair with the French advanced guard, commanded by Marshal Macdonald, at Bischofswerda, during which that town was burnt down, Miloradovitch, whose corps still acted as rearguard, retired to Bautzen, and occupied the town and the high ground on our left of it, on the right bank of the Spree. At the same time Kleist (whose division had been frequently engaged), bringing up the rear of the Prussian columns, crossed the Spree and occupied some high ground on the right of Bautzen.

A well-connected chain of videttes posted along the line of the Spree, and supplied by picquets which were stationed on the left bank, now covered the whole of the right wing and centre; to these the light cavalry of the enemy's advanced guard opposed a similar chain; and these two lines of videttes in presence, three or four miles in extent, in a large proportion composed of lancers, had a very remarkable and picturesque appearance. Relying upon the vigilance of these advanced posts, the other corps of the Allied Army, already in position, remained seven or eight days in their respective bivouacs in a state of the most complete repose, well provisioned, and enjoying the most beautiful summer weather.

Until his arrival at Dresden, it would appear that Napoleon had not expected that the Allies would attempt to make a stand before they could rally upon the Oder. His combinations appear to have had the occupation of Prussia in the first instance more in view than the active pursuit of the Allied Army through Lusatia and Silesia; with that intention he had sent off large detachments to his left, and the 2nd, 3rd, 5th, and 7th French corps had been directed upon Berlin; but as soon as he was convinced of the determination of the Allies to offer battle in the position at Bautzen, he gave a new direction to the 3rd, 5th, and 7th corps, united under the command of Marshal Ney, that they might be brought to bear immediately upon the right of the position occupied by the Allies. He concentrated all the remaining columns on Bautzen, with the exception only of the 2nd corps, com-

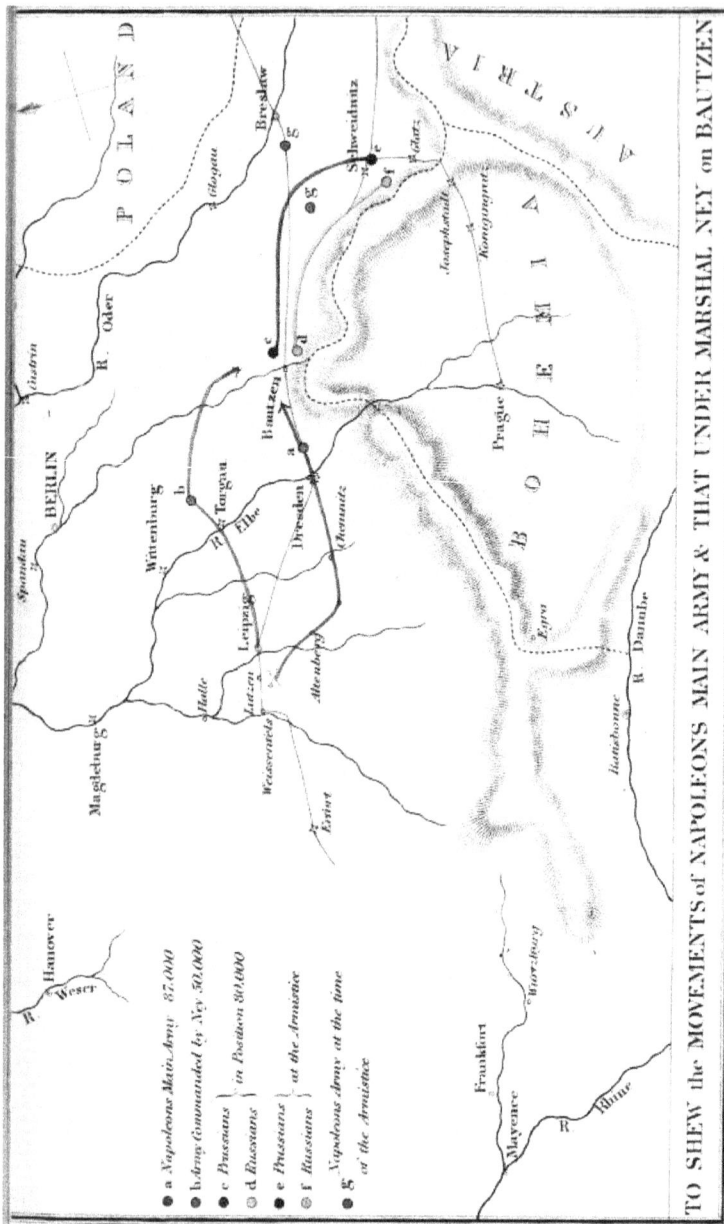

TO SHEW the MOVEMENTS of NAPOLEONS MAIN ARMY & THAT UNDER MARSHAL NEY on BAUTZEN

AUSTRIA

POLAND

BOHEMIA

BERLIN

Spandau
Custrin
R. Oder
Glogau
Breslaw
Schweidnitz
Gldatz
Josephstadt
Konigingratz
Prague
Magdeburg
Wittenberg
Torgau
R. Elbe
Bautzen
Dresden
Chemnitz
Eger
Ratisbonne
Danube
Halle
Leipsig
Lutzen
Weissenfels
Altenberg
Erfurt
Wurtzberg
Hanover
R. Weser
Frankfort
Mayence
R. Rhine

a Napoleons Main Army   82,000
b Army Commanded by Ney 50,000
c Prussians ⎫
d Russians ⎬ in Position 80,000
e Prussians ⎫
f Russians ⎬ at the Armistice
g Napoleons Army at the time
     of the Armistice

manded by Victor at Magdeburg, and of Davoust, who took the chief command on the Lower Elbe, and he delayed his attack to give time for this combination to be accomplished.

Some intelligence of this flank movement of Marshal Ney's corps having been received by the Allies, General Barclay de Tolly, who had lately arrived with a reinforcement of about 15,000 men, composed chiefly of the blockading corps at Thorn, which the surrender of that fortress had released, was detached by the order of the Emperor of Russia, with his corps and that of General Kleist, to feel for Marshal Ney's columns, to engage them in detail, to delay them, and with a sort of roving commission to take advantage of any favourable opportunity that might offer. This may have been done partly for the sake of giving Barclay and his corps something to do, as, although senior to Wittgenstein, it had been settled that he was not to take the command of the Allied Army till after the battle.

Accordingly, he made a night march on the 18th in two columns, fell in with a French division next morning near Königswartha, which had been detached for the purpose of communicating with the corps of Ney, defeated it, and brought back to the Allied position that night six pieces of the enemy's cannon and 1,000 prisoners, among whom were three general officers. General d'York was also detached, and fell in with a French force sent out from their main army to communicate with Ney; after a desultory engagement near Weissig, which he prolonged till nightfall, he retired again into the Allied position.

Napoleon himself quitted Dresden on the 18th, and arrived before Bautzen on the morning of the 19th; it appears that he employed the day in reconnoitring and making his dispositions for the attack.

The distribution and relative circumstances of the two armies in bivouac on the night before the first battle, were these:—

In the Allied Army, General Wittgenstein was to retain ostensibly the chief command during the battle, although he was junior to General Barclay de Tolly; ostensibly, because the Emperor Alexander in fact assumed the supreme direction of affairs. At first it was intended that General Blücher should command the united cavalry for the day; but the nature of the country, bounded by the river, intersected by the brook, and otherwise full of obstacles, being unfavourable to the free employment of that arm, the arrangement was altered, and he was entrusted with the chief command of the several corps of the Prussian Army forming the right wing of the Allies.

Barclay de Tolly being senior to both, was to act independently

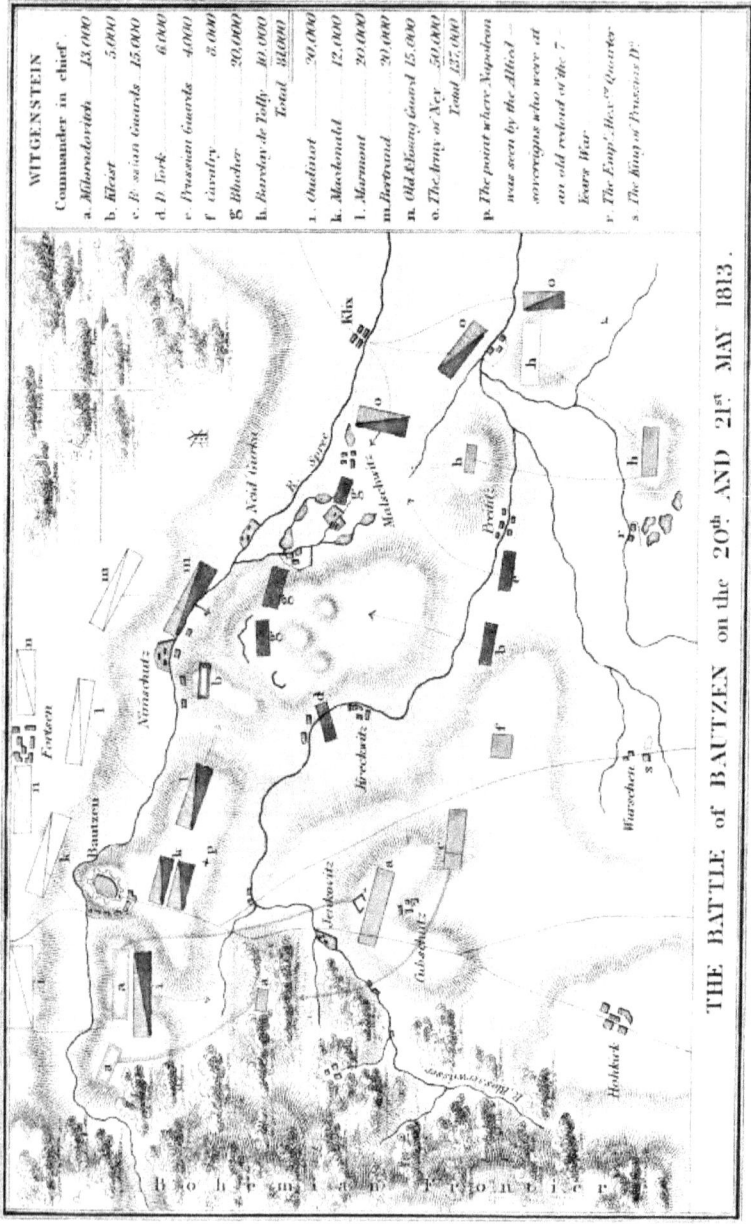

WITGENSTEIN
Commander in chief

a. Miloradovitch — 13,000
b. Kleist — 5,000
c. Russian Guards — 15,000
d. D'York — 6,000
e. Prussian Guards — 4,000
f. Cavalry — 8,000
g. Blucher — 20,000
h. Barclay de Tolly — 10,000
Total 81,000

i. Oudinot — 20,000
k. Macdonald — 12,000
l. Marmont — 20,000
m. Bertrand — 20,000
n. Old & Young Guard — 15,000
o. The Army of Ney — 50,000
Total 137,000

p. The point where Napoleon
   was seen by the Allied
   sovereigns who were at
   an old redout in the 7
   Years War
r. The Emp.rs Head Quarter
s. The King of Prussia's D.o

THE BATTLE of BAUTZEN on the 20th AND 21st MAY 1813.

with his corps, and employ it as a "*colonne mobile*" according to cir-cumstances, for the security of the extreme right, which it was always expected the enemy would attempt to turn. Whether he declined the chief command, because Wittgenstein had made all arrangements be-fore he arrived, or whether the emperor so ruled it, is of little conse-quence; but never did general perform more active, able, and zealous service, so far as his small means would allow, in aid of the army in position whilst they could maintain their ground, or in covering the retreat when they were obliged to abandon the field.

The distribution of the several Allied corps was as follows:—

Miloradovitch with the corps, formerly that of Wittgenstein, 13,000 men, still occupied Bautzen and the high ground to the left of the town, with the river in his front; but after rendering the passage of the Spree as difficult and destructive to the enemy as he could, it was intended that he should fall back to his place on the left of the general position, with his right near the great road to Görlitz, occu-pying the high ground behind Klein Jenkowitz, and his left crossing the ravine formed by the stream of the Blösaer-Wasser, and extending to the woody mountains. Prince Eugene of Würtemberg's division, consisting of 3,000 men, was detached into the woody hills to cover the left flank.

The left wing of the Allied Army being now under the command of Miloradovitch, since Wittgenstein had been invested with the chief command, the Russian guards and grenadiers to the number of 15,000, were placed in second line, or reserve, near Kubshütz, in rear of that wing. This position of the left wing was strong in itself, and from the nature of the ground, being thrown forward and forming an angle with the centre of the Allied position, it effectually protected the centre so long as it could be maintained.

Kleist being still in advance with 5,000 men, occupied some strong high ground on the right bank of the Spree, about a mile and a half below Bautzen, and with a numerous artillery well posted behind field-works, was directed to dispute the passage of the river as long as possible. If forced, he was then to retire into the main position, where his place might be designated as the right centre.

General Blücher's own corps, consisting of 20,000 men, occupied the small hills to the right of Krekwitz and constituted the right wing, which, from the nature of the ground, was also thrown forward. His right flank was secured by some swampy fields and ponds, as well as by the villages of Pliskowitz and Malschwitz, which he occupied with a detached brigade under General Tschaplitz.

The centre, like a curtain between two bastions, was much retired, and therefore required to be but slightly occupied in proportion to its extent, which might be about two English miles. The corps of D'York, amounting to 6,000 men, was appointed for that duty, and occupying the passes of the brook and swampy ground in his front with light infantry, the rest of his corps remained on the rising ground, to support the two wings and maintain the connection between them.

The whole reserve cavalry of 8,000 men were assembled in rear of the centre; but the intervention of the brook and its unfavourable banks rendered that arm of little service.

The Prussian guards, 4,000 men, were in reserve in rear of the right wing.

Barclay de Tolly, with his independent command of about 10,000 men, having thrown out detachments to impede the advance of Marshal Ney, occupied, in the first instance, with his main body, a position near Glein, beyond the extreme right and in echelon to it. He stationed the division of General Langeron in front of Preititz, to preserve his connection with General Blücher's right, and advanced other detachments to watch for the approach of Marshal Ney.

The distribution and force of the French Army, on the night before the battle, were as follows:—

Oudinot with the 12th corps of 20,000 men was on their extreme right, and stationed on the bank of the Spree, above Bautzen, opposite to Miloradovitch. Next stood Macdonald on his left, with the 11th corps of 12,000 men, in front of Bautzen. Then, to their left, was Marmont, with the 6th corps of 20,000 men, extending nearly to Nimschütz; and to Marmont's left was Bertrand with the 4th corps of 20,000 men opposed to Kleist.

Napoleon's headquarters on that night were at Förstgen, in rear of the centre, surrounded by the Old and Young Imperial Guards, amounting to 15,000 men. Macdonald had the chief command of the 11th and 12th corps, which composed the right wing, and which, as we have computed, amounted together of 32,000 men. Soult commanded in chief the other corps above enumerated, which constituted the centre of the Grand Army; his force, including the guards in reserve, consisted of 55,000 men. Ney had the chief command of the three corps destined to form the left wing, but they had arrived only that evening at the following stations:—

Lauriston, with 10,000 men, was the most advanced in position, near Weissig, having been engaged with D'York.

Ney, with his own corps of 30,000 men, was at Maukersdorf.

Regnier, with 10,000 men, was about a league farther to the rear, having passed with his whole corps through Hoyerswerda.

Ney's headquarters and the centre of his command were that night at Maukersdorf, about fifteen English miles from the extreme right of the Allied position, and about the same distance from the left centre of the French Grand Army, which extended to the Windmühlenberg, immediately opposite our extreme right. The left wing of the French Army, amounting to 50,000 men, could not, therefore, be brought into action till too late to take part in a battle on the next day; but Napoleon sent orders to Ney to hasten its march upon the village of Klix, where he was to cross the Spree, and his whole force would then out-flank the right of the Allies, and would proceed to envelope and take them in reverse, if they should continue to hold their ground on the 21st of May.

The right and centre of the French Army, actually in presence on the night of the 19th, occupied a line of bivouacs alone equal in extent to the front of the Allied position. At the very lowest computation their numbers amounted to 87,000 men, and this exclusive of the left wing under Ney.

The total Allied force, including Cossacks, has never been estimated to exceed 80,000 men, at the highest computation; Napoleon, therefore, risked nothing when resolving to commence the attack on the following morning, the 20th of May, without waiting for the approach of Marshal Ney, and it is probable that he may have been led to this decision by a desire to prevent the possible escape of an enemy whom he may, while considering the disparity of numbers, have viewed without presumption as an easy prey almost within his grasp.

The round numbers above are carefully computed, with every allowance for the well-known difference which is ever found to exist between the men on paper and the men under arms on the day of battle. Still, if they are overrated as to the actual combatants on either side, they are equally so on both, and, therefore, the relative strength of the contending armies remains the same.

The author both here and throughout this work, has preferred the use of round numbers to the affectation of greater precision, supposed to arise from the adoption of any particular set of returns, because the truth cannot be known with exactness from that source; but they are not given at random, for he has compared them with all the most authentic estimates set forth in such means of information as he has been able to examine, and adopts them as the nearest approximation to the truth he can arrive at.

Having thus detailed the position, comparative force, and relative circumstances of the hostile armies on the 19th, the events of the two following days are easily explained.

More than a week we had been in daily expectation of a battle, sleeping in our clothes and with our horses saddled. All baggage of every description had been sent a day's march to the rear. The Emperor Alexander and the King of Prussia, with their personal staff, made daily visits to the outposts, and rode frequently over the position.

The information as to the movements of the enemy was very imperfect; in this respect the *"état major"* of the Allied Army was by no means so well organised as it ought to have been, or as it afterwards became later in the campaign.

On the 20th of May Wittgenstein intended to make a reconnaissance in force; but as some movements in the enemy's bivouac appeared to indicate a similar intention on their part, he relinquished his design. Neither the strength nor exact position of the hostile force immediately in presence was accurately known, though the attitude and circumstances of the three corps composing the left wing under Marshal Ney had been clearly ascertained from the reconnaissance made by Barclay de Tolly, and from the prisoners taken by him. It was, therefore, expected that Napoleon was about to attempt only a reconnaissance, and that a general action would not take place till the next day, when the left wing of the French Army might be able to take part in the contest.

About noon a cannonade was heard, and on hastening to the field we found that the enemy was pushing down heavy columns to attack the town of Bautzen and the corps of Miloradovitch and at the same time that of Kleist. Each of these movements was supported by heavy batteries of artillery.

These demonstrations of course foreboded a forced passage of the Spree, which, though not a large river, is, as far as the author recollects, not easily fordable in many places, after it enters the plains of Lusatia, although at this time the dry weather had reduced it to its smallest dimensions.

Napoleon, as it appears, stationed himself on the commanding eminence on which a windmill stands, to the right of the road leading to Bautzen, and directed that whilst Marshal Macdonald commenced his attack on Miloradovitch and the town of Bautzen, Oudinot should pass the Spree and turn his left flank, while Marmont should force a passage about a mile below Bautzen, and thus place himself between the corps of Kleist and that of Miloradovitch; while Bertrand with the 4th corps should attempt to cross the river in presence of Kleist.

The old stone bridge at Bautzen had not been destroyed; but being well flanked and commanded, it was vigorously defended.

After repeated attacks and great sacrifice of lives Marshal Macdonald was unable to gain it till late in the evening. Oudinot had no less difficulty, but ultimately succeeded in forcing a passage higher up, and established his pontoons under cover of a very heavy *tiraillade* and cannonade, in presence of the Russian division of General Emanuel, who occupied the left of the advanced position held by Miloradovitch. Marmont met with less difficulty, there being no troops immediately in front of the central point at which he crossed; he was molested only by the well served, fire of a Russian light battery, supported by some cavalry.

As soon as the division of General Campan, which was a part of Marmont's corps, had crossed the Spree, the French commenced the assault of Bautzen, on the weak side of the town, and about six in the evening the enemy succeeded in obtaining possession of it.

No sooner had Oudinot effected the passage of the river, than he commenced a vigorous attack with extended infantry on the Russian light battalions, posted in the woody hills on the extreme left of Miloradovitch, as if with a determination to dislodge them. As the French appeared to be gaining ground, Miloradovitch having been thus forced, in conformity with his instructions withdrew the troops, and fell back into his place in the main position, leaving General Emanuel to cover his retreat. To arrest Marshal Oudinot's further progress on the left flank, Miloradovitch also detached a reinforcement to the light troops stationed in the woody hills to his left. These movements were executed about sunset, without hurry or inconvenience.

The attack made upon General Kleist by Bertrand, with the 4th French corps was less successful. Having been foiled in all his attempts, he was unable to effect the passage of the river in presence; and although the bridge at Nieder Gurka had not, I believe, been destroyed, even there the enemy found it impossible to pass the river, and deploy in face of the well posted Prussian batteries, and the *tirailleurs* of General Ziethen's brigade. Marmont, however, who had by this time passed nearly the whole of his corps, by means of his pontoons, to the right bank of the river, immediately below Bautzen, and had gained possession of the town, detached the division of Bonnet about eight o'clock in the evening to his left, to take Kleist in flank, who was thus obliged to retire at nightfall into his place in position, according to the preconcerted disposition that has been already detailed.

On that night Napoleon was said to have slept in his tent, which was pitched in front of Bautzen, and in the centre of the corps of Oudinot. The French Army continued to pass the Spree at or near Bautzen, and to establish themselves on the right bank—a dangerous operation if the Allies had been in force sufficient and in sufficient heart to attempt a vigorous general attack at daybreak upon an enemy not yet formed, and posted disadvantageously with a river in their rear. But under existing circumstances such an attempt would almost have amounted to an act of desperation.

The Emperor Alexander and the King of Prussia, accompanied by Lord Cathcart and their suite, returned to their former quarters in rear of the centre; and the Allied Army lay that night under arms, on the ground they were to occupy in their defensive position on the following day.

The King of Prussia was accompanied in all these campaigns by his sons, Prince William and Prince Charles, and by his nephew, Prince Frederick of Holland.

The prince royal was already of an age to be entrusted with a command, and was therefore less frequently present at the royal head-quarters.

CHAPTER 4

Battle of Bautzen—Second Day

It was a fine summer morning on the 21st of May; all was still, and even the sound of an occasional musket-shot, discharged along the distant line of advanced sentries, was scarcely to be heard. At daybreak we were in the field, and the Emperor of Russia and King of Prussia were already on a height in front of the centre.

However, the enemy were in motion, and appeared to be assembling, in force, on the rising ground immediately in front of Bautzen, menacing our left, or centre. Napoleon himself was very distinctly to be seen, accompanied by his staff, and apparently superintending the assembly of his troops. Whilst his preparations were in progress, he dismounted and walked about with his hands behind his back in conversation with officers of his suite. All our glasses were directed towards him; and one, belonging to Lord Cathcart, which proved to be the best there, was in great request, and was employed, on this occasion, by the Emperor Alexander and the King of Prussia.

Although the two hostile staffs were not out of the range of each other's artillery, and though Napoleon himself was quite within the reach of the Russian batteries, the Allies were too courteous to disturb his meditations by a shot. Berthier and others were recognised, but one person in the group with whom Napoleon seemed to have much conversation, and while discoursing with whom he frequently consulted his map, puzzled the Allied headquarters very much; he was in a bright yellow uniform, and after various conjectures it was agreed that it could be no other than Murat, who delighted in dress, and was occasionally to be seen in all sorts of costumes.

This was important, if the belief were well founded; because the presence of Murat argued, that the Italian levies were in a state of forwardness; besides that, the personal exertions to be expected from his well-known activity and skill as a cavalry officer, would require increased vigilance on our side. This belief was entertained till much later in the day, when it was ascertained from prisoners or deserters, that the man in yellow was no other than a Saxon postillion employed as a guide, of whom Napoleon was asking the names of the different villages.

During this period of suspense, a large body of troops, apparently upwards of ten thousand men assembled, "*en masse*," on the "plateau" in front of Bautzen, and appeared to form one hollow square. The author has since heard it said, that this was the corps of Oudinot getting under arms, which Napoleon had caused to bivouac in that order, and in the centre of which he had passed the night. The square when formed, not only appeared to move by the front face, but by the angle. Whether this was to give an idea of the discipline of his army, whether he expected some great cavalry movement on the part of the Allies, or whether he wished to attract attention to this part of the field, while the more important movements of his left wing were in progress, could not be known; possibly he may have had any or all of these objects in view.

Attention was now drawn to a more serious affair which had commenced in the woody hills to our left, where Oudinot had pushed forward numerous light battalions, well supported and under cover of a heavy cannonade. In various points also along the whole line, a cannonade had commenced, of which the emperor and the king received their full benefit, though with little apparent concern, wherever they presented themselves. On the left, the hills were maintained with great obstinacy during the whole day, by a part of Miloradovitch's command, and it even became necessary to send some battalions of the corps of grenadiers to their support.

A gallant attack was made at this time by three battalions of the Pavlofsky regiment, who were then grenadiers, but have since been made guards. They were led forward in line through the broken ground and coppice wood *à pas de charge*, preserving their line and formation with as much regularity as such ground would permit, and arrived in sufficiently close and good order to enable them to drive all before them, with considerable loss to the enemy. But their own subsequent loss was far more severe when extended as light infantry in the wood and maintaining the ground they had gained, their conspicuous brass grenadier-caps rendering them ill adapted for that particular duty. However, during the whole day they maintained their ground, until the final retreat was ordered, and were then obliged to leave behind them in the wood a very large proportion of killed and wounded to the mercy of the enemy.

But these operations against the left wing of the Allies can only be considered as false attacks or feints to gain time, to divert attention and prevent the detachment of large supports from the left to the right wing, the point upon which a grand and overwhelming operation of the enemy was in progress, an operation which the arrival of Marshal Ney's corps could not fail to render decisive.

In the early part of the day Napoleon did not press the attack on Marshal Blücher's corps in his front, with much vigour: it remained strongly posted in the heights above Krekwitz and in the villages, apparently, with a firm resolution to defend them to the last; but the cannonade on both sides was unremitting.

The three corps constituting the French left wing under Marshal Ney had, however, begun to cross the Spree at Klix, and were working their way round the extreme right of the Allies with slow, but irresistible progress. Barclay de Tolly, disputing the ground and checking their advance as efficiently as his small numbers rendered possible, was at length obliged to occupy a strong post, retired and in echelon, to the right, and this attitude had the good effect of compelling Ney to detach a large part of his force, to show front towards him and cover his own movement.

As soon as Ney had sufficiently accomplished his flank movement round the right, which was not till about ten o'clock in the morning, and then only with the heads of straggling columns, he moved forward to attack the villages of Malschwitz and Preititz, in the hope of taking the Allied right wing in reverse. At the same time Napoleon caused the fourth French corps, composed chiefly of Germans, to attack it in front, and moved Marmont's corps to its left upon Basankwitz, to bear upon Blücher's left. A part of the troops which had assembled in front of Bautzen were also seen taking ground to their left, to support this formidable attack.

Ney gained possession of Preititz about eleven o'clock in the morning, and at that time the right wing of the Allied Army was nearly enveloped on all sides by the enemy. The Prussians, however, under their resolute and skilful general, were not to be disheartened. The repeated attacks of the enemy's fourth corps were repulsed, and the numerous well-posted and well-protected Prussian batteries continued to deal destruction among the French columns.

In this precarious situation it became of the utmost necessity to dislodge and repulse Marshal Ney from Preititz. The corps of Kleist and a brigade from General Blücher's corps were sent to support General Langeron's division in this quarter, and Barclay de Tolly, with the remainder of his corps, made a simultaneous movement against the corps of Ney. After much hard fighting, Kleist recovered possession of the village of Preititz. Marshal Ney was obliged to abandon his attack for a time, and fall back to concentrate his corps in a defensive attitude, to show front to Barclay de Tolly and gain time for his troops to assemble.

This success gave momentary hopes to the Allies, and some reinforcements were sent to General Blücher. Nevertheless, it was soon evident that this retrograde movement of Marshal Ney, however involuntary on his part, could only in the end verify the proverb, "*reculer pour mieux sauter;*" especially when the great superiority of his force was considered, which amounted to nearly 50,000 men, and had now ample time to assemble. The Allies were not in a condition to assume the offensive against an enemy who had an advantage in numbers of nearly two to one, and whose principal columns were now concentrated towards a focus, and brought to bear simultaneously on the corps of General Blücher in his salient and exposed position, with six hours of daylight still remaining.

A retreat in good order was evidently the most favourable result the Allied Army could expect. To prolong the affair would only have occasioned an increased loss on both sides in killed and wounded, which the enemy could afford better than the Allies; and enough had been done to show that the determination of the Allied sovereigns remained unchanged, to persevere in the great struggle in which they were engaged. These considerations induced the Emperor Alexander and the King of Prussia, at about three in the afternoon, very reluctantly to sanction the order for a general retreat, with an army neither disheartened nor disorganised, but though somewhat diminished in numbers, still prepared to dispute another position with equal resolution.

It was fortunate that they came to this decision in good time, or it would have been too late for General Blücher to extricate his corps from its perilous situation. As it was, he manifested a little too much reluctance in obeying the order to commence his retrograde movement, and his troops suffered severely in consequence.

As this probable result had been anticipated, all dispositions for the general retreat of the army had been duly prepared, and the ground for the night fixed for each corps and division. All the rearguard posts that were capable of being disputed, had been well considered; and good discipline and a superiority in cavalry, through a country generally favourable to that arm, secured a safe and orderly retreat, which was made in two columns, the left wing, by Hochkirch, on Löbau, and the right, by Weissenberg, on Reichenbach. Barclay de Tolly and Kleist took up a position near Cunnewitz, to enable General Blücher to disengage himself; and if he had delayed his retreat half an hour longer, it may be doubted whether his post could have been maintained against Marshal Ney; if lost, the right wing of the Allies would have been infallibly cut off.

The *tirailleurs* of Ney were now again gaining ground in all quarters round our right, like the influx of a tide; and Barclay de Tolly and Kleist had no longer power to check their progress. The French *tirailleurs* had gained possession of the ground and enclosures about the house which had been the Emperor Alexander's headquarters, near Würschen, about two miles in rear of the centre of the original position, just as Blücher, retiring in echelon from the right, had succeeded in completely disengaging his corps. He had united several batteries of light artillery, which were supported by all his cavalry, including the Prussian cavalry of reserve, and so effectually kept the enemy at bay, that Ney was obliged to have recourse to a similar disposition, and assembled a battery of sixty guns to oppose to him.

The Prussian infantry retreated, in the meanwhile, in perfect order, molested only by a distant cannonade. To check the rapid advance of the French in his rear, and to collect his own forces, General Blücher made a stand on the commanding ground near Belgern, and then moved off, by Weissenberg, on Reichenbach, according to the route assigned to the right column. Barclay de Tolly retired in the same direction, and Kleist was left, with a large proportion of cavalry and light artillery, to form the rear-guard and cover the retreat.

The main body of the French Army halted on the ground previously occupied by the Allies. Marshal Ney took possession of Würschen immediately after Blücher had retired, but did not press the rear-guard under General Kleist any farther that evening.

Napoleon did not follow the rear guard of Miloradovitch beyond Hochkirch, and on that evening his tent was pitched near the inn at Klein Burschwitz, in advance of the right wing of his army, on the road by which our left column had retired, and there he passed the night surrounded by his guards.

The Emperor of Russia rode by Hochkirch towards the rear, and went on to Görlitz. Lord Cathcart slept at a farmhouse on the hill in front of Reichenbach, which had been his quarters on the former occasion.

CHAPTER 5

Termination of the Campaign by an Armistice

The routes of the two retiring columns of the Allied Army converged on Reichenbach, and the commanding ground in rear of that defile was occupied by the Allies with purpose of resistance, and therefore more in force than an ordinary rear-guard post.

The columns of the enemy were in motion before daybreak on the 22nd of May. About noon their cavalry and artillery commenced a most vigorous attempt to force the position of Reichenbach; but two Russian light battalions held the entrance of the defile; and a powerful Russian battery on the high ground, supported by a strong force of cavalry and well posted infantry, was not easily to be forced or turned, and continued in the meanwhile to deal destruction on every French column that presented itself. For a long time, the French attack was unsuccessful.

In the afternoon Napoleon arrived at the farmhouse which had been our quarters the preceding night, and which was situated on the bank opposite to the Allied position, and under a very heavy fire he continued thence to direct the attack. We were told that Marshal Duroc was killed at this time and place, but it appears that event happened later in the day, and nearer Görlitz. In one of the attacks a regiment of cavalry, consisting of the lancers of the Dutch guard in the French service, which had passed the village of Reichenbach, was cut off, and nearly every man and horse killed or taken. The French cavalry of the guard was engaged, and at length prevailed. The rear-guard of the Allies retired in good order upon Görlitz.

It would be tedious and unnecessary to detail the daily affairs of rear-guard which took place during the remainder of this campaign. They were of importance only in evincing the superior discipline and unbroken spirit of the Allied troops, in whose favour they generally terminated, and who, though retreating from almost all of them, carried off trophies and left none.

Lord Cathcart, after leaving Reichenbach on the morning of the 22nd of May, was obliged to ride to the rear to overtake his baggage, in order to write his despatches and send off a messenger.

Barclay de Tolly, as senior to Wittgenstein, had now assumed the chief command.

After quitting Görlitz the two columns again diverged a little; the right column, commanded by Blücher, retreating by Siegersdorf, Buntzlau, Haynau, and Liegnitz, on the great road to Breslau; and in fact, the main line of operations. He was followed closely by Ney, and, after an interval of a day's march, by the main French Army.

The left column of the Allies was composed of the Russians, the reserves, and headquarters. The baggage and incumbrances of all sorts, which had been kept well in the rear, preceded this column in its retreat, by Löbau, Löwenberg, Goldberg, Jauer, and Striegau, upon the well-known fortress of Schweidnitz, where also an entrenched position was in preparation, and the fortress had been put into a state of defence, as far as time had allowed. During this retreat, the most remarkable affair was one which took place at Haynau, between Marshal Ney and the rear-guard of the right column; it had been preconcerted by Blücher in person, and is one of the most brilliant cavalry affairs of modern days, since the improvement of firearms, and the use of the bayonet, have deprived that arm of much of the influence it possessed in times less removed from the age of chivalry in which it was paramount.

The Prussian general having passed his main column across the bridge and through the defile of Haynau, still defended the entrance to the village with the *tirailleurs* of his rear-guard; but finding that the nature of the ground in rear of Haynau favoured his purpose, he formed five regiments of cavalry in mass behind the village of Baudmansdorf, in a situation completely concealed from the enemy's view by the village and an intervening rising ground. This ambuscade was formed obliquely to the line of retreat of the main column, which traversed an unenclosed country, and to the southward of that line.

When all was arranged, the three regiments forming the rear-guard gave up the bridge at Haynau and retired, following the main column to a good rear-guard position on the direct road to Liegnitz, and a few miles from Haynau. Here they halted and showed front, inviting an attack.

As soon as Ney's advanced guard had passed the defile, entered the plain, and deployed to attack the Prussian infantry rear-guard, a preconcerted signal was given—the burning of a windmill. The Allied cavalry, masked till that moment, now deployed in two lines on the right of the enemy, and moved rapidly onwards to attack them in flank. The success of the cavalry was complete. The French lost 1,500 men and eleven guns. Ney himself, it is said, narrowly escaped. Colonel Dolf, who commanded the attack, was unfortunately killed. But the loss of the Allies did not amount to 100 men.

After passing through Liegnitz, Blücher quitted the Breslau road, and marched upon Schweidnitz, where the army was to assemble.

Napoleon appears to have imagined that the Allies were in full retreat upon Breslau, and that it was their intention to fall back by their regular military communication, and halt behind the Oder. He pushed on the corps of Ney through Wohlau to Breslau, which he occupied. But when he discovered that the Allies had moved to a flank, and were now concentrated and prepared to defend a strong entrenched camp, having its right near the fortress of Schweidnitz, and its left resting on the Bohemian mountains, circumstances were completely changed, and a new disposition became necessary. The Allied Army awaited the attack; and if Napoleon had struck the blow, the ulterior fortunes of Europe might have been reversed. The headquarters of the Allied sovereigns were for some days in Schweidnitz, but on the 28th were removed to Gröditz, a few miles in rear of the position.

Political events, however, now brought the campaign to a conclusion far more advantageous to the Allies than could have resulted from a victory on their side. On the 29th of May the Russian General Schowalof and the Prussian General Kleist were sent to the outposts with a flag of truce to meet General Caulincourt; the subject of the interview was an armistice, the overtures for which had been made by Napoleon. In the meantime a cessation of hostilities for thirty-six hours was mutually agreed to, and the necessary orders were immediately issued from the respective headquarters.

The essential particulars of this armistice were adjusted without much difficulty or delay on either side, in the names of the Prince de Neufchatel, as Vice-Constable of the French Armies, on the one side; and Barclay de Tolly on the other, as Commander-in-Chief of the Allies. They were as follow:—

A total cessation from hostilities until the 20th of July, and six days' notice to be given by either side before the rupture of the armistice. The lines of demarcation to extend from the Bohemian frontier to the Oder, as laid down in the Atlas, leaving an intervening neutral ground in which Breslau is included.

The Lower Elbe to be the line of demarcation between Davoust and Prussia, but Magdeburg and all other fortresses at that time in possession of the French to continue in their hands, with a small circumference of neutral ground around each. The troops to occupy their ground, according to the compact, by the 12th of June.

This armistice was ratified on the 4th of June. The armies went into cantonments. The headquarters of the Emperor of Russia and King of Prussia removed to the neighbourhood of a town called Reichenbach, where the former occupied the *château* of Peterswaldau; Napoleon went to Dresden.

CHAPTER 6

The Armistice

It would be foreign to the purpose of these military notes to enter further into diplomatic affairs, than is necessary to explain and connect the several campaigns to which they refer.

With regard to the armistice concluded in Silesia, on the 4th of June, 1813, two questions appear to be of importance:—

Why the campaign of Lützen and Bautzen was terminated by a suspension of hostilities at that particular juncture, and in the manner, we have seen?

Why the conferences at Prague which ensued, did not lead to a peace?

First, then, to account for Napoleon's forbearance in refraining from an attack upon the Allied Army, that had prepared to offer him battle in its defensive position at Schweidnitz, the author can only suppose it to have arisen from disinclination to hasten the decision of Austria, whose neutrality must have been brought at once to an end, if he had fought the army of the Allies, and forced it back upon the Austrian frontier under cover of Glatz; for this would evidently have been its only base, and with reference to apparent political circumstances it was an insulated base. He may well have supposed that the Allies would not have abandoned their regular line of operations, the direct road through Breslau to the Russian frontier, and as it were, have placed their backs to a wall, unless there already existed a secret understanding with Austria, that a door should be opened in it to receive them in case of defeat.

The Allies could not fail to derive strategic advantages from a new line of operations opened to them within the Bohemian frontier, besides an actual increase of force from an Austrian contingent, and this in addition to the moral effect which an Austrian declaration of war would have upon all the disjointed members of the old Germanic empire, whose spirit of nationality had not been extinguished by subjugation, and whose contingents were a large part of Napoleon's force These were strong inducements for him to pause before striking a blow which might have reversed the fortunes of Europe, if Providence had not stayed his hand, and may explain his preference for an armistice, which prolonged the hope of bribing or cajoling the Emperor Francis to persevere in his neutrality; a cautious, but, as it proved, mistaken policy.

As to the second question, why the conferences at Prague did not lead to a peace. To arrive at a distinct answer, we must glance at the policy and fortunes of Austria, since the Treaty of Alliance was concluded with Napoleon against Russia, on the 12th of March, 1812. By that treaty Austria was bound to supply Napoleon with an auxiliary force of 30,000 men, to co-operate as he should command. The abject condition of Austria, after the defeats at Austerlitz and Wagram, and the preponderance of French influence which she was unable to shake off, compelled her to submit to the conditions of this treaty.

The conduct of Prince Schwartzenberg, who commanded the stipulated contingent, and the care he took to keep his troops as inactive as possible, without losing all regard for appearances, show the reluctance of Austria to fulfil the terms of that treaty.

When Napoleon commenced his retreat, and when the failure of his expedition to Russia was apparent, a retrograde movement of the Austrian contingent suffered Tschichagof to disengage his army and remove it to the Berezina. No sooner were the disasters of the French irrecoverable, than the Austrian Army withdrew from the contest, as far as the necessity of avoiding a premature rupture with France would permit. The Emperor of Russia and the British government had already secretly received unequivocal assurances of the real sentiments of Austria; but towards Napoleon dissimulation was still considered necessary, and was practised with success while the treaty of 1812 nominally remained in full force.

There can be no doubt that Prince Metternich and Count Stadion were fully aware of the only true line of policy that their country ought to pursue; but although they possessed the confidence of the Emperor Francis in the highest degree, French influence had not yet lost its sway at Vienna. It was not till the happy moment, when the rapid advance of the Russian and Prussian Armies gave encouragement to the Austrian court, and before it was even contemplated that Napoleon could have reorganised the large force with which he was already in the field, that the war party in the council of Vienna gained the ascendancy, and induced the Emperor Francis to take arms against Napoleon, and join the Allies in the contest for the recovery of the independence of Europe.

The Austrian Army had been suffered, perhaps from necessity, perhaps from policy, to decline at this time to the lowest and most inefficient condition. From the peculiar fiscal system of its component states, as well as from their geographical position which permits little foreign commerce at any time, and none in time of war, the Austrian empire had not the means which commercial nations possess of raising those necessary supplies which are required for the instant organisation of an army, and the more recent system of national loan contractors was yet in embryo. It was found that an army of 60,000 men could not be brought into the field before the end of July, if indeed it could be organised so soon.

To gain time, therefore, Prince Schwartzenberg was sent on an embassy to Paris to express the desire of his sovereign for a general pacification, but still to renew to Napoleon an assurance of the firmness of his attachment, and his intention to adhere to the existing treaty of 1812. This was questioned by the Duke de Bassano; but, in obedience to his instructions, Schwartzenberg repeated the assurance, and declared that General Frimont, whom he had left in temporary command of the Austrian contingent, was still prepared to obey the orders of Napoleon. He continued to repeat this assurance until the departure of Napoleon from Paris, on the 22nd of April, to join his army in Saxony.

Not satisfied with these assurances, Napoleon sent the Count de Narbonne to Vienna, to supersede Count Otto as ambassador. On the 21st of April, the day on which the new ambassador presented his credentials, he addressed a note to Count Metternich, the chief purport of which was to demand an explanation on the subject of the auxiliary corps, and it was expressed in terms which left but little opening for an evasive answer.

This produced a reply from Count Metternich, dated the 26th of April, professing, on the part of the emperor his master, an earnest desire for peace; but now openly stating, for the first time, that the geographical position of Austria, with reference to the present seat of war, would not allow her to continue a mere auxiliary, and therefore the stipulations of the treaty of alliance with France, dated the 14th of March, 1812, must cease; that circumstances prompted Austria to assume the character of a mediating power, and with that object a larger army was now required; that this step should in no respect prejudice the basis of the treaty; on the contrary, it was hoped that it would be in conformity with the views of his majesty the Emperor of the French, who had expressed an opinion " that the development of a more imposing force, directed to one single end—peace—was the best and most efficacious means of obtaining it."

The Austrian General Count Bubna was despatched soon after to Napoleon's headquarters, to keep up the deception as to the project of mediation, which he described as the cause of the preparations of Austria, though they were really intended as hostile to the French; and Count Stadion was sent to the headquarters of the Allies, to renew the secret, but more sincere, assurance of military support to the two Allied sovereigns, as soon as the army and finances of the Austrian empire should be in a condition to render it practicable. The earnest endeavours of both these envoys in their respective missions were directed in the first instance to conclude an armistice as an immediate object, in order to gain time, and in this they were successful.

Napoleon appears to have forgotten his Russian disasters, and to have become as confident as ever of ultimate success, after the Battle of Lützen had proved that his exertions to restore the numerical superiority of his army had fully succeeded. He was unwilling to believe that the Emperor Francis and his subjects, after the severe defeats of Austerlitz and Wagram, their subsequent humiliation, and their present deplorable condition, both as to forces and finances, would dare to take arms against him. He cared little for the co-operation of the Austrians, if he could only secure the continuance of their neutrality. He made no objection to the proposal for a congress at Prague, in which Austria undertook to assume the dignified attitude of an armed mediator.

To gain time was no doubt in some respects desirable to him, for the haste with which the campaign had been opened had not allowed time for the completion and organisation of his several corps, and the prospect of carrying the war beyond the Oder rendered it necessary to secure an intermediate base along the line of the Elbe; a month at least was therefore required for the formation of magazines and other commissariat arrangements.

As to any serious idea that Austrian mediation could lead to any settlement of the affairs of Europe that would satisfy his ambitious views, he had none. He was too well aware that for him, personally, the end of war could not be peace. The demon he had unchained and let loose upon the world, if deprived of its prey, would have turned inevitably in vengeance on the hand which should attempt to curb it. On the other side, the Allied sovereigns, as well as Count Metternich, were too well acquainted with the character, the views, and political position of Napoleon, to entertain any hope that negotiations could end in that desirable result; but to them the advantage of gaining time by an armistice was greater and more obvious than it could be to their adversary.

There is sufficient evidence that as early as the month of May, both Narbonne at Vienna and Caulincourt at Dresden had doubted the sincerity of the Austrian cabinet, and anticipated no other event than the ultimate dereliction of Austria from the interests of France, and her active co-operation with the Allies. Both the envoys frequently endeavoured to awaken the attention of Napoleon to this impending danger; but he, too confident in his own foresight and his own power, held their just apprehensions in contempt, and became the dupe of the skilful Metternich: "*J'ai Metternich dans ma manche, qui a l'Empereur dans sa poche*," said he, ("I have Metternich up my sleeve, who has the emperor in his pocket,") although the retreat upon Schweidnitz might have led him to suspect a secret understanding between Austria and the Allies more mature and menacing than he permitted himself to believe.

This mock congress assembled at Prague. On the part of Russia, Baron Anstedt, and on that of Prussia, Baron Humboldt, were sent to attend it by their respective sovereigns. Counts Metternich and Stadion were present on the part of Austria, while England took no share in the proceedings. On the 30th of June a convention was concluded, accepting the mediation of Austria; the armistice was to be extended from the 20th of July to the 10th of August. The 5th of June had been appointed for the opening of the Congress, but Caulincourt did not arrive till the 25th; diplomatic delays and formalities sufficed to pass the time till the 10th of August, and then no progress whatever had been made in the business for which it had professed to assemble; but the military preparations of Austria being in a sufficient state of forwardness, the conferences terminated with a denunciation of the armistice, and a declaration of war by Austria against Napoleon.

Diplomatic formalities, which are so convenient when delay is desired by either of the contracting parties disappear when both are of one mind, and sincerely wish to come to the point. The preliminaries of treaties of alliance between Austria and the Allied sovereigns were settled in a few days, and although the treaties were not concluded till the 28th of August at Töplitz, yet long ere that formality took place, the armies had joined in actual hostilities, and the campaign of Dresden had been fought.

Although Napoleon had no desire for peace, it must not be supposed that he neglected to employ all the art and persuasion in his power to induce Austria to remain neutral in the contest; but the Emperor Francis continued firm to his purpose of seizing the opportunity which now offered of shaking off the yoke of France.

In vain did Napoleon try to avail himself of his family alliance, and endeavour to turn to account the affectionate regard of the Emperor Francis for his daughter, promising him at the same time, that if he would only remain neuter until the end of the war, all things should be settled according to his desire and in favour of Austria; in vain did he specifically promise, as a bribe for non-intervention, that since Prussia had merited dissolution as the penalty of her defection, the best share in the partition of her territory should fall to Austria, including even Silesia, that old hereditary subject of contention; the Emperor Francis was fortunate in possessing a clear-sighted, patriotic and faithful minister for foreign affairs, worthy of the implicit confidence he enjoyed; through his exertions an Austrian Army was placed in the field against Napoleon, and that preponderance ultimately established which enabled those who fought, not for conquest but for peace, to terminate the war and accomplish the pacification of Europe.

Whilst upon this subject, it may be desirable to advert to the leading points of the several treaties by which the Allied Powers bound themselves to act together for the attainment of their common object—a lasting and general peace. These being public documents, all who desire the minute details will find them in full in the usual well-known books of reference. During the armistice, at the Allied headquarters of Reichenbach, two important treaties were concluded on behalf of Great Britain; one with the Russian and the other with the Prussian court. When the King of Prussia at length resolved to break with Napoleon and join the Emperor of Russia, a treaty, offensive and defensive, between those powers was concluded at Kalisch on the 1st March, 1813, and overtures for a reconciliation with Great Britain were then transmitted without delay.

In anticipation of these, however, the British government, which had been made aware of the actual state of things, from the despatches of the British Ambassador and other sources, had lost no time in sending large supplies of arms and warlike stores to the coast of Germany; and Colonel Lowe, afterwards Sir Hudson, who was a good man of business in practical matters of military finance, was sent out to Lord Cathcart, and joined him at Kalisch, to be employed under his orders, and with the concurrence of the Allied sovereigns, in organising a German legion, to be formed of those willing and ardent spirits who were well known to be ready to rally in defence of the good cause as soon as opportunity and means should offer.

The next step was to send out Lieutenant General Sir Charles Stewart, the present Marquis of Londonderry, as minister plenipotentiary to the court of Berlin, to conclude the treaty of peace with that court, and he arrived at the Allied headquarters at Dresden, a few days before the Battle of Lützen. The treaty he was empowered to negotiate with Prussia and Sweden offered two millions sterling for the war in the north of Germany, to be conducted by the Prince Royal of Sweden, and he was the bearer of the tender of a like sum for the service of the Grand Army of the Allies, upon certain stipulations being agreed to; the more important of which were that Russia should maintain 200,000 men in the field, and Prussia 100,000, exclusive of garrisons; the whole being for the service of the year ending the 1st of January 1814.

It will be evident from the foregoing narrative that as Sir Charles Stewart could only have communicated his most welcome and important stipulations so shortly before the battle which took place near Lützen, there was no time for diplomatic arrangements till the comparative repose afforded by the armistice which terminated that active campaign. At Reichenbach, therefore, the several treaties were formally negotiated and concluded.

In a convention of subsidy with Russia, signed at the emperor's headquarters at Peterswaldau, on the 16th of June, 1813, by Lord Cathcart on the part of Great Britain, and by Count Nesselrode and Baron Anstedt on the part of Russia, 1,133,334*l.* sterling were assigned to Russia, to be paid by monthly instalments, towards the maintenance of an army of 160,000 men in the field, exclusive of 500,000*l.*, which were allowed for the support of the Russian fleet, which had been placed at the disposal of His Britannic Majesty for the purposes of the general cause.

There was also a convention by which Great Britain engaged to provide the expenses of a Russian German legion of 10,000 men; the preliminaries of this had been negotiated at Kalisch in the month of March, and it was signed at Reichenbach on the 24th of June, on the part of Great Britain, by Lord Cathcart, and on that of Russia by

Baron d'Alopeus. This Russian German legion subsequently formed part of the Russian contingent to the Army of the North, and, as regarded British interests, was transferred to the management of Sir Charles Stewart.

The Prussian treaty was concluded by Sir Charles Stewart on the part of Great Britain, and Count Hardenberg on that of Prussia, on the basis already stated; to continue for the remainder of the year, that is to say, towards the maintenance of a force in the field of 80,000 Prussians, a subsidy of 666,666*l.*, in monthly payments, should be granted.

A stipulation was inserted in each of these treaties that British officers should accompany the operations of the army.

There were other conditions in the Prussian treaty, especially as to prospective territorial acquisitions to Prussia and Sweden, as well as respecting Hanover, which ultimately formed the basis of the negotiations at the Congress of Vienna: but, as they have no reference to the subject of these commentaries, we will not enter into them.

But there were secret transactions carried on at Reichenbach of far more immediate interest. Count Stadion, the Austrian Minister, made frequent visits, and although the negotiations of Prague were still pending, yet nothing had been officially concluded between the Austrians and the French. Various and most salutary arrangements were hypothetically made in the event of an Alliance offensive and defensive between the Allies and Austria, an event of which there was little doubt. Count Stadion, a statesman of great ability and eminence, was known to be personally hostile to the French Alliance, and therefore his presence at the headquarters of the Allies, during the armistice, plainly manifested the leaning of Austrian policy, and did not escape the suspicious penetration of Napoleon.

CHAPTER 7

The Austrians Join the Alliance

Before proceeding to the active business of the campaign, let us take a comparative view of the advantages and losses on both sides during the suspension of hostilities; and, first, as to the forces actually in the field at the expiration of the armistice. In forming this estimate we will not adopt the exaggerated or premature statements circulated at the time, though they may appear to bear the sanction of authority, for it was not always considered advisable at the moment to publish the true statement, and sometimes recourse was had to exaggeration, and sometimes to concealment, of the real numbers. In the following estimate, those forces only which were really and truly effective, and within reach to take an active part in the campaign, are included; and their strength is rated, it is hoped, as near the truth as round numbers will allow, after a careful comparison of all the various authorities with notes that were written at the time.

NAPOLEON'S FORCE IN GERMANY.

July, 1813.

FRENCH GRAND ARMY.

		Men.	
Old Guard	- - - -	6,600	
Young Guard	- - - -	32,000	
Cavalry of Guard -	- - -	10,000	
Vandamme	- - - -	25,000	
Victor -	- - -	21,000	
Marmont -	- - -	30,000	
Poniatowski	- - -	15,000	
St. Cyr -	- - -	31,000	
Latour Maubourg, cavalry	- -	10,000	
			180,600

The corps of Poniatowski was allowed by the Austrian Government to pass through Bohemia without arms, during the armistice.

July, 1813.

ALLIED GRAND ARMY.

Russians.

	Men.
Wittgenstein's corps reviewed by the Emperor at Landshut, in Silesia, before marching to join the Austrians in Bohemia - - - - -	45,000
Miloradovitch, Russian guards and grenadiers - - - - -	24,000
Cavalry of reserve, Grand Duke Constantine - - - - -	11,000
300 pieces of artillery, &c.	
Total Russians - - -	80,000

Prussians.

	Men.
The corps of Kleist - - -	25,000

Austrians.

The army in Bohemia ready to take the field, and which marched to attack Dresden.

	Men.
Infantry - - - - -	35,000
Cavalry - - - - -	8,000
Artillery, &c. - - - -	2,000
Total Austrians - -	45,000
Total of grand army - - -	150,000

FRENCH ARMY OF SILESIA,

Intended to be opposed to the army under General Blucher.

	Men.	
Ney's corps, in his absence commanded by General Souham - - -	32,000	
Lauriston - - -	35,000	
Macdonald - - -	21,000	
Sebastiani } cavalry - - - Milhaud }	13,000	
		101,000

ALLIED ARMY OF SILESIA,

To be left for the defence of Silesia and the main communications, under the command of General Blucher.

	Men.	
Blucher's army, composed of Prussians and including a disciplined Landwehr, about	45,000	
Russians, under General Langeron -	33,000	
		75,000

84

Undisciplined Landwehr and the levée-en-masse cannot be put upon paper, but must be allowed a certain value on this side.

FRENCH ARMY OF THE NORTH.

Napoleon's army on the Lower Elbe and on its right bank, opposed to the army of the north.

					Men.
Bertrand -	-	-	-	-	21,000
Regnier -	-	-	-	-	20,000
Oudinot	-	-	-	-	24,000
Arrighi } cavalry Kellerman		-	-	-	10,000
					75,000

Army of Davoust, newly formed by making two corps out of the 1st corps, viz. the 1st and 13th, completed with recruits and 8,000 Danes; intended for the defence of Hamburg and to dispute the passage of the Lower Elbe - - - - 35,000

110,000

Grand total of the whole disposable force of } Napoleon between the Rhine and the Oder } - - 391,600

ALLIED ARMY OF THE NORTH.

Under the chief command of the crown Prince of Sweden, Bernadotte.

					Men.
Swedes -	-	-	-	-	25,000
Bulow, Prussians -	-	-	-	20,000
Winzingerode, Russians	-	-	-	8,000
Woronzof, Russians	-	-	-	4,000
Walmoden, Germans	-	-	-	9,000
German Legion -	-	-	-	5,000
Tanenzien	-	-	-	5,000
					76,000

Grand total of the whole allied force be- } tween the Rhine and the Oder - - } - - 301,000

In this computation no notice is taken of the garrison of Dantzig on the one side, or the blockading force on the other. In the same manner the Austrian corps of Frimont is considered as paired off with that of Wrede on the Bavarian frontier. Thus it appears that the total available force of Napoleon, at the termination of the armistice, exceeded that of the Allies by 90,000; but, by way of compensation, we must remember that, in his arrangements for occupying the fortresses on the Elbe, including Hamburg, Napoleon had placed at least 40,000 men *hors-de-combat* as regarded active operations in the field; and, on the other hand, the national character which the war had assumed on the right bank of the Elbe had already, by the armament of *landwehr* and *levée-en-masse*, produced something more than a moral influence in favour of the Allies; although it would be premature to give it any more physical importance in this campaign, in point of disciplined force, than we have already done in swelling the Prussian corps to the numbers we have given.

To show the difference between men on paper and men in the field, and how little reliance can be placed by historians on returns which bear the sanction of authority at the time, without careful sifting and comparison, a return made before the cessation of the armistice is subjoined, which will be found in some of the accounts of this campaign. It was intended merely as an estimate, and could not be realised.

EXAGGERATED STATEMENT PUBLISHED BY AUSTRIA.

	Men.	
Russians in Silesia - - -	80,000	
Prussian troops of the line - - -	40,000	
Landwehr picked and exercised - -	30,000	
		150,000

This is rated below the truth.

CORPS OF THE PRINCE ROYAL.

Army of the North - - - - -	85,000

This may be near the truth.

RUSSIAN RESERVES.

Tolstoi - - - - -	60,000	
Doctorof - - - -	14,000	
Labanof - - - -	30,000	
		104,000

No part of this force as yet arrived at the Oder.

AUSTRIANS.

	Men.
Troops of the line in Bohemia and other parts -	150,000

Only 45,000 were ready to march for the campaign of Dresden, at the largest computation, and not more than 50,000 took the field with the Allies at any time during the war in Germany or France. Exclusive of this force, they had, however, an array in Italy, in 1814, and other corps in process of formation.—

Austrian reserves (nil) - - -	100,000
The rest of the Prussian Landwehr - -	90,000

The Russian reinforcement already march-
ing to join their army   -   -   -   107,000
No part of this reserve was available.

Total   -   -   -   -   -   777,000

Although many of the arrangements were in progress that are implied in this exaggerated, or at least premature, Austrian report, yet
all were not fully carried into effect even at the termination of the
war. Lord Burghersh's account of the campaign in France in 1814, in
which he was present, is decidedly the best that has been published;
but not having witnessed personally this war in Germany, he was led
to remark, upon the faith of this Austrian report, that:

> Although the whole amount as therein stated may not actually
> have been present under arms, it would certainly be within the
> truth to estimate the Allies at 550,000—a vast superiority over
> the enemy, who never were rated at more than 357,107.

Whereas the truth is, that the available Allied force never exceeded
300,000 men; and until Napoleon crossed the Rhine he had, or might
have had, always the advantage in point of numbers.

Having already shown that in this campaign a superiority in the
field did not exist on the side of the Allies, but that, if we even adopt
Lord Burghersh's numbers in stating the French force, which are only
less than the above because he omits the army of Davoust, there remained a superiority, on the side of Napoleon, of about 90,000 combatants, available, if brought into the field—his numbers amounting to
390,000, while those of the Allies did not exceed 300,000.

We can only regard the premature and exaggerated statement
above, as one which gives a very fair insight into the vast resources of
the Allies, and the great exertions they were capable of making; and
we cannot but perceive the little chance Napoleon had of ultimate
success, when we consider his diminished resources; for he could no
longer boast, as he is said to have done in 1812, that he had a yearly
income of 100,000 recruits: his expenditure of late had far exceeded
that assumed revenue of human lives.

Besides arranging his supplies, and completing the organisation of
his armies, Napoleon had employed the time in securing the line of
fortresses on the Elbe. Hamburg was put into a good state of defence,
and the army of Davoust was formed to protect it; but when it is
necessary to secure such large cities, they become in fact entrenched
camps, and require armies for their defence. The political consequence

of Hamburg as the centre of commerce, and the focus of all the mercantile wealth and resources of the north of Germany, was even greater than its value as a strategic point, although its bridge across the Elbe, so near the mouth of the river, was of no small military importance.

Magdeburg, Wittenburg, and Torgau, with their bridges and *têtes-de-pont*, were able to resist a besieging force. The bridge of Dresden had been repaired, as well as the defences on both sides of the river; and although this city, like Magdeburg, required a large force for its defence, yet 30,000 men might be considered competent to secure it from the *coup-de-main* of any army that could be brought against it. Lastly, Napoleon formed an entrenched camp at Pirna, for the security of a bridge at that point.

These defences on the Elbe constituted an intermediate base, and were prepared, no doubt, in consequence of the sanguine expectation that he entertained, when hostilities were suspended in the month of June, of being able, in his next campaign, to carry the war through Prussia and Silesia into Poland. That expectation was not unreasonable, considering that he then had a decided superiority in point of numbers in the field—that the head of his columns had already reached Breslau—that he occupied Custrin, Stettin, and Glogau, on the Oder, and that the Poles were favourable to his interests; while he flattered himself with the hope of securing at least the non-intervention of Austria, if not its active support, and is known to have entertained this hope almost to the period when the conference at Prague terminated.

During the armistice the Allies were not remiss in bringing forward their reinforcements, and increasing their strength. This fact is shown by comparing the force with which they opened the campaign of Lützen, which amounted to little more than 100,000 men, with the force actually in cantonments at the end of the armistice, and ready to take the field in the country between the Elbe and the Oder, which, including the Swedish Army, the Prussian levees, and the Russian reinforcements, amounted to upwards of 250,000.

In this we do not include the large reserves which had already crossed the Niemen, amounting to upwards of 80,000 men, which might be available in less than two months, but which we will notice no further till they arrive, for they had no direct influence on the campaign of Dresden.

The general outlines of the plan of campaign adopted by the Allies, and in readiness to be carried into effect on the expiration of the armistice, were as follow:—

THE GRAND ARMY.

Immediately upon the declaration of war by Austria against Napoleon, a force of about 100,000 men, consisting of Russians and Prussians, was to march out of Silesia through the chain of mountains which defines the northern boundary of Bohemia, and to proceed secretly and suddenly westward along their southern base, through the dominions of the Emperor Francis, towards the left bank of the Moldau; there to join the Austrian Army, and from that new base to act upon Napoleon's communications in Saxony, and in rear of the line of the Elbe.

THE ARMY OF SILESIA.

A force of about 80,000 Russians and Prussians, partly composed of Landwehr, was to remain in Silesia, under the command of General Blücher, to keep possession of that province, and cover the great line of communication through Poland with Russia. On this road, large but still distant Russian reserves were coming up to support that well-chosen commander, to whom instructions were given to avoid a general action in the meantime, especially against superior numbers.

THE ARMY OF THE NORTH.

This force was composed of various and unequal materials, Swedes, regular Russians and Cossacks, Prussians, chiefly *Landwehr*, and Germans of all denominations. It amounted in all to about 80,000 men, and was placed under the chief command of Bernadotte, the Crown Prince of Sweden. About 10,000 of these men were acting as partisan corps under various enterprising but almost independent commanders. The duty of this army was, in the first place, to cover Berlin; and if the movement of the Grand Army should draw the war into the countries on the left bank of the Elbe, then to pass the river, and co-operate by closing upon the enemy's left.

The partisans were to cross the Elbe, harass the enemy's rear, and endeavour to excite the Hanoverians, Hessians, and other German people to join in national hostility against the French. Towards the close of the armistice the prince royal came to a council of war that was held at Trachenberg, a small town about thirty miles north-east of Breslau, where these combinations were arranged.

With regard to the chief command of the Allied Grand Army, the Emperor of Russia and the King of Prussia, intending to be present in the field, conceded to Austria, that it should be placed under an

Austrian Field-marshal; although the effective force which his nation was able to contribute bore but a small proportion to that which was to be brought out of Silesia by the two sovereigns.

Prince Schwartzenberg, the Commander-in-Chief of the Allied Army, was an officer who, when very young, had been much distinguished in the campaigns in the Netherlands in 1795; but whose services had since been more of a diplomatic than military character. In point of conciliating manners and high rank, both hereditary and military, Schwartzenberg was well qualified to maintain harmony and cordiality among his newly united officers and troops of various nations; and since, at the opening of the campaign, the Austrian dominions were to furnish the base of the operations of the Grand Army, and the supplies were to be drawn from them, it was desirable to the Austrian Government to retain, in their own hands, as much as possible of the arrangement of those essential details.

We may here notice the arrival of General Moreau at the headquarters of the Allied Army. Whether he received any invitation, or what may have been the motive and inducement which led him forth, from his retreat in America, to enter once more into the public affairs of Europe, we will not stop to inquire; but the arrival of so renowned a general at headquarters, at this juncture, could not be matter of indifference to the newly appointed Austrian commander-in-chief.

Moreau's principal friend and patron was the Emperor Alexander, who placed great value on his military opinion; and it is said that the post of *Chef-d'État-Major* was contemplated for him,—a post similar to that held by Berthier under Napoleon: but Moreau prudently preferred to remain a Russian general officer without any specific appointment, and was willing to give his services and advice in the manner in which they might be most useful to the cause of the Allies, who had for their object the restoration of peace to Europe. An object which implied hostility to Napoleon and his armies, but not hostility to France.

General Jomini, the celebrated author of several well-known military treatises, had been hitherto on the *état-major* of the French Army, but at this time came over to the Allies; he was received into the Russian service, and employed on the staff. The correct information he was enabled to give, as to the strength and distribution of the enemy's forces, could not fail to be of great advantage on the side of the Allies.

TO SHEW the RELATIVE CIRCUMSTANCES at the RESUMPTION of HOSTILITIES in AUGUST 1813.

CHAPTER 8

March Through Bohemia

On the 10th of August, the very day on which the armistice expired, the author was present with Lord Cathcart, who was in attendance upon the Emperor Alexander, at a review of the corps of Count Wittgenstein, assembled on the heights between Landshut and Trautenau, which are on the borders of Silesia, and prepared to pass the defile into Bohemia on the following day. This force, which marched past the emperor, was perfectly appointed, and in excellent order: it consisted of

	Men.
24 Squadrons	2,000
84 Battalions	41,000
160 pieces of cannon	———
	43,000

On the 14th the Imperial Headquarters crossed the frontier with the reserve, under the command of General Miloradovitch, consisting of

	Men
The Guards	12,000
The Grenadiers	12,000
	———
	24,000

Followed by the cavalry of reserve, commanded by the Grand Duke Constantine,

	Men
53 squadrons *cuirassiers* & 18 light	11,000
124 pieces of artillery.	

Total Russian force marched through Bohemia 80,000

———

The Prussian corps of General Kleist had preceded us, and marched by Joseph Stadt on the 13th. This corps amounted to about 25,000 men.

Thus, the whole of the force which proceeded out of Silesia, to become part of the Grand Army on the Saxon frontier, amounted to about 80,000 effective men, with upwards of 300 pieces of artillery, and every other requisite to complete it for the field in the same ample proportion. It is unnecessary to detail the precise routes of the several columns on their march; they were duly arranged with reference to the possibility of interruption from the inroad of any French force that might be pushed through the only practicable defiles of Zittau or Friedland, and were kept near enough to support each other. So prompt was the movement, and such was the secrecy preserved, that Napoleon was not aware of it in time, and they arrived at their destination, on the left bank of the Moldau, without being molested.

A small Austrian force had been stationed in the mountains, to observe the two defiles from Lusatia that had been alluded to, and not without cause; for this force was eventually attacked by Poniatowski, whom Napoleon charged with that duty, when he first heard of the movement of the Allies. It appears to have been more a reconnaissance than to have been made with any intention of forcing the pass; and although Vandamme moved to support it, and Napoleon, soon after he left Dresden, went to the headquarters of Prince Poniatowski to be present at this reconnaissance, it was not persevered in, as it did not take effect before the Allied columns had all gone by, and was then of importance no longer.

We have already estimated the force which the Emperor Alexander and the King of Prussia left behind in Silesia, under the command of General Blücher, at about 75,000 men; in these, 33,000 regular Russian troops, commanded by General Lanzeron, formed the essential component.

Before the 18th of August, the Emperor of Russia and the King of Prussia arrived at Prague, whither the Emperor Francis had come to meet them, with Prince Schwartzenberg and his general staff. Lord Cathcart also hastened to Prague, to give that timely support to Austrian credit which he had it in his power to do, as His Britannic Majesty's plenipotentiary. He immediately arranged with Count Stadion an advance of half the subsidy hypothetically stipulated by that minister in a secret article of the treaty of Reichenbach, to be paid immediately on the event of Austria joining the Allies: he took upon himself, under the discretionary powers that had been vested in him, to draw bills on the British treasury, to the amount of 250,000*l*., on account of secret service money; trusting to approval and subsequent arrangements at home. This advance was of less importance from its real amount, than from the moral effect which the appearance of British public bills of exchange could not fail to produce in the money market in favour of Austrian credit; and it tended very materially to enable the force that Austria could prepare for active service, immediately to take the field.

The Russian and Prussian columns arrived on the left bank of the Moldau on the 17th, 18th and 19th of August, passing over the bridge of Leutmeritz and pontoon bridges in that neighbourhood. As to the Austrian force, at this time actually assembled on the Saxon frontier, and ready to take the field as part of the Grand Army, the truth is not to be found in the official returns allowed to be published at the time, as we have already shown. Circumstances, explained above, rendered the several *corps d'armée* unavoidably small, incomplete, and, generally speaking, ill appointed. To have done much with small means should enhance the merit of success, or excuse a less fortunate result; and it is not always considered expedient at the time to betray the weakness of an armed force, or to expose the nakedness of the land.

The distribution of the Austrian Army that actually took the field, was as follows:—

Assembling on the Eger, near Laun, three *corps d'armée*, a corps of reserve, and three divisions of cavalry, *viz.*:—

		Generals of Division.
1st Corps, Count Colloredo	-	Hardegg. Wimpfen. Greth.
2d Corps, Marq. de Chasteller	-	Lederer. F. Alois. Lichtenstein.
3d Corps, Count Giulay	-	Crenville. Murray. Prince Philip of Hesse Homburg.

RESERVE.

The Hereditary Prince of Hesse Homburg.

DIVISION.

Grenadiers	-	-	Weissenwolf. Bianchi.

CAVALRY.

Prince Maurice Lichtenstein.   Count Bubna.

RESERVE CAVALRY.

Count Nostitz.

94

Besides this army there was a fourth corps of Bohemian levees, which had only formed two divisions, Mesko and Prince Hohenlohe, though it was dignified with the name of an army. It had been hastily got together by General Klenau in the neighbourhood of Tilsen and Carlsbad, and was chiefly composed of very young recruits. It might amount to 20,000 men; but was not much to be depended upon as yet; nor was it capable of manoeuvring with the precision that characterizes the movements of the Austrian regular armies.

As an Austrian *corps d'armée* at this time seldom averaged more than 8,000 effective men, we overrate the total effective strength of that contingent which took the field in August 1813, when we estimate it at 50,000 men, the treaty of Reichenbach stipulated for only 60,000. Considering the very recent forced marches of the Russians and Prussians, through Bohemia, we may therefore regard the effective strength of the Grand Army on the Moldau, collectively, as something less than 150,000 men.

Next, as to the views and movements of Napoleon—it appears that, on the 10th of August, when the armistice expired, Napoleon was at Dresden, engaged in reviewing his guards and providing other pageants in honour of his birthday, which he had ante-dated on this occasion, being probably aware that on the 15th, which was the proper day, he would have other things to do.

After waiting some time for the return of the Comte de Narbonne from Prague, and having given him a hasty audience on his arrival, Napoleon entered his carriage on the 15th, accompanied by Murat, and left Dresden by the Pirna road. After inspecting the works of Sonnenstein and the bridges, at midnight, he proceeded by Stolpen to Bischofswerda. It is supposed that he chose this circuitous road more for the sake of concealing his real intentions than from any curiosity respecting Sonnenstein. It appears that Caulincourt, returning from Prague, did not join him till he was at Görlitz, on the 18th, and it is doubtful if he was fully apprised of the general plan of campaign intended by the Allies, and of their movements through Bohemia, until that day. On the 19th Napoleon went to Zittau, and caused the reconnaissance of the Bohemian pass to be made by Poniatowski, to which we have before alluded.

By this time the Grand Army of the Allies had assembled behind him on the Saxon frontier, menacing his communications with his proper base, and the sovereigns had actually departed from Prague to join the troops. This unexpected and doubtless unwelcome news ought to have convinced Napoleon that it was no longer for him to persevere in the offensive from the advanced base of the Elbe, but that he had been, in fact, suddenly placed in an unforeseen dilemma. According to the principles of strategy (which in this, as in all other instances, are in clear and manifest accordance with the dictates of common sense,) he should have suspended his offensive plans beyond the Elbe, till he had removed the Grand Army of the Allies from his communications, or otherwise disposed of it by concentrating a superior force, on his part, and bringing it to action.

If he could not succeed in doing this, the sooner he should trust solely to the Rhine for his base, and withdraw all unnecessary garrisons from the Elbe, the better it would have been for him. But so sudden a revulsion in the ambitious mind of Napoleon, from visions of conquest to cautious strategy, was not in his nature. We have already pointed out what those visions of conquest were, which were now so seasonably interrupted. During the armistice his attention had been directed onward to Silesia and Berlin. The storm gathering in Bohemia was not sufficiently observed, or not expected so soon to burst upon him.

In full expectation of continuing to hold the advantage of the offensive in the ensuing campaign, which he had recovered at Lützen and had not lost at Bautzen, he had made the arrangements necessary for the concentration of the 1st, 2nd, 3rd, 5th, 6th, 8th and 11th corps, with the guards and three corps of cavalry, for the purpose of a general battle with the Grand Army of the Allies, which he still expected to encounter in Silesia. If this force could have been brought into action, and if the campaign had been resumed exactly where the former campaign had terminated, Napoleon would now have possessed a force of nearly 200,000 men, including 30,000 cavalry, to oppose to 175,000—the utmost that the Russians and Prussians in Silesia could have brought against him.

His experience at Lützen and Bautzen, and the offer of battle at Schweidnitz, could leave him in no doubt whether the Allied sovereigns would accept the combat or not, with that disparity of numbers against them; and he probably reckoned with confidence upon gaining a decisive victory over his northern foes, before Austria could offer any serious hostility to him, even if it should be the ultimate intention of that court to do so, which he was still reluctant to believe.

These were his views in Silesia; but he had prepared a simultaneous invasion of Prussia by the 4th 7th, and 12th corps, and a corps of cavalry. This force, amounting to something less than 70,000 men, was directed on Berlin, and was to be supported by the army of Davoust from Hamburg. The army, which the Crown Prince of Sweden might be able to concentrate for the defence of Berlin, could not be expected to exceed 60,000 men. If the French Army could not accomplish the conquest of Prussia at once, by defeating the Army of the Crown Prince, even in despite of his Russian reverse Napoleon looked, no doubt, with the confidence of one more accustomed to victory than defeat, to the prospect of being able to detach such reinforcements to the north, after his anticipated victory in Silesia, as would render the final subjugation of Prussia an inevitable consequence.

CHAPTER 9

Investment of Dresden

The greater part of the French Army was concentrating in Silesia, and Napoleon quitted Dresden, on the 15th of August to proceed to Görlitz. As soon as this was known to the council of war assembled at Prague, it was agreed that no time should be lost by the Grand Army of the Allies in making a demonstration in favour of the small army of Blücher. The first intention is said to have been merely to occupy a position which should command Napoleon's communications through Leipzig, and that the movement upon Dresden was an afterthought, suggested by the necessity of a more immediate and pointed demonstration, and the supposed inadequacy of its garrison, which may have given hopes of a successful assault.

On the 19th the two emperors and the King of Prussia departed from Prague to review about 8,000 Austrian cavalry and other troops on their way to join the army; and on the 21st the Imperial and Royal Headquarters were at Kommotau. On the 22nd of August the Allied Grand Army debouched into Saxony, in four columns, through the only four practicable passes in that continuous range of thickly wooded mountains that divides Bohemia from Saxony.

Although it is not perhaps so lofty here as in its more eastern extent, (which has been already described, where the same chain of mountains marks the Lusatian and Silesian frontier,) it is, in this place, impracticable for the passage of large columns, except by a few well known and established defiles. Towards Bohemia the declivity of these mountains is more abrupt than towards the north; and, as they sink into the plain on the Saxon side, small roads and villages become more frequent; yet, as the same tracts of woodland continue, their intricacy is rather increased than diminished until the fertile and cultivated low grounds are reached.

The general disposition for opening the campaign was this:—

Commencing from the right, the first column, composed of the corps of Wittgenstein and Kleist, was to pass the defile of Nöllendorf and Peterswalde, and follow the great road from Töplitz to Dresden—which is parallel to the course of the Elbe, though not close to its bank. This route required an attack on the entrenched camp at Pirna, and called for sufficient precautions for blockading the small fortress of Königstein, and observing the bridges on the Elbe—which were too well protected by the neighbourhood of that fortress and other works to be easily molested.

The second column (composed of the Russian reserves, both infantry and cavalry, and the headquarters of Barclay de Tolly, who was in chief command of the Russians), was to march by the defile of Altenberg and Bärenstein.

A third column, composed of the main Austrian Army and the Imperial and Royal Headquarters, to march by Kommotau, and to enter Saxony by the great Leipzig road—a much more circuitous route than the other two.

A fourth column (composed of the corps of General Klenau, consisting chiefly of new levies which had been assembled in the country behind Carlsbad, and had not previously joined,) was to arrive by Annaberg, and, marching on the extreme left, to continue its route by Freyburg upon Dresden.

As soon as the Austrian main column had passed the defiles and reached Marienberg, its direction was changed suddenly towards the right, by Zöblitz and Sayda, upon Dresden.

On the 22nd of August Wittgenstein with the right column, was met by a detachment from the corps of St. Cyr, which his advanced guard engaged twice, and drove from their posts. In the evening he attacked the lines of Pirna with the bayonet, and carried them, driving from them the division of General Bonnet. A part of his opponents retired upon Dresden, and part by the bridges across the Elbe. Nothing further occurred that was worth recording till the afternoon of the 25th, when the several columns, with the exception of that of General Klenau, which was still a day's march distant, had reached the valleys behind the sloping hills that form an amphitheatre on the western side of the old town of Dresden, on the left bank of the Elbe.

The advanced guard of Wittgenstein had already followed the enemy to the suburbs between the Elbe and the Grosse Garten; Kleist had also driven the outposts that he found on the Pirna road, behind the walls of that extensive garden or park, the chief place of public recre-

NAPOLEON AT DRESDEN

ation near Dresden. These enclosures reach about a mile and a half to the southward of the town, and afford a strong hold for skirmishers.

A chain of picquets was established, and the Emperor Alexander, the King of Prussia, and Prince Schwartzenberg passed some time, in the calm of a fine summer's evening, on a hill which afforded a distinct and beautiful bird's-eye view of the plain that was so soon to become a field of battle. At a distance of not more than two miles from us, Dresden stood in the centre of the plain, with the broad and winding Elbe flowing through the city, and dividing it into the old and new town. On the opposite bank our prospect was bounded by the woody hills of Lusatia.

No doubt the subject that occupied the thoughts of the Allied chiefs at that moment was not the beauty of the scene so much as the important question whether to commence an immediate attack or not; but it was considered that the new redoubts and other defences, as well as the repairs that had been made in its once formidable ramparts, and the reestablishment of its wet ditches, placed it in a state of defence sufficient to render any hasty and rash attempt to carry it by assault quite unwarrantable at that late hour in the evening, especially with an army that was tired with marching; for the garrison of Dresden was known to amount to 30,000 men at least. The Allied Army therefore bivouacked for the night.

On this occasion, while the important conference of sovereigns and chiefs was going on at a little distance from us, General Moreau (who, from motives already stated, was either not invited to join it, or perhaps studiously held himself aloof from it,) was conversing familiarly in English (which he spoke perfectly), and smoking his cigar with the author and some others of the suite. We asked him whether the town was to be attacked. He told us that he was glad to say the town was not to be attacked, and that the intention had been given up;—

For, its fortifications are in good repair, and within the town as well as in the *faubourgs*, houses have been loop-holed. There is a garrison of 35,000 men; and notwithstanding this, if attacked with determination by the superior forces at our disposal, it might be taken, but with a loss of 5,000, perhaps even 15,000 men. We are already on Napoleon's communications; the possession of the town is no object; it will fall of itself at a future time.

The author gives a place to this conversation here, as he finds it in his notes, written immediately on arriving at Töplitz—not only because it is to him a favourite recollection, but because there is to be found a sneering insinuation, in the French official accounts of the day, that Moreau was more responsible for the arrangement of the campaign, as well as for the details of the attack upon Dresden, than is justified by facts. He was, in truth, placed in a delicate situation, and had not yet time to become at home in it.

His arrival at headquarters was looked upon, naturally enough, by the commander-in-chief "*in esse*" with some degree of jealousy; the consequence of which was a disinclination to admit his interference; and therefore Moreau's advice had no influence whatever over the decisions or dispositions of the Austrian commander-in-chief, unless imperceptibly through the medium of the Emperor Alexander, whose confidence he appeared to possess;—whether to the benefit or disadvantage of the cause, the author does not attempt to judge. It should also be remembered that the interval between his arrival at headquarters, and the moment when he received his mortal wound, was scarcely a fortnight.

Early in the morning of the 26th of August, a contest between the Prussian and French outposts, about the extremity of the Grosse Garten, which adjoins the suburbs, brought on a more serious affair in that quarter, and led to an attempt by the corps of General Kleist to gain possession.

In the afternoon the Austrian Army got under arms, and began to advance in several columns upon Dresden, presenting certainly a very menacing aspect; but Prince Schwartzenberg (in his bulletin, dated Altenberg, the 29th of August,) calls them strong reconnoitring corps despatched, in the direction of Dresden, to examine the works erected in the avenues to the city, and to ascertain the force and distribution of the enemy. The corps of Count Colloredo, under cover of a heavy cannonade, descended into the plain, preceded by Croats and other light infantry in extended order. Halting to support them, he deployed his reserves, and detached a sufficient force to storm a redoubt which commanded the Dippodiswalda approach, and which was gallantly carried; but being well flanked, and commanded by neighbouring houses filled with musketry, it was soon abandoned.

Sir Charles Stewart and Sir Robert Wilson accompanied the storming party, and entered the redoubt. On the right, Kleist made great progress in dislodging the enemy from the Grosse Garten, and Wittgenstein advanced on the plain to the right of it; but as that space was commanded most effectually from the higher ground on the opposite bank of the Elbe, he could do little in that quarter but return a cannonade across the river.

Of the corps of General Klenau, which was advancing by the Freyburg road, only the division of Mesko had as yet arrived. This division, with part of the corps of General Giulay and of the reserve, was engaged in making the reconnaissance on the Freyburg approach. The Austrian artillery dismounted the guns, and destroyed a redoubt near Lobda; and the division of grenadiers of Weissenwolf took that village, and held possession of it.

There is a small river named the Welsseritz, which runs through the village of Plauen, and forms a deep ravine at the village and above it. Passing through the suburbs of Friedrichs-stadt this stream falls into the Elbe immediately below Dresden. The Welsseritz, and especially its deep ravines, separated the troops on its left bank from the rest of the army, so as to render mutual support, if not almost impossible, at least tardy, and only to be effected by circuitous routes. Although the enemy made a sortie in considerable force on the same evening from the suburb of Friedrichs-stadt against this unsupported left wing, it not only repelled the attack, but retained possession of the village of Lobda.

On the part of the Allies, the events of the day terminated without any important result, and the formality of the proceedings gave it more the appearance of a field-day than of anything more serious. The several lines and columns retired to their places in position on the heights surrounding Dresden, and bivouacked for the night.

The Grosse Garten, of which Kleist had at one time gained possession, could not have been maintained without a corresponding advance of the rest of the line; the greater part of it was, therefore, abandoned at nightfall.

On that day the force of the French did not amount to more than 30,000 men; but while these events were passing on the side of the Allies, a more important operation was in progress on the opposite approaches to the city. Information was received that Napoleon, with his guards and other considerable reinforcements, had arrived at Dresden. In confirmation of this, considerable columns were visible towards the evening on the right bank of the Elbe, arriving by different routes, and entering the new town of Dresden. This sudden re-appearance of Napoleon in Saxony, who, from other recent information, was known to have been in Silesia, appeared almost incredible; but the interesting account of the Baron d'Odeleben, who was an "*officier d'ordonnance*" at the French headquarters, explains it thus:—

After a sanguinary but indecisive engagement, in which Napoleon had endeavoured with superior numbers to overwhelm General Blücher, whom he had encountered on the River Bober, and brought to an action near Lowenberg, (but in which, by skill and hard fighting, the latter had not only extricated his inferior force, but even in retiring gained some advantages,) Napoleon first heard of the immediate intention of the Allied Grand Army to march upon Dresden. He received this information on the 22nd of August, and was then about ninety miles distant from Dresden.

It will be remembered, that on the same day the Allied Grand Army entered Saxony; and although it is true that the route taken by the Austrian columns was circuitous, yet the points at which the two right columns passed the frontier are only twenty English miles from the capital.

Of course, Napoleon knew not of this invasion as an event that had already occurred; but his information was sufficiently clear as to the intention of the Allies to induce him to give instant orders to his guards to commence their retrograde march to the Elbe that very night; and next morning, the 23rd, he set in motion the corps of Victor and of Marmont, with the cavalry of General Latour Maubourg for the same destination. Leaving the greater part of the cannon of his army in Silesia to Marshal Macdonald, and accompanied by Murat and Ney, he hastened to superintend and accelerate, by every means in his power, the forced marches of his reinforcements towards Dresden; and at nine o'clock on the morning of the 26th he had arrived at the head of his guards.

The troops he brought with him might amount to nearly 80,000 men, which would raise the total of the defending army to 110,000; and (after making forced marches of some thirty English miles on an average in the four and twenty hours of three consecutive days,) nearly the whole of this force passed through Dresden, and assembled on the field of battle, to the westward of it, by sun-set on the 26th.

While he was making these arrangements for the relief of Dresden, he sent orders to Vandamme to cross the Elbe at the bridges of Sonnenstein, and march upon Töplitz—that by entering Bohemia he might cut off or molest the communications of the Allies; and he expected that this movement would prove an effectual counter diversion.

Towards dusk on the evening of the 26th we heard a heavy cannonade, and distinctly saw the flashes in the neighbourhood of König-stein, about twelve miles in our rear. This afterwards proved to be the corps of Vandamme, who, in obedience to his orders, had passed the Elbe, and was checked for a time in his progress by the gallant resistance of Count Ostermann Tolstoi, whom Wittgenstein had left behind, to observe that point, and to keep open his communications.

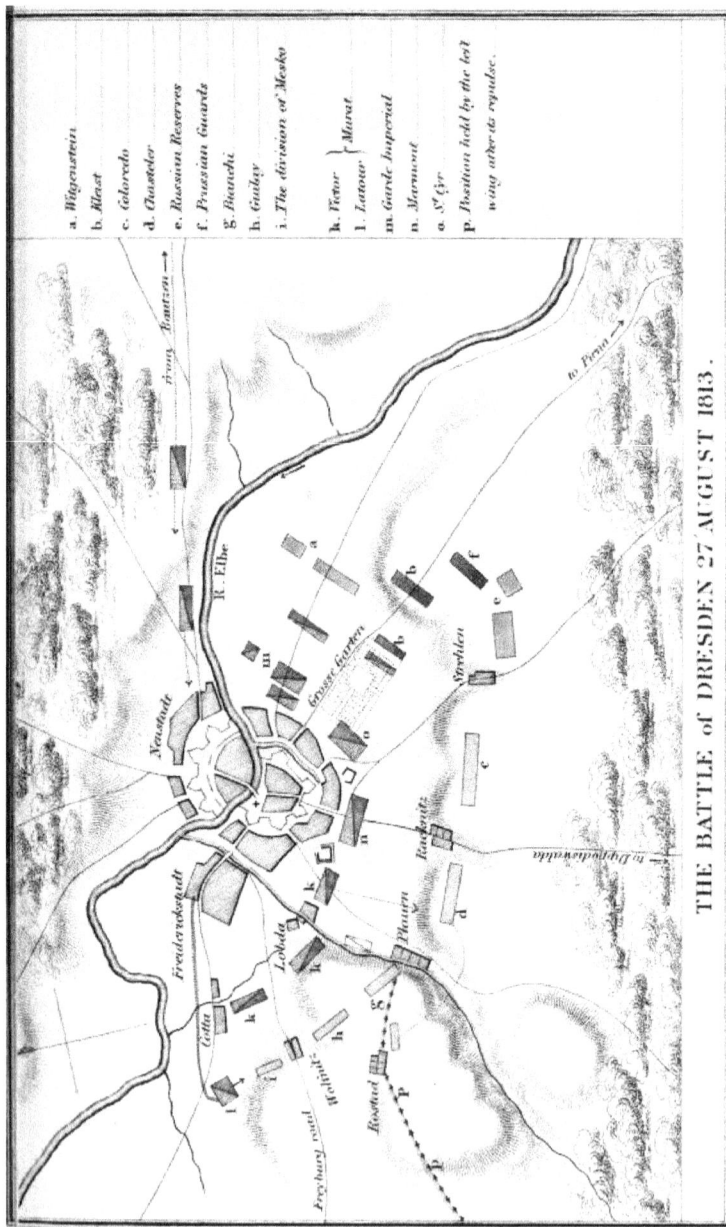

THE BATTLE of DRESDEN 27 AUGUST 1813.

a. Wigenstein
b. Kleist
c. Colordo
d. Chasteler
e. Russian Reserves
f. Prussian Guards
g. Bianchi
h. Gulay
i. The division of Mesko

k. Victor ⎫ Murat
l. Latour ⎬
m. Garde Imperial
n. Marmont
o. St. Cyr
p. Position held by the left wing after its repulse.

CHAPTER 10

Battle of Dresden

The position occupied by the Allied Army on the 27th of August, before Dresden, was as follows:—On the extreme right, in the plain between the Pirna road and the Elbe, the corps of Wittgenstein; next to him, on the Pirna road, and with an advanced brigade in possession of a part of the Grosse Garten, the Prussian corps of Kleist. Next to Kleist, between Strehlen and Rackniz, the Austrian corps of Colloredo; and between Rackniz and Plauen the corps of General Chasteller.

In front of the village of Leubniz (that is, in rear of the right centre) were posted the Russian reserves both of cavalry and infantry. The Austrian reserve was to have been stationed in the rear of Plauen, to support Chasteller; but the want of force, in proportion to the extent of front, demanded its services elsewhere. Through Plauen flows the rivulet with steep banks, named the Welsseritz. Beyond this rivulet, and between it and the Freyburg road, were the divisions of Bianchi and the corps of Giulay. Prolonging this line beyond the Freyburg road, and forming the extreme left of the whole line, was the division of Mesko, the only part of the corps of Klenau in the field.

This extreme left, though thrown forward and already too much extended, derived no "*appui*" from the Elbe, as there was still upwards of an English mile of plain intervening; it rested therefore upon nothing, and was without a sufficient support of cavalry in a country favourable to that arm, and requiring the use of it—a trying situation, it must be allowed, for very young troops.

Napoleon, whose force, either close at hand or already there, amounted to about 100,000 men, had lost no time in passing it through the city to the front of Dresden, and made the following distribution. Seeing the extension and exposed attitude of the Austrian left, he gave the King of Naples orders to attack it with his right wing. The troops placed at Murat's disposal for this purpose, already on the left bank of the Welsseritz, consisted of about 20,000 infantry of the corps of Victor, and 10,000 cavalry of various nations which composed the cavalry corps of Latour Maubourg.

The left wing of the French Army, composed of the Young and Old Guard and the cavalry of the guard, he caused to assemble near the Grosse Garten, and to the left of it.

In the centre Napoleon stationed the corps of Marmont, near the redoubt on the Dippodiswalda road, which had been assaulted the evening before. At this point he placed himself at six o'clock in the morning, and remained there the greater part of the day.

Between the centre and the left wing St. Cyr formed his corps "*en masse*," to connect and support the line, and was stationed close to the walls of the town, and to the French right of the Grosse Garten. Although this column appeared strong, his whole corps could not have been present, as, without doubt, many of the duties and defences of Dresden, that were not otherwise provided for, were still furnished by it.

Thus, the positions occupied by the two armies may be described as two corresponding segments of circles; one within the other, having Dresden for a common centre, and the Elbe for a common base. In proportion, therefore, as Napoleon's army was nearer to that centre, the extent of front occupied by it was smaller. The concave arc on which the Allied Army was formed was nearly six English miles from right to left; and the convex arc on which Napoleon stood was less than three.

The Allied line, except at the two extremities, had the advantage of an eminence; but Napoleon's forces stood with their backs to the defences of Dresden, sheltered by regular redoubts, and the loop-holed houses of the suburbs were at hand. This was an attitude in which a much smaller force would have been secure from attack so long as it chose to stand on the defensive; while its concentration placed it in a favourable attitude for assuming the offensive against any weak part of the extended line of the Allies.

Having given this detailed account of the relative positions, a few words will suffice to describe the events of the day.

Under cover of the thick weather and heavy rain, which commenced about midnight, and continued without intermission during the whole day of battle, Murat issued in force, in obedience to his orders, from the Friedrichs-stadt suburb, at about seven in the morning; but his movements were concealed by the mist. By about eight in the morning Victor had pushed a heavy column, up the left bank of the Welsseritz, through Lobda, the village that had been taken the preceding evening by the Austrian grenadiers, but abandoned when the rest of the army retired into position. This column commenced a vigorous attack upon the division of Bianchi, while the rest of the Austrian left wing was sufficiently engaged in front.

Murat, in the meantime, at the head of the cavalry, issued from the northern extremity of the Friedricks-stadt suburb, unperceived till too late, and forming two columns, passed near the village of Cotta, and, by a circuitous route, gained the rear of the extreme left of the Austrians, and proceeded to make his attack. The result of this affair was, that the whole left wing then in line was defeated with great loss, and nearly all the officers and men of the division of Mesko were either killed or taken prisoners. Two distinguished regiments of the reserve were also broken in square, and suffered severely. The Austrian loss amounted to General Andreossi and 30 officers killed, 138 officers wounded; General Count Mesko, General Szesen, 59 other officers, and upwards of 10,000 rank and file were taken prisoners.

The division of Prince Alois Lichtenstein, detached from the corps of Chasteller across the Welsseritz, at length arrived to give support; and, by a judicious disposition and a steady front, that officer succeeded, with his small force, in arresting the farther advance of the enemy in that quarter, and enabled the remains of the left wing to rally. With reference to the line, this wing now stood with its left thrown back, and the Freyburg road was in possession of the enemy.

While these events were occurring on the left of the Welsseritz, Napoleon caused some batteries to advance against the other parts of the line, with sufficient supports, which were answered by our batteries and a cannonade extended along the whole front. Some desultory attacks were made by the French, particularly against Plauen; but they were repulsed, and they were probably made with no more definite object than merely to occupy attention. At Plauen they were gallantly repelled by the division of Austrian grenadiers, who received the attack in line; but as soon as Napoleon heard that Murat was engaged, and gaining ground on his right, he went in person to his left wing, and ordered the attack of the Grosse Garten in force, and a general advance against the right wing of the Allies.

By overwhelming numbers, Mortier gained possession of the Grosse Garten, although it was most resolutely defended by the Prussians, and he advanced on the Pirna road, as well as on the plain to his left of the Garten, against Wittgenstein. St. Cyr also moved a large supporting mass forward into the plain, to his right of the Grosse Garten.

In the annexed plan it will be seen that the Allies' right wing was in much greater force than the other parts of the line, and that the whole of the Russian and Prussian forces, consisting of good, and for the most part experienced, soldiers, in the highest state of discipline, stood opposed to Mortier and St. Cyr; and that this force, amounting to at least 80,000 men, was concentrated behind a line of front less than two English miles in extent.

The enemy attempted to advance, but Wittgenstein held his ground in the plain to the right, and in several charges of cavalry he had a decided advantage—on one occasion taking 500 prisoners.

The gallant Prussians, who formed the corps of Kleist, also maintained their ground with their usual steady valour; nor were they likely to give way, when the king's brother, Prince William, was fighting in the front with his brigade, and when the king himself was among them to encourage the soldiers with his presence, as he never failed to do in times of need.

The Russian reserves, including 10,000 splendid cavalry, under the command of the Grand Duke Constantine, were close at hand, but had not been brought into action; and at this period of the battle, orders were sent to Count Barclay de Tolly to move forward, and do something decisive. A large French column had advanced into the plain so far as to be thought assailable; and it was supposed that the cavalry might have time to break into it before it could retreat to the cover of the suburbs and defences of Dresden. There is now reason to think, this was a part of the corps of St. Cyr, although General Jomini said at that time it was the Young Guard.

Prince Schwartzenberg, who no doubt, with the emperor's concurrence, had given the orders, went, in the meantime, to look after the unfortunate affair on the left, concerning which the most discreet concealment was at the time, and long afterwards, observed. The King of Prussia, as we have said, was with his own people. The Emperor Alexander (in conversation with Lord Cathcart and General Moreau—the one on his right, and the other on his left,) was riding slowly along the front towards the right, where the intended attack was to take place.

When somewhere between Rackniz and Strehlen, and not far from the hollow road which passes through the latter, they turned directly to the front, attracted by a movement of Russian cavalry, when a cannon shot struck Moreau, (who at the moment might have been half a horse's length in advance of the emperor,) in the right leg, and going through his horse shattered his left knee. The horse plunged forward about thirty yards and fell dead. Moreau, though suffering great torture, said to those who had hastened to extricate him from his wounded horse, "Tell the emperor that I am willing to sacrifice my limbs in his service, for his cause is just."

The author here will endeavour to correct one prevalent though not very important mistake, as to whence the shot came; about which, however, Napoleon evinced much curiosity, and was certainly misinformed.

The Emperor Alexander, who was generally in front of his lines, had on this day been long exposed to the cannonade of shot and shells coming directly from the front; but just before the shot which proved fatal to Moreau, the author distinctly saw one of those field-batteries of the enemy, which preparatory to, or during an advance, are shifting their ground, and gaining any advantageous post, to fire into any collected body of their opponents. As it arrived on the crest of an opposite eminence obliquely on our right, he could distinctly see through the mist the bustle of preparing for action, and therefore it could not have been more than a quarter of a mile distant.

The smoke of the first round hid it from our view, and must have concealed us from them; but there is not a doubt it was a shot, in the first round from that battery, directed at the leading horsemen of the group, which took effect upon Moreau; for it was not of large calibre, and came obliquely from the right. It therefore could not have been a chance shot from one of the redoubts near Dresden, where Napoleon was present; for they were either directly in front or obliquely to our left, and at least a mile distant; and that version was entirely a poetic licence to give point to a bulletin.

The shot continued to fall thick and fast among us, coming obliquely from the right all the time we continued on that spot, and killing or wounding several of the escort; but the ground being wet and on the side of a hill, the balls buried themselves, and did comparatively little mischief after the first unlucky round.

The emperor rode at once to the spot where Moreau was lying, and caused the Cossacks of his guard to form a "*brancard*" for the removal of the wounded general, by passing their pikes through some cloaks; he then turned his horse, and proceeded at a walk, in conversation with Lord Cathcart, towards the high ground to the right of Strechlen, where he could best superintend the contemplated attack with the reserve. He seemed, naturally enough, much affected by the calamity which had befallen his new but apparently much esteemed friend, and had not gone far before he was met by General Jomini, who had been the bearer of the order to General Barclay de Tolly to make the attack with the reserve, and was now the bearer of his answer.

Barclay submitted the inexpediency and fruitlessness of the attempt against the heavy masses of the enemy's infantry, posted as they were under the shelter and protection of the defences of Dresden; observing also that if he should take his artillery down into the plain, which he must do to support his attack, and if a retreat should be necessary, which, he might well know, had from various causes become inevitable, the difficulty would be much increased by having to extricate his guns. The emperor, no doubt, saw the justice of Barclay de Tolly's opinion. The advance was countermanded, and all further thoughts of making an attack were abandoned.

The emperor halted, and dismounted on the top of a hill behind Strehlen. A bivouac fire was lighted for him; the rain fell more heavily than before, and hostilities seemed almost suspended by it. At length the King of Prussia arrived, and Prince Schwartzenberg soon joined the two Allied sovereigns. They resolved to make a general retreat, and orders were given to commence it, while the troops in front were to keep a good countenance till night fall, and then to retire covering the rear.

This retreat had now become no easy operation for so large an army, since the Pirna road was known to be cut off by Vandamme on our proper right, and the Freyburg road was in full possession of Murat on our proper left, and the only line of retreat remaining for the whole army was that by the central route through Dippodiswalda, besides such mountain roads and paths as could be found converging on the single defile of the Altenberg road through Eichwald to Töplitz. The fatigue which the French Army had previously undergone, and the good services of the Cossacks and irregular troops in a country peculiarly suited to them, rendered this movement practicable, though it was not performed without some confusion and loss, as many guns were unavoidably abandoned to the enemy.

The Emperor of Russia slept for some hours at Dippodiswalda; Napoleon returned to Dresden about six o'clock, satisfied with his day's work, and well knowing, that in the exhausted condition of his troops nothing further could be done that day; but he was not then aware of the retreat of the Allies.

In this battle, and during the retreat, the total loss of the Allies has been a subject of much exaggeration; but it would be correct I believe to estimate it at upwards of 30,000 men "*hors de combat.*" The French loss is said to have amounted to 8,000 or 10,000 men.

The ill-fated Moreau, after having had both legs amputated, was carried all night in a litter on men's shoulders. Soon after day-break, he was brought to the house that had been Lord Cathcart's quarters at Dippodiswalda, where we had passed the night. By this time the rear-guard was already close to the town, and we were about to depart; so that there was only time to dress his wounds, and again, carried on men's shoulders, the fatiguing march was resumed. In this disadvantageous manner he passed three or four days and nights after his severe and painful wound.

CHAPTER 11

Battle of Kulm

We have before noticed, that on the 23rd of August, when Napoleon set off from Silesia to relieve Dresden with the second and third
corps and his guards, &c, he sent orders to Vandamme, who was at
Rumburg, in command of the first corps, as a support to Poniatowski,
observing the pass of Zittau, to return to the Elbe, and crossing at the
bridges of Sonenstein, to proceed, by the road through Nöllendorf, to
Töplitz, to gain the entrance of the defiles into Bohemia, in our rear,
and thus cut off our communications and supplies. Vandamme's corps
certainly amounted to 25,000 men, and it was to be supported by the
division of Bonnet, which had been driven across the Elbe by Wittgenstein's advance; this division amounted to 10,000 men.

In the account of the events on the 26th, it is stated that in the
evening of that day we had heard and seen the flashes of a heavy
cannonade, accompanied by musketry, in the direction of Königstein,
about twelve English miles in rear of our right. This was probably
some preparatory operation to clear a front for the passage of the
river, and remove the division of the guards under Count Ostermann
Tolstoi and the division of Prince Eugene of Würtemberg, which had
been left as a blockading force to Königstein, and as corps of observation opposite the bridges: for early in the morning of the 27th Prince
Schwartzenberg received intelligence that the enemy had pushed a
large body of troops across the Elbe in the night.

For some time, it was believed at headquarters that Victor was with
Vandamme. If this supposition had been true, an army of upwards of
50,000 men would have been placed on our communications, and our
circumstances would have been more critical than they really were:
but we have seen that Victor was at Dresden.

The two Russian divisions were, however, opposed to nearly four
times their numbers. When Count Ostermann Tolstoi discovered the

intention of the enemy, he was with his division of guards on the north side of Königstein, and immediately taking his resolution he forced his way, not without some hard fighting, through their advanced troops, and placed his corps so as to cover the road to Bohemia.

These mountain roads afford a strong defensible point at every turn, and as they rise gradually towards the summit level on the Bohemian frontier, and then fall abruptly into the vale of Bohemia, the ground favoured the retiring troops, who took every advantage it offered to delay the advance of the enemy. Such operations, however, against the wide-spreading advanced guard of a superior force are often intricate and hazardous; and on the 28th of August, Prince Eugene of "Würtemberg (who, though young for his rank, was one of the most experienced and distinguished officers in the Russian service,) fell into some embarrassment with his division; he was forced, and lost five guns and nearly 2,000 prisoners.

By the 29th Count Tolstoi had descended into the plain below Nöllendorf, keeping hold of the woody ridge on his proper left, with some *tirailleurs*, probably the remains of the division of the Prince of Würtemberg, who continued to render the most essential services throughout these gallant affairs; but having been unfortunate was not even named in any of the accounts.

Vandamme followed Count Ostermann into the plain, with ten battalions at first; but finding he could make no impression upon the Russians with that force, he proceeded to bring the rest of his corps down from the hill of Nöllendorf, and probably would have prevailed, if the King of Prussia, and the Emperor Alexander soon after, issuing from the mountains by the Dippodiswalda road through Eichwald, had not arrived in the same plain by this time; and, seeing the state of affairs, sent orders to the division of Russian grenadiers and the cavalry of reserve, which had already reached the defile of Eichwald, to hasten and support Count Tolstoi. This aid restored full confidence.

The Russian guards not only repulsed the attack of Vandamme, but forced him back upon Kulm. Here he took up a position for the night, in which he assembled his whole corps, as it came down from the mountains. Though he was not aware of the general retreat of the Allies from Dresden, Vandamme might have observed the force opposed to him growing stronger every hour, and he ought to have been upon his guard. Whether his intelligence was intercepted by Cossacks, or from some other cause, he was not apprised of the retreat of the whole Army of the Allies upon Töplitz, which commenced on the

BATTLE OF KULM

evening of the 27th, and now threatened to overwhelm him like a vast avalanche.

This is the more remarkable, as it would appear, from the account of the Baron d'Odeleben, that Napoleon himself went as far as Pirna on the 28th, which is within fifteen miles of Nöllendorf; and Mortier, with the Young Guard who arrived there that night, remained "*en bivouac*" on the 29th.

The position occupied by the French 1st *corps d'armée*, on the morning of the 29th, was as follows:—

The centre was at Kulm, where there was a large country house or *château*; the ground in front sloping to some swampy meadows. The right was towards the woody ridge, and the left on the village of Neudorf. The country was arable and unenclosed, and traversed by small streams capable of turning a mill; but, generally speaking, these were not obstacles of much military importance. Immediately in rear of this position rose the Nollendorf heights, whence only one practicable road descended, to which the enemy could look for reinforcements, or in case of need, for a retreat.

Nevertheless, Vandamme seems to have expected support, and in the meantime, assuming that he had a superiority of numbers, he little doubted that now he had concentrated them in an open country, he could easily repulse the force opposed to him, and gain the town of Töplitz which was in sight. On his arrival there, it appears that he was to have opened his brevet of field-marshal, which was already sealed and in his pocket.

In the course of the evening of the 29th, a great part of the Allied force issued from the mountains. Some had passed on, but others were halted in their progress by the two Allied sovereigns, who fortunately, on this emergency, took matters a good deal into their own hands. The responsible commander-in-chief was still occupied with the re-treating columns; and, if the author recollects aright, he did not come out from the mountains till late in the evening. The King of Prussia sent orders to Kleist, who was still in the hills, to apprise him of the state of affairs, and to urge him to use all diligence in endeavouring, by the mountain paths, to gain the hill and defile of Nöllendorf in rear of the enemy.

The command of the troops that were available for the intended attack, on the part of the Allies, was given to Barclay de Tolly, and the following disposition was made:—

The Austrian division, under Prince Philip of Hesse Homburg, was

THE BATTLE of CULM 29ᵗʰ AUGUST 1813.

FRENCH

a. Corps of Gen¹ Vandame

ALLIES

b. Division of Prince Philip of Hesse Hombourg

c. Russian troops the division of Count Ostermann

d. Division of Gen¹ Bianchi

e. Corps of Count Colorado and Russian brigade of General Knorring

f. Russian Guards

g. General Kleist.

on the right, supported by the division of Bianchi, in second line. On the left, was the Russian division of grenadiers, with some battalions *"en tirailleur"* in the woody hills on their left. The Russian guards were in reserve in rear of the centre, where a battery of nearly 100 pieces of artillery was collected.

Count Colloredo, with the 1st Austrian corps, had orders to make a flank movement to the right, and then to turn and attack the enemy's left. This flank movement was executed with precision and vigour, by both infantry and cavalry, and attended with complete success.

Whilst the rest of the Allied line attacked to its front, Kleist's *tirailleurs* appeared in the hills at the proper moment, and the head of his column was soon after seen issuing from the woods of Nöllendorf, in rear of the enemy, and in possession of the only road for their retreat.

The result of this combined attack on an isolated corps, by so superior a force, was such as might be expected. General Vandamme, with six other general officers, sixty pieces of cannon, and upwards of 7,000 prisoners, remained in possession of the Allies. The killed and wounded must have been very numerous; and, although the neighbouring forest afforded the means of escape to the rest, yet few returned to serve again under Napoleon's banners; and the original first *corps d'armée* ceased to exist.

In the retreat of the main army, and the pursuit by the French, Murat, with the corps of Victor and his cavalry, had pushed on by the Freyburg road, and penetrated into the hills as far as Sayda. Marmont, with his own corps and the French cavalry of the guard, followed the main column of the Allies by Dippodiswalda, on the route to Altenberg. St. Cyr was in the frontier mountains, nearest to the Moldau.

The fortunate victory at Kulm conferred advantages that are beyond all calculation. It was more than a compensation for the disasters of the army at Dresden, and in the retreat. It raised the spirits of the disappointed soldiers and the confidence of their commanders, exactly at the right moment and in the right place. If it had not occurred precisely when and where it did, it is very doubtful if the Allies would have rallied in the plain of Töplitz, and become conscious of their power to guard the defiles, and prevent their opponents from issuing from the mountains, otherwise than in detail and at so great a disadvantage in the face of their concentrated force, as to render it certain ruin for the French to seek a battle under such circumstances.

On the other hand, when we look at the annexed sketch, and consider the crowded, embarrassed, and ill-provisioned state of the Allied retreating columns, on the 28th, we cannot but admit that if Vandamme had been able, one day sooner, to enter the vale of Töplitz, and also been properly supported, all these advantages might have been his; and the Allied Army, being too much entangled to be capable of a vigorous effort to cut its way out of the toils that surrounded it, might very possibly have been reduced to starve or capitulate in the Saxon mountains.

After the Battle of Kulm the Allied Army rallied in the vale of Töplitz, occupying a position opposite to the defile of Nöllendorf, and observing that of Eichwald; but the roads by which the main army had retired in the worst possible weather, were so encumbered and broken up, that the route by the pass of Eichwald was almost impracticable.

The Allied sovereigns made Töplitz their headquarters for the next six weeks, and remained there in perfect security, preparing for ulterior and more matured operations. Although this interval was not by any means passed in military inactivity, yet the affairs which took place in the mountains, and at the defile of Nöllendorf, partook more of the character of "*la petite guerre*" than of strategy; and although they were often very interesting and instructive, we will not interrupt the narrative of the decisive operations of the war, by entering minutely into their details at present.

It is important, previously, to refer to the valuable co-operation which had been rendered, and was still given, by General Blücher, in Silesia, and by the Crown Prince of Sweden, with the Army of the North; that we may be able to judge how far the pointed movement of the Grand Army upon Dresden, was essential, and how far it was effectual as a diversion. In doing this, if the author gives only the outlines of the achievements of the cooperating armies, it is not because he undervalues them, but because he is anxious to avoid complication, and to adhere steadily to the plan of detailing only the operations of the main army with which he was present.

CHAPTER 12

Battles of the Katzbach and Gross Beeren

During the period comprised in this book, Blücher was left in Silesia to retain and cover the great communication by Breslau. He had an army of Russians and Prussians amounting to about 75,000 men; and although it contained a proportion of young troops and *landwehr*, it was a good and efficient regular army, hearty in the cause; its Prussian contingent burning with a desire to avenge the wrongs of their native land, and already inspired with confidence in their gallant and popular commander. But we must not omit to notice that in this spirited but new army, the 30,000 steady Russians, under General Langeron, formed a valuable ingredient, and afterwards rendered good service. Blücher's orders were to avoid a general action, and to retire before superior numbers; but he was to keep the enemy constantly occupied, and to seize any advantage that might result from the diversion intended to be made by the Grand Army.

The French force, concentrated in Silesia and opposed to Blücher, might already exceed his army in the proportion of two to one; and although nothing would have suited Napoleon better, or have been more gratifying to him, than to have given a decisive "*coup de patte*" to the army of Blücher in the first instance; yet the movement of the Allied sovereigns through Bohemia, to concentrate the Grand Army on the southern frontier of Saxony, had so changed the whole aspect of affairs, that he could no longer expect, or even have time, for a decisive campaign in Silesia. Accordingly, we find that, after his reconnaissance at Zittau, and the arrival of Caulincourt with full intelligence of the preparations and warlike intentions of the Allies in Bohemia, he hastened to give battle to Blücher, whose several corps had been busy since the commencement of hostilities, and with considerable success.

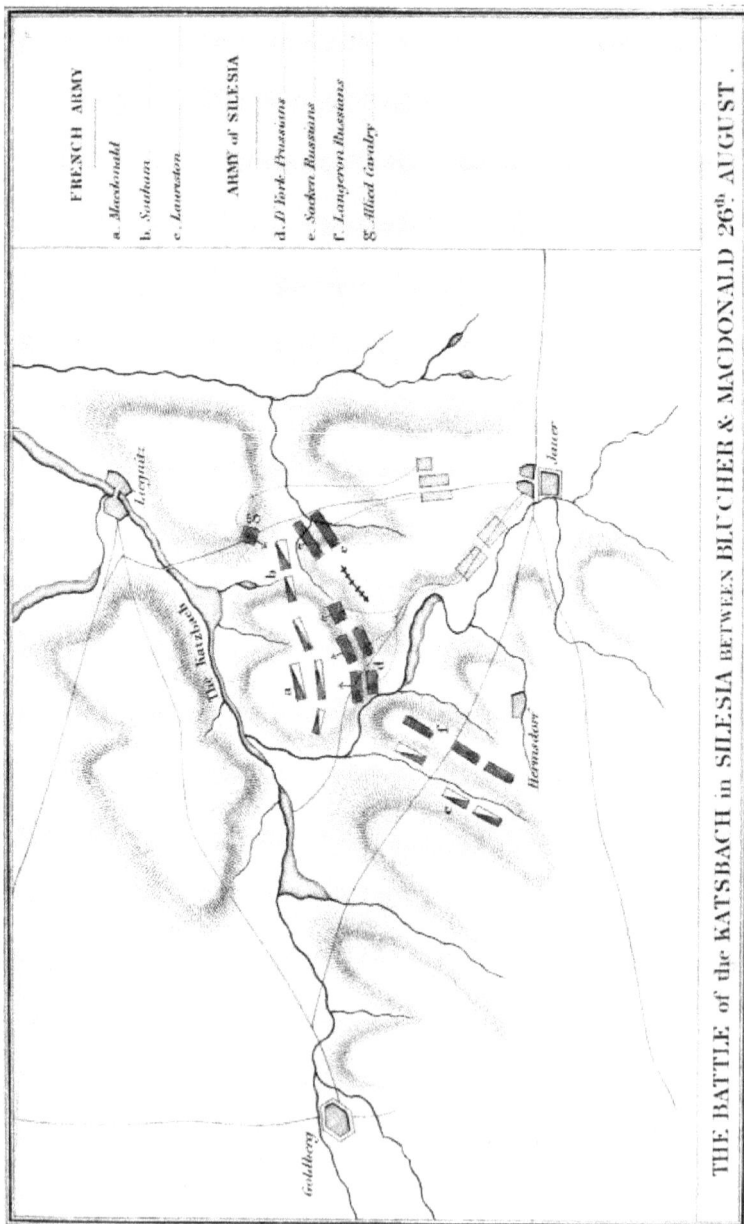

FRENCH ARMY

a. *Macdonald*
b. *Sebbura*
c. *Lauriston*

ARMY of SILESIA

d. *D York Prussians*
e. *Sacken Russians*
f. *Langeron Russians*
g. *Allied Cavalry*

Liegnitz

The Katzbach

Jauer

Hemsdorf

Goldberg

THE BATTLE of the KATSBACH in SILESIA between BLÜCHER & MACDONALD 26th AUGUST.

By the 20th of August, Napoleon had concentrated a force sufficient for his purpose, and met with Blücher, who was preparing to advance across the River Bober. If Napoleon had allowed the Allied troops to pass the river, it might have been difficult for Blücher to extricate himself, and concentrate his force in an attitude to meet his enemy on fair terms. As it was, the Prussian general took warning from the menacing movement of the French, and caused his several corps to retire, and again assemble in a good position, between Adelsdorf and Pilgramsdorf, about two miles in advance of Goldberg. Napoleon attacked on the following day, and a hard-fought battle ensued, in which the Prussians inflicted severe losses upon their enemies, but were forced to retire beyond Goldberg.

Without doubt Napoleon was aware of the intentions of the Allied sovereigns, yet did not believe it possible that Austria could be in a state to take the field. Former examples had not given to that power a character for rash and premature undertakings, and it was therefore with some surprise, that, on the day of his success against Blücher, he learned that the Grand Army of 140,000 men was not only assembled on the Saxon frontier, at a distance of little more than twenty-five English miles from Dresden, but that the Allied sovereigns had quitted Prague to join it, and that an immediate movement into Saxony was to be expected.

This news reached him on the 22nd, as we have already stated, and he made instant arrangements for the support of Dresden, from which he was then about three times as far distant as the invading army which threatened it. The force which he left in Silesia, under the command of Marshal Macdonald, consisted of the 3rd, 5th, and 11th corps, and a corps of cavalry; still this may have amounted to 80,000 men; and at all events it was fully equal in numbers to that of General Blücher.

The Prussian general, who had retired to Jauer, was no sooner aware of the departure of Napoleon, and consequent diminution of his enemy's superiority, than he determined to make a general attack upon their position, on the River Katzbach; and on the 26th of August he carried his intention into effect. This battle terminated in one of the most brilliant and decisive victories recorded on behalf of the Allies.

An opportunity for this co-operation, on the part of the Army of Silesia, had been prepared by the expeditious and well-timed diversion made by the Grand Army; and, on the other hand, in order to show the importance of the co-operation of General Blücher, it is only necessary to state, without entering into details, that on the 1st

BATTLE OF THE KATZBACH

of September his headquarters were advanced to Lowenberg, on the River Bober, and by that time he had gained, by his victory and its consequences as set forth in his general order, three eagles, 103 pieces of cannon, with much ammunition and baggage, and taken prisoners one general of division, two generals of brigade, and 18,000 men. The killed and disabled were doubtless in full proportion. The French 11th corps were nearly destroyed, and the miserable remnant, mostly without arms, afterwards incorporated in others. The Battle of the Katzbach was fought on the day Napoleon reached Dresden.

Army of the North.

Marshal Oudinot, in chief command of the Northern Army of France, which was composed of the 4th, 7th, and 12th French corps, and a corps of cavalry, was entrusted to carry into effect the designs of Napoleon against Prussia.

At the termination of the armistice, Bernadotte, the crown prince, took post with his Swedes at and near Potsdam. The Russians were in cantonments to his right, and the two Prussian corps of Bülow and Tauenzien were detached to his left, to cover the approaches to Berlin from the south.

The country in which the Allied Army of the north was thus stationed is, generally speaking, very flat, and the small rivers which intersect it, and are tributary to the Havel and the Spree, as well as those two larger rivers, are dammed up by nature as well as by art, forming important obstacles to the manoeuvres of an army advancing to Berlin in the presence of an enemy. The intervening country, though generally plain and unenclosed, is also interrupted by occasional swamps and woods. These defensive advantages had been improved in many places, and it must be acknowledged that the capital of Prussia ought not to be easily approached, if covered by a competent force.

Oudinot lost no time in preparing a combined advance upon Berlin with his three *corps d'armée*. On the 22nd of August he came in contact with the advanced corps of Bülow and Tauenzien, whom he found posted in the country between Mittenwalde and Trebbin—two towns through which two great roads approached Berlin from the south. The result of the various affairs which ensued on that day was the ultimate retreat of both the Prussian corps into more advantageous positions within ten English miles from Berlin. The corps of General Bülow was now near Gross Beeren, and the corps of General Tauenzien, about three miles to his left, separated from him by a mo-

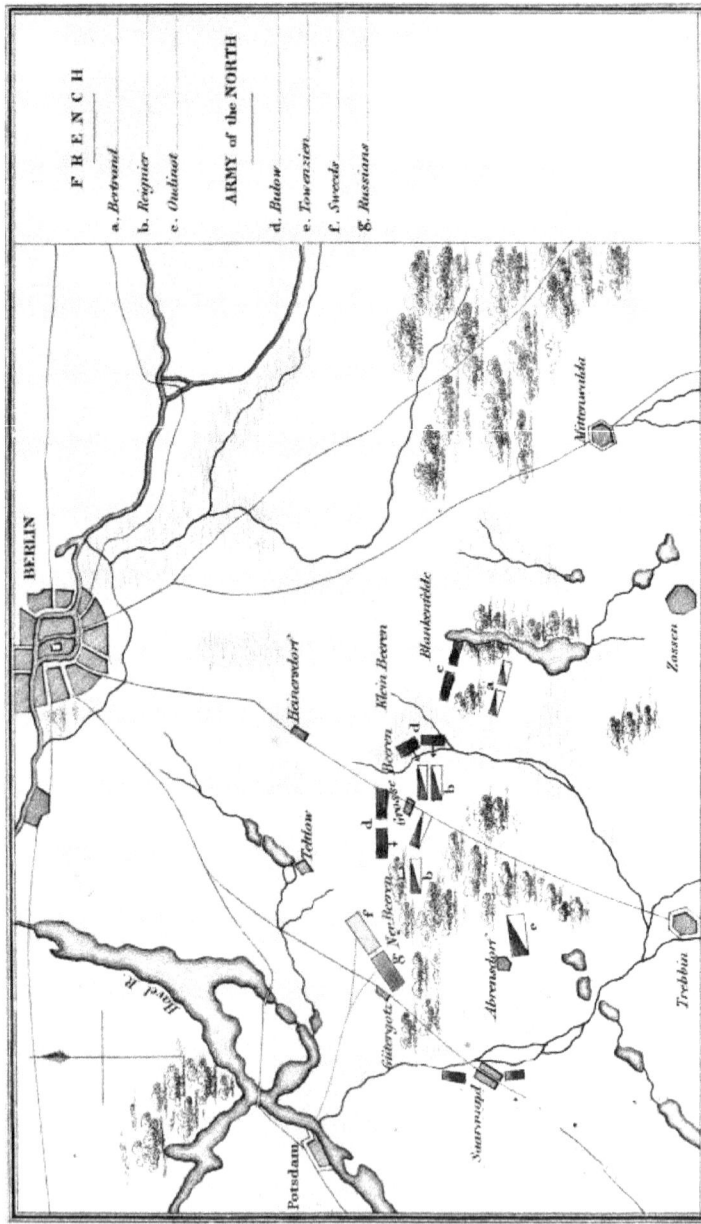

FRENCH

a. Bertrand
b. Reynier
c. Oudinot

ARMY of the NORTH

d. Bulow
e. Tauenzien
f. Sweeds
g. Russians

BERLIN

Wittenwalde

Blankenfelde

Zossen

Klein Beeren

Heinersdorf

Grosse Beeren

Tehlow

Ahrensdorf

Gütergotz

Neu Beeren

Trebbin

Sputendorf

Potsdam

Havel R.

BATTLE of GROSSE BEEREN IN WHICH Mr. OUDINOT WAS REPULSED by the ARMY of the NORTH 23d AUGst.

rass, but securely posted with a morass on each flank.

On the 23rd the attacks on these two corps were renewed by the 4th and 7th French corps. The 12th French corps remained in echelon two or three miles in rear of the left of the other two, and took no part in this day's action. The passive attitude of the French 12th corps may have been occasioned by a knowledge of the Allied force stationed at Potsdam, which was not above six miles from their left; and as no Swedes or Russians had yet appeared in that quarter, this caution was certainly not unwarrantable.

After much perseverance and gallantry, Bülow had retaken Gross Beeren, and was beginning to prevail against General Regnier's corps, while Tauenzien was holding his ground manfully against that of General Bertrand, when the crown prince, with his Swedes and the Russians, made their appearance, and formed on the right of Bülow, but did not come into action. This attitude sufficed to decide the affair of Gross Beeren in favour of the Allies. The French corps were repulsed, and pursued by the Prussians with energy sufficient to compel them to retreat with some loss upon the Elbe.

Thus, the first attempt upon Berlin, since the armistice, was foiled, even before the attack on Dresden.

SECOND ATTEMPT ON BERLIN.

After the Battle of Dresden, Napoleon, by no means satisfied with the conduct of Oudinot in the campaign of Gross Beeren, sent Marshal Ney to supersede him in the chief command. With a view to his altered circumstances, he had then formed the plan of making Dresden a common centre for his armies; acting from which, instead of from a more orthodox base, he might bring concentrated and superior forces, to bear against each of his three separate opponents in succession, and thus he hoped to beat them in detail: a fault in strategy of which he decidedly paid the penalty.

This principle of military action, when a general places himself, with collected forces, in the centre of a hostile circle, can only be justified in the case of small armies in desperate circumstances, such as in civil war, where no other strategic base than the metropolis can be found; the possession of this by either party may then be decisive; and if the foe can be brought to battle without delay, a victory may be attended with a favourable and conclusive result. But in Napoleon's case, his subsequent failures will serve as a sufficient commentary on the uncertainty of that unscientific mode of warfare, and the danger

BATTLE OF GROSS BEEREN

that attends it in the operations of large armies.

When the French Northern Army was defeated at Gross Beeren it retreated upon Wittenburg. Ney's instructions required him to re-assemble this army, and place it more directly on the line of communication between Dresden and Berlin; and in proceeding to effect this primary operation, according to his own account, by a movement upon Dahme, his columns were interrupted by the two Prussian corps of Bülow and Tauenzien, and forced to show front to the left, when they were on their route from Wittenberg to Jüterbock, their advanced guard having reached the village of Dennewitz.

Here a battle took place on the 26th of September, not very unlike the battle at Gross Beeren, since the two Prussian corps bore the brunt of the battle; and the crown prince, with the Swedes and Russians, arrived in position on their right, in time to decide the victory by an attitude, without giving to his Swedes, in either case, any active part whatever in the fight. But on this occasion General Winzingerode, at the head of about 10,000 Russian and other cavalry, followed up the advantage with so much effect that some 10,000 prisoners and 80 pieces of cannon were taken; and the proportion of killed, disabled, and dispersed, caused without doubt a diminution of Napoleon's forces to the amount of not less than 25,000 men.

THE ARMY OF DAVOUST.

Hamburg.

Marshal Davoust did not neglect to attempt a diversion from Hamburg, as far into the country of Mecklenburgh as he was able, consistently with a due regard to the external and internal security of that important place. With about 15,000 men, who were probably all he had disposable for the purpose, he took the field, on the 17th of August, against Walmoden; and, advancing with great caution, he was in the neighbourhood of Hagenow by the 20th, menacing Schwerin. Walmoden contented himself with hanging on his flank, and observing him closely, but was not in sufficient force to warrant the risk of a battle.

After the failure of Oudinot, Davoust returned to Hamburg, and soon after Napoleon withdrew from him a large draft to assist in repairing the losses of his other armies. From that time Davoust could attempt little more than the protection, or rather subjugation, of Hamburg, and could not even restrain the numerous partisans of the Allied Army of the North in their enterprises against him.

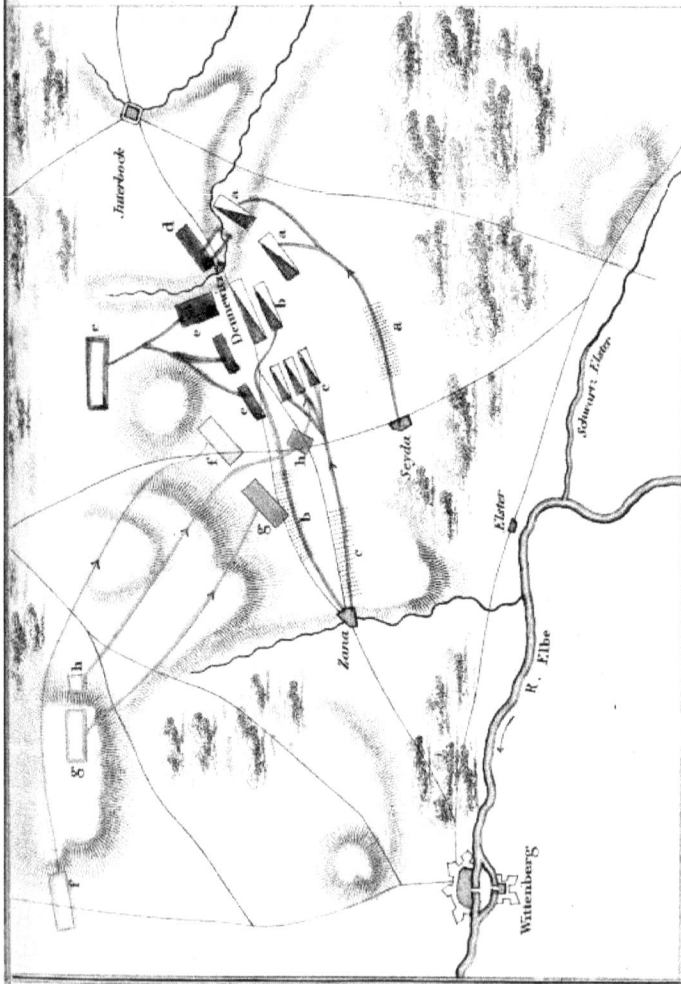

BATTLE OF DENNEWITZ
6TH SEPT 1813.

a. M'Oudinot
b. Bertrand
c. Regnier under the Chief
command of Marshal
Ney and on the March
to Jutterbock
d. Gen! Tauenzien
e. Gen! Bulow
f. Swedes
g. Wintzingerode
h. Gnudry

THE BATTLE of DENNEWITZ. MARSHAL NEY DEAFEATED by the ARMY of the NORTH.

To sum up the results of the campaign of Dresden, and its immediate consequences, we may compute the total loss of the French in
killed, prisoners, and disabled (in short, "*hors de combat,*") at not less
than 80,000 men, to the date of the 26th of September, while, by a
similar computation, the total loss, on the part of the Allies, cannot
have amounted to 50,000. The French also lost nearly 300 pieces of
artillery; and although artillery was lost or abandoned by the Allies, in
the Saxon mountains and other places in this campaign, amounting
perhaps to more than fifty pieces, yet the loss of ordnance was of much
greater consequence to the French than to the Allies, not only on
account of its extent, but of the difficulty they found in replacing it.

Moreau, in his letter to his wife, which was dictated after the battle
of Dresden, says of this campaign, "*Quoique l'armée ait fait un mouve-
ment retrograde, ce n'est nullement par revers mais par decousu*" ("Although
the army has made a retrograde movement, it is not by reverse but
by disjointedness"); and Maret, Duc de Bassano, states no more than
the truth in his official report, where he says that the Austrian Army
quitted its frontier before its organisation was finished, and before its
equipment and clothing were complete.

A delay of six months, and an expenditure of some millions of
money, which Austria had not at her disposal, to equip the troops,
were indispensable to enable her to open such a campaign with any
prospect of success. Admitting the truth of this remark, we must yet
acknowledge that Prince Schwartzenberg was not unwarranted in
pointing, in his general orders, to the great advantages gained by the
Army of Silesia, and the Army of the North, as the consequences of
the well-timed diversion of the Army of Bohemia in its movement
upon Dresden.

CHAPTER 13

First Excursion of Napoleon Against the Army of Silesia

The author is anxious, at this particular period, to invite the attention of the reader to the first principles of strategy, which, like the elements of all sciences, are, when duly recognised, clear and self-evident truths. In point of theory, the admirable work of the Archduke Charles, or, for practical illustration, the base of Torres Vedras covering Lisbon, and the glorious achievements which emanated invariably from it, will be consulted and considered with advantage by those who desire a thorough knowledge of this science; but, for the present purpose, it will suffice to point out that the elements may be reduced to the three following postulates:—

1st—A base of operations, being that locality from which the supplies of the army are to be furnished.

2ndly.—The objective, being an object or goal, the attainment of which must render the campaign decisive, and to which, therefore, all movements must have reference.

3rdly.—The line of operations, being the most favourable route or communication leading from the base to the decisive point or objective.

It follows of course that the base of the defending army must either be the decisive point itself that is menaced by the opposite party, or some other point covering it, and that the line of operations must be common to both.

Bearing these principles in mind, it will be found in the history of modern warfare, conducted by regular armies on both sides, that in every instance where they have been lost sight of, or departed from (and there are many), victory has led to no good result, and defeat has proved an irretrievable disaster. Whereas, where they have been duly attended to, each success has become a point gained in the progress of the campaign; and though partial failures may have retarded operations, and even occasioned retreats, yet such failures have not proved decisive.

In the following chapter it will be found that Napoleon, through obstinacy, like a headstrong gambler playing a losing game, contrary to his own experience and former practice, determined to cling to Dresden, and make it a centre of operations. Under existing circumstances, this was a wilful departure from the principles of strategy; for by doing so, he left the line of communication with his true base, the Rhine, at the mercy of his powerful enemy.

The author is the more desirous of calling attention to this subject, because a popular, and in most cases accurate, writer of general history has characterised this policy of Napoleon's as profoundly conceived, and most ably carried into effect! He trusts that the events recorded in this book alone will suffice to justify the true principles of strategy, and prove the worthlessness of the mis-called "profound conception" of operations with large armies radiating from an insulated centre, without reference to the true base and line of communication.

Napoleon, after following in person the first day's retreat of the Allied Army from Dresden, halted not far from Pirna, on the eve, as it happened, of the battle at Kulm, which was only fifteen miles from that place. He ordered his Young Guard to bivouac near Pirna, and then entered his carriage, and returned to Dresden, flattering himself, no doubt, that his bright star was still in the ascendant, and supposing that all would continue prosperous; judging, too, that Murat on the right, and Vandamme on the left, would suffice to follow up the retreat. At Dresden he soon received unpleasant tidings from the Katzbach, and worse news still from Kulm.

Through the woody mountains some eight thousand fugitives, starving and without arms, found their way to Dresden from the wreck of the corps of Vandamme. His first care was to prepare the frame-work of a new corps, in lieu of that which had perished. For this purpose, he not only assembled a proportion of officers, noncommissioned officers, and men, but guns, and all other things needful, by drafts from other corps, and particularly from that of St. Cyr; and to this new corps he appointed the Count de Löbau as chief, still naming it the First corps.

A few days sufficed for these, and perhaps for other equally important affairs relating to his empire; and on the 3rd of September we find him proceeding from Dresden to the eastward, again to take the field in person against General Blücher.

Second Attempt of Napoleon in Person Against the Army of Silesia.

On the 3rd of September Napoleon left Dresden by the Bautzen road. He was much disturbed by the many convincing proofs of the calamity of the Katzbach; for he witnessed the miserable debris of the eleventh corps, which he met upon the road before he reached Bischofswerda. Near this place he halted for the night; and next morning, accompanied by Macdonald and Murat, whom he had ordered to join him at Dresden, he hastened forward to the troops that were in Silesia. Arriving at Hochkirch, he found the armies in presence.

General Blücher occupied a strong position in the hills, called Stromberg and Vohlaerberg. Napoleon caused it to be attacked, and after a protracted resistance, which the nature of the ground rendered more expensive to the attacking than to the defending party, the Allies retired, covered by light troops and Cossacks, which in that woody and broken country rendered it impossible to press or hurry them.

Their retreat was followed, slowly and cautiously, beyond Reichenbach; but there, Napoleon saw plainly that Blücher, whose forces were not very disproportionate to his own, was acting on a systematic plan of avoiding a general action, and retiring, to entice him farther from his centre of support and supplies, into a country rendered very intricate by its woods and broken ground, and totally exhausted of forage and provisions. He therefore reluctantly abandoned, for a time, the vain hope of disposing of the Army of Silesia in the summary manner he had wished.

Much dejected at this new failure in Silesia, and after an absence of only four days, he went back to Dresden on the 7th. The news of the signal defeat of his Northern Army at Dennewitz met him on his return. Thus, two of the great blows that he would have struck from his central *appui* were already parried.

CHAPTER 14.

Expedition of Napoleon in September, 1813, Against the Bohemian Frontier

After the Battle of Kulm, the Allied sovereigns had no sooner resumed their position within the Bohemian frontier, and been informed of the satisfactory proceedings of their armies in Silesia and the north of Germany, than they took active measures to bring forward reinforcements, and make other arrangements preparatory to a renewal of hostilities. Considering their immense resources, these arrangements, if duly matured, could not fail to place the advantage so entirely on their side as to render success almost certain; and in this confident hope they determined, in the interim, to restrict their own forces and the other co-operating armies to a system of defensive resistance, which the false position wilfully assumed by Napoleon enabled them to do.

The Russian and Prussian contingents of the Army of Bohemia had not sustained more loss than is the unavoidable consequence of such a campaign as that of Dresden. They were experienced troops, and their discipline and equipment were unimpaired. Still the wear and tear of an army under such circumstances is great; and, without reckoning those who from temporary causes, sickness and slight wounds, were absent from the ranks, and allowing merely for their actual loss, we cannot compute their effective strength, in the beginning of September, at above 60,000 men. This force occupied the position of Kulm and the neighbourhood of Töplitz.

The Austrians had been less well prepared to take the field at the sudden opening of the campaign, and had of late been out of practice in actual warfare; hence their commissariat and other essentials to an army in the field were very defective; and although they had suffered severely from the enemy, they were inconvenienced nearly as much by their own imperfect organisation. After the battle of Kulm they retired across the Elbe at Leütmeritz, ostensibly to be prepared to repel an apprehended invasion of Bohemia by the defiles of Zittau and Friedland; but as there was no sufficient cause for this apprehension, it is not impossible that their disappearance immediately after the Battle of Kulm may be ascribed, in part, to a very natural and judicious wish to profit by the calm that promised to succeed the recent stormy events, in which their organisation had been somewhat shattered, and to gain a quiet opportunity of refitting, so as to return to the front in perfect order at the time their services should be required.

On the Pirna road the enemy had not followed the retreat from Dresden in force, probably relying upon Vandamme for that duty; and, after the Battle of Kulm, Napoleon's attention being turned to Silesia, that road remained comparatively unguarded. During this interval, Wittgenstein did not continue in indolent security in the position at Kulm, where he was entrusted with the outpost duties, but pushed a reconnaissance through the defile of Nöllendorf, and reached as far as Pirna. On the 7th of September, the day of Napoleon's return from Silesia, his advanced guard, commanded by General Ziethen, was within a few English miles of Dresden, and remained in that advanced position all night.

Napoleon's thoughts were now directed towards Bohemia, and on the next day, the 8th, he marched out of Dresden, on the Pirna road, with his guards and his newly formed 1st corps; the 6th corps making a corresponding movement by the roads leading to the defiles of Eichwald, the 14th corps supporting it.

Wittgenstein retreated of course, but having advantageous ground, and well knowing the management of supports alternating or judiciously placed in succession, with confidence derived from the certainty of a secure reserve behind him in the position at Kulm, inflicted severe loss on those who attempted to press him, and did not withdraw from the last mountain position of Nöllendorf, into the plains of Kulm, till the evening of the 10th.

Napoleon followed his retreat as far as the verge of the mountains, and some light infantry made their appearance in the hills of Groupen, which commands the defile of Eichwald, with the confidence of troops whose reserves were at hand. A disposition was made to oppose any attempt of the French to issue from the pass of Eichwald, as well as from that of Nöllendorf; but no serious attack was made by the enemy at either point.

The force Napoleon had with him at that time could not have been adequate to the invasion of Bohemia, if the whole Allied Army had been assembled to oppose him; yet there is no doubt he would have attempted it, if he could have forced his way into the plain. He was probably aware of the temporary absence of the Austrians, and therefore thought the moment favourable; but till then he was not fully aware of the nature of the obstacles. He spent that day and the next in examining the defiles, particularly that by Eichwald; but he found the road so broken up and destroyed, and by nature so unfavourable to his purpose, that he abandoned the enterprise, and returned to Dresden on the 13th of September.

On the same day the Austrians began to return to the plains of Kulm, and the Allied Grand Army, including troops in position, and those within supporting distance, may have amounted soon after to something more than 100,000 men, well fed and well supplied in every respect. Although they had long been and were still for the most part *"en bivouac,"* and in unfavourable weather, and that the luxury and encumbrance of tents were alike unknown in these armies at any time, yet their condition, in point of nourishment, health, and comfort, was infinitely superior to that of the enemy, who remained in the miserable and exhausted country above them.

The impossibility of supplying the wants of a concentrated army from the local resources of that wild country, even for a few days, and the great difficulty of transport, rendered it impossible for Napoleon's army to remain long in force upon the frontier line of hills. A considerable portion of it fell back into more convenient quarters; and, as soon as this was discovered, Prince Schwartzenberg planned a combined reconnaissance.

The "abattis" at Nöllendorf was cleared, and on the 14th of September Wittgenstein again advanced on the Pirna road, pushing forward a division through the mountains on the enemy's left, in the hope of cutting off a part of his force; the Austrian corps of Colloredo, and the division of Prince William of Prussia, were to effect a similar operation on the enemy's right.

Although these combinations did not completely realise the intentions of the commander-in-chief, as must sometimes happen in an intricate country, yet some advantages were gained with little loss, except that of Colonel Blücher, a son of the general, who was wounded in a charge of cavalry, and captured by the enemy. The Duke of Cumberland, now King of Hanover, who had lately arrived at Töplitz, was

137

present in this affair. The Allies held the hill of Nöllendorf that night, and returned into their position the next day.

The alarm of this advance by the Allies brought Napoleon back to Pirna. He slept there on the 15th, and on the 16th made arrangements for the concentration of the 1st, 2nd, and 14th corps, two corps of cavalry, and his guards, at Nöllendorf; the 6th corps being already at Altenberg.

On the 17th Prince Schwartzenberg had drawn the advanced posts, from the abattis and base of the hills, closer to Kulm, and stood prepared to dispute the entrance into the plain. The enemy then advanced in force, and endeavoured to extend at the mouth of the defile; they were opposed by a heavy cannonade, and Napoleon sent some of the cavalry of the guard into the plain, who attempted to charge the batteries, but without success.

The Austrian field-marshal having previously occupied Aussig, which is on the Elbe, and on the extreme right, directed General Meerfeldt, now at the head of the corps which at Dresden had been commanded by General Chasteller, to advance from that place through the defile formed by the Elbe, supported by Colloredo, and gain the dominant heights of Nöllendorf, in rear of the enemy. Hitherto Wittgenstein's duty had been confined to maintaining his position in the plain, and preventing the French from issuing from the mountains; in the evening he was ordered to attack, which he did with his accustomed energy and judgment, at the same time causing the Prussian brigade of Ziethen by mountain paths to gain the enemy's right flank.

These attacks prevailed at all points, and the appearance of the Austrians in the hills, in rear of the French left, produced a panic among them. One general, seven cannons, and upwards of 2,000 prisoners were taken. The fog and the approach of night alone prevented a defeat possibly equal to the former catastrophe at Kulm.

It did not enter into the plan of the Allies to pursue this advantage, and follow the French into the mountains. Meerfeldt and Colloredo withdrew, and the enemy were suffered to recover and retain their position at Nöllendorf on the 18th. The Austrians employed that day in relieving the corps of Wittgenstein in the position at Kulm, and in taking up the outpost duties.

On the 19th the enemy retired of their own accord, and unmolested, to the position of Gishübel near Königstein. Napoleon slept that night and the next at Pirna, and on the 21st he returned to Dresden, having made a fruitless campaign.

Third Campaign of Napoleon, Based Upon His Centre of Dresden, and Directed Against the Army of Silesia.

After his failure against the Army of Bohemia, Napoleon again only allowed himself one night's rest on his return to Dresden; and the next day, which was the 22nd, he started for Hartau near Bischofswerda, where he had caused the 3rd, 5th, and 11th corps to assemble, with some cavalry; being determined to make one attempt more to bring General Blücher to a battle.

This excursion proved as unsatisfactory as the preceding in its result; for, in conformity with the preconcerted plan of forbearance, Blücher declined the combat and retired. Thus was Napoleon again foiled; he had been unable to interrupt the regular progress of those arrangements of the Allies which now wanted only a few days for their completion, and which, when completed, could not fail to render his precipitate abandonment of Dresden and the Elbe inevitable. Yet he still clung to that false base, and neglected to secure in time a position for his army more in conformity with the obvious rules of strategy.

Having penetrated little beyond the forests in the neighbourhood of Bischofswerda, without coming to any regular action, Napoleon again returned to Dresden on the 24th, and thus ended the fifth and last of those unavailing excursions in which he had been wasting his strength and time since the armistice.

As soon as he had withdrawn, Blücher resumed the offensive, and pushed his advanced posts to the environs of Dresden. Count Bubna, who commanded the Austrian corps which had been entrusted with the defence of the defiles of Zittau, advanced into Lusatia, and joined the left of the Silesian Army. The Russians and Swedes of the Army of the North were assembled opposite Dessau, communicating with Tauenzien, who was opposite Wittenberg; and Bülow at Elster completed the communication with the army of Blücher; so that the whole right bank of the Elbe, with the exception of the two fortresses of Wittenberg and Dresden, and certain *têtes-de-pont*, might be said to be in possession of the Allies.

The Grand Army of Russia, Prussia, and Austria, amounting to upwards of 100,000 men, was assembled in the neighbourhood of Töplitz, and the several divisions of the corps of Beningsen (which was the reserve formerly alluded to, as being expected from the Russian frontier, which in all were said to amount to 40,000 men, exclusive of reinforcements, to complete the Russian corps to the proper numbers of the establishment,) began to arrive by Leutmeritz and Aussig, and join the Grand Army.

Klenau, with about 12,000 men, had been left all this time in the entrenched position of Sebastiansberg, where he had taken post to guard that defile after the battle of Dresden, and had thrown up some field-works for its defence; but that route was too intricate and too distant from Dresden to enter into Napoleon's plan of operations so long as he continued to act from a centre, and therefore Klenau had been undisturbed.

Numerous partisans, including the Hettman Platof with eight or ten thousand Cossacks, were doing good service, on the great road to France, in the country between the Elster and the Saale, by impeding the progress of supplies, and cutting off communications.

The attention of the reader is directed to the diagram, in order to judge, in one comprehensive view, of the circumstances in which Napoleon allowed himself to be found on or about the 30th of September, at which time the first movement of the campaign of Leipzig aroused him, like a stag from his lair, where he had lain too long to escape from the toils which the hunters had drawn round him.

CHAPTER 15

Circumstances of the Armies at the Opening of the Campaign

To ascertain the force, on the side of Napoleon, that was available for the Battles of Leipzig, we must deduct 26,000 men for the corps of St. Cyr and Count Löbau left at Dresden. This leaves a force of 182,000 men available for the campaign. In this computation, the corps of Davoust, and the unattached and provisional battalions in the several garrisons on the Elbe, are not noticed; but these, with the garrison of Dresden, would make the troops remaining on the Elbe amount to 60,000, and Napoleon's whole force in Germany to 242,000.

Of the French loss, upwards of 50,000 are accounted for, as prisoners taken by the Allies during the two months which intervened between the dates of the comparative statements annexed. The rest were killed, disabled, sick, and deserters, who became daily more numerous among the foreign components of Napoleon's army.

The campaign, which had caused this loss to Napoleon of about one-third, comprised, as we have seen, three signal defeats of the French, and a constant succession of harassing and fruitless marches; whilst to the Allies it had been a period of comparative repose. And now Napoleon's resources were well-nigh exhausted, whilst those of the Allies were only beginning to be developed. There had been no great fault in the tactics of the French Armies—no disgraceful defeat—but the whole was the result of an unpardonable fault in strategy of their chief.

No. 1.

Statement of the Forces of Napoleon, at the opening of the Campaign of Leipzig, compared with their former Strength at the opening of the Campaign of Dresden:—

Corps.		Men. (In July, 1813.)	(In October, 1813.)	Men.
	Old Guard -	6,600	- -	4,000
	Young Guard -	32,000	- -	24,000
	Cavalry of the Guard -	10,000	- -	6,000
1.	Vandamme -	25,000	Afterwards Mouton, Count Lobau.	6,000
2.	Victor - -	21,000	- -	18,000
3.	Ney (Souham) -	32,000	Ney at Leipzig -	22,000
4.	Bertrand -	21,000	- -	14,000
5.	Lauriston -	35,000	- -	10,000
6.	Marmont -	30,000	- -	20,000
7.	Regnier - -	20,000	- -	8,000
8.	Poniatowski -	15,000	- -	10,000
11.	Macdonald -	21,000	- -	14,000
12.	Oudinot - -	24,000	Broken up.	
14.	St. Cyr - -	31,000	- -	20,000
	Latour Maubourg	10,000	- -	6,000 ⎫
	Sebastiani ⎱ Milhaud ⎰	13,000	Sebastiani ⎱ Milhaud ⎰	6,000 ⎪ 3,000 ⎬ Cavalry.
	Arrighi ⎱ Kellerman ⎰	10,000	Arrighi - Kellerman - Augereau -	3,000 ⎪ 4,000 ⎪ 10,000 ⎭
	Total -	356,000	Total -	208,000

Loss of strength during August and September, not made up, 148,000.

No. 2.

Statement of the Forces of the Allies at the opening of the Campaign of Leipzig, compared with their former strength at the opening of the Campaign of Dresden:—

(In July, 1813.)	Men.	(In October, 1813.)	Men.	Men.
Wittgenstein -	40,000	- - -	16,000	⎫
Russian Reserve -	24,000	- - -	18,000	⎪
Cavalry of Reserve -	11,000	- - -	8,000	⎪
Kleist - -	25,000	- - -	29,000	⎪
Colloredo - ⎫				⎬ 120,000
Chasteller (Meerfeldt) ⎪		Meerfeldt -		⎪
Giulay ⎬	50,200	- - -	49,000	⎪
The Reserve ⎪		- - -		⎪
Klenau ⎪		- - -		⎪
Blucher (D'York) ⎭		- - -		⎭
Langeron - ⎫		- - -		
Lacken - ⎬	75,000	- - -	82,000	
Sherbatof* - ⎭		- - -		
Swedes - ⎫	25,000	- - -	20,000	⎫
Winzingerode ⎪	12,000	- - -	17,000	⎪
Bulow ⎬	20,000	- - -	24,000	⎬ 71,000
Tanenzien - ⎪	5,000	- - -	10,000	⎪
Beningsen - - ⎭		- - -	20,000	⎭
Tolstoi *		- - -	20,000	
Nostitz (Bubna) -	6,000	Bubna - -	10,000	
Total -	293,000	Total -	323,000	

Deduct about 60,000 for the corps marked * left on the right bank of the Elbe, and the disposable force will amount to 263,800.

The increase of force, as estimated in the foregoing tables, over and above the numbers required to replace the loss incidental to an active and harassing campaign, amounted to 33,000 men; therefore, the whole amount of new troops brought into the field in that period cannot have been less than 120,000. This renovation of strength was chiefly accomplished by the vast exertions made by Prussia, in organising and bringing forward *landwehr*, and drafting from that source for the completion of regular corps.

Russia had also done her part nobly, considering that from the Niemen to the Elbe is a distance of about eight hundred miles.

As regards the war in Germany, the Austrians, although they were at home, had only been able to keep their small force efficient, and to replace the loss they sustained in the campaign of Dresden; but their attention had also been directed towards Italy during this period.

The plan of campaign adopted by the Allies had for its basis a general concentration of all their armies on the main communications of Napoleon with France. This was the principle advocated by Moreau and others at the outset of the preceding campaign; and although it implied the abandonment, on the part of the Allies, of the main communication with the Russian territories, yet little was to be apprehended on that account; for the exhausted condition and national hostility of the countries to the east of the Elbe, and the important but precarious stake which Napoleon still held in those to the west, rendered the maintenance of a direct communication with his only proper base, the Rhine, an object of vital importance to him; whilst the Allies, having adopted the Bohemian frontier for their base, were in a great measure independent of the line of operations through Silesia, which they were about to abandon.

To carry this plan into effect, it was agreed that the Prince Royal of Sweden, with the Army of the North, about 61,000 men, and General Blücher, with that of Silesia, about 65,000, should cross the Elbe north of Dresden, and, acting in concert, move down upon the Saale at Halle or Merseburg; whilst the Grand Army, amounting to about 120,000 men, should move out of Bohemia, by its left, upon Lützen or Weissenfels. When the three armies should be united near these points, in rear of the defiles caused by the Rivers Pleisse, Elster, and Saale, they would be in complete possession and command of Napoleon's communications, and their united forces would amount to about 246,000 men. Besides these, the troops left to defend the Bohemian passes, or observe Dresden, including the army of Beningsen, amounted to about 60,000 men, otherwise disposable according to circumstances. These operations were to commence, on all sides, with the month of October.

The apathy of Napoleon at that time has never been satisfactorily explained or excused. He appears to have been unprepared with any plans, but remained at Dresden, and took no decisive measures till the 6th of October. By this time the movements of the Allies had rendered it no longer possible for him to concentrate his forces, and assume a defensive attitude behind the Saal, covering the great road to France. The recovery of that advantage, then lost by his delay, implied nothing less than a victory to be gained over superior forces in a position of their own choice. Instead of attempting this recovery of his lost communication in the first instance, when he did, at length, leave Dresden, he directed his principal forces towards the north, still clinging to the Elbe. His motives are thus explained in the fifteenth bulletin:—

> The emperor's intention was to pass the Elbe, to manoeuvre upon the right bank between Hamburg and Dresden, to threaten Potsdam and Berlin, and to assume Magdeburg for the centre of operations, which had been supplied with provisions and warlike stores for this purpose.

With regard to Napoleon's conduct on this occasion, it has been said, first, that he stayed too long at Dresden; secondly, that the position of Leipzig was ill chosen, with a river in his rear; and, thirdly, that he should have retired behind the Saale.

As to the first remark, there cannot well be two opinions. The second would be equally just, if the battle in front of Leipzig had not become ultimately a matter of necessity, and not of choice. With regard to the third remark, the military circumstances of the country, implied by the phrase "behind the Saale" (so well understood, and so constantly employed, by all military men who treat of war in Germany), require some explanation to enable others to appreciate its important connection with the dilemma in which Napoleon found himself placed at the beginning of the month of October, 1813.

The River Saale rises in a "spur" from the western extremity of the Bohemian frontier chain of mountains which may be said to connect that gigantic ridge with the Thuringer Wald. It soon becomes a considerable river, and its general course is northerly. After being joined by several tributaries, it falls into the Elbe, about fifteen miles above Magdeburg. Jena, Weisenfels, Merseburg, Halle, and other wealthy and important towns, are seated on its banks.

The great road which traverses central Germany from east to west crosses the Saale near Naumburg, and passes on through Erfurt, Gotha, Eisenach, and Frankfort towards Mayence, where it crosses the Rhine into France. This was Napoleon's line of operations, or main communication with France, when he occupied Dresden; indeed, it formed a link in his main communication when at Moscow, and it was at all times of vital importance to his armies. To those who look upon a sufficient map, it will be obvious that the course of this great road is influenced, in a remarkable manner, by geographical circumstances, which cannot fail to render it the best, if not the only available, line of operations for an army that has the Rhine for its base, and that threatens a war of invasion against Saxony or Prussia, and the countries beyond.

The diagram prepared for the purpose, may however assist in pointing out more clearly the remarkable manner in which the Harz mountains to the north, and the Thuringer forest, also a mountainous tract of country to the south, geographically contract the intervening space to a degree which, with reference to the operations of the large armies we have at present in our contemplation, may be considered to constitute a grand defile.

In the centre of this defile, and at the most convenient strategic point on the great line of road, stands the town of Erfurt, containing 16,000 inhabitants, and regularly fortified; of sufficient size to be capable of sheltering a large garrison as a place of arms in case of need, and of sufficient strength to require a regular siege. It is secured and controlled, moreover, by the small commanding citadel of St. Petersburg, which is in itself as strong and complete a fortress as art can contrive.

This whole extent of country, with the points to which we have adverted, and many others which cannot fail to strike a military observer, must be included in the idea conveyed by the phrase "behind the Saale," and not merely the defensibility of that little river itself, or any particular position on its bank.

It will be admitted, that in a narrow and well flanked country like this, full of good positions, and guarded by a fortress at the best-chosen strategic point, a comparatively small defensive army might bar the passage against a superior force. A large manoeuvring army, assuming such a country as its proximate base, might therefore act from it with freedom and security. No doubt, this country may be turned by a road to the south, through the Thuringer Wald, which is not impracticable, though difficult by nature, and, like all mountain and forest roads, more easy to defend than to force. Any attempt, however, to manoeuvre by these roads, under circumstances approaching to equality of force, without previously dislodging the hostile army by a battle somewhere in the country of Saxe Weimar, would expose the flank of a lengthened column to a concentrated attack, and to inevitable dismemberment and destruction in detail.

The same observation would apply to the road on the other flank, by Sondershausen, or between the Unstruth and the southern base of the mountainous district of the Harz.

The roads leading more widely to the southward, as those by Saalfeld, Hof, Würzburg, and Ratisbon, could not properly enter into the views of a general whose base was the Rhine, and whose decisive object was placed beyond the Elbe, as permanent lines of operation, although by these roads Napoleon advanced unexpectedly upon Jena in 1806, and placed his whole force between Prussia and the Prussian Army; but this was a surprise, and the Prussian Army should not then have been found on the left bank of the Saale. On that occasion, however, Napoleon had no sooner gained Erfurt, which had been in possession of the Prussians till then, than he took measures to open and establish his line of communication permanently by that road which passes through it, with a view to operations beyond the Elbe. As regards the present question, the southern route is too far removed from the seat of war, supposed in this argument, to have any direct reference to it.

Any operation by the Allies against a French Army established in position behind the Saale, to turn altogether the northern barrier—that of the Harz mountains—would have implied the removal of the war into the north of Germany, and abandonment of all the southern interests.

Now, when it is said that Napoleon should have retired behind the Saale, it must be meant that he should have done so immediately after repelling the attack of the Allied Grand Army upon Dresden in August, instead of waiting till the end of September. By this time their movements had made it too late for him to contemplate such a measure of precaution; and the loss of time could only be retrieved by force of arms.

Let us, then, consider what might have been the state of affairs if, during the armistice, he had at once adopted the measure of retiring with his main army behind the Saale, and combined it with the project hinted at in his fifteenth bulletin, for the disposal of his forces in the north. Suppose him at that time, when his whole force in the field, including his garrisons on the Elbe, amounted to nearly 400,000 men, to have divided that force into two great armies, one for the north of Germany, the other for the Saale.

The troops might have been withdrawn from Silesia, the garrisons of Dresden, and all other places on the Upper Elbe, except Wittenberg, might have been sent, with all stores and supplies, down the river to Magdeburg. The line of base for the Northern Army would have been contracted to the Lower Elbe, between Magdeburg and Hamburg. Wittenberg might have been retained as an outpost, and for the sake of its bridge, but would not have been essential to that base. So stationed, 200,000 men would, in truth, have threatened Potsdam and Berlin.

Suppose, next, that he had concentrated his remaining 200,000 men in the country behind the Saale, securely covering his main communication, and occupying a position from which he might have acted with confidence and vigour against any force that could be brought out of Bohemia to oppose him. In that case, both his armies would have been placed at the same time in the midst of plenty, with every facility for securing ample and regular supplies from the rear, and in an attitude equally well prepared for offensive or defensive operations.

When we recollect that this state of things was certainly at Napoleon's option at the period to which we allude, and that it must have passed through his mind, his apathy and indecision at Dresden appear more like infatuation, or morbid obstinacy, than the result of any error in judgment, of which a mind like his could have been capable when in its usual health and vigour.

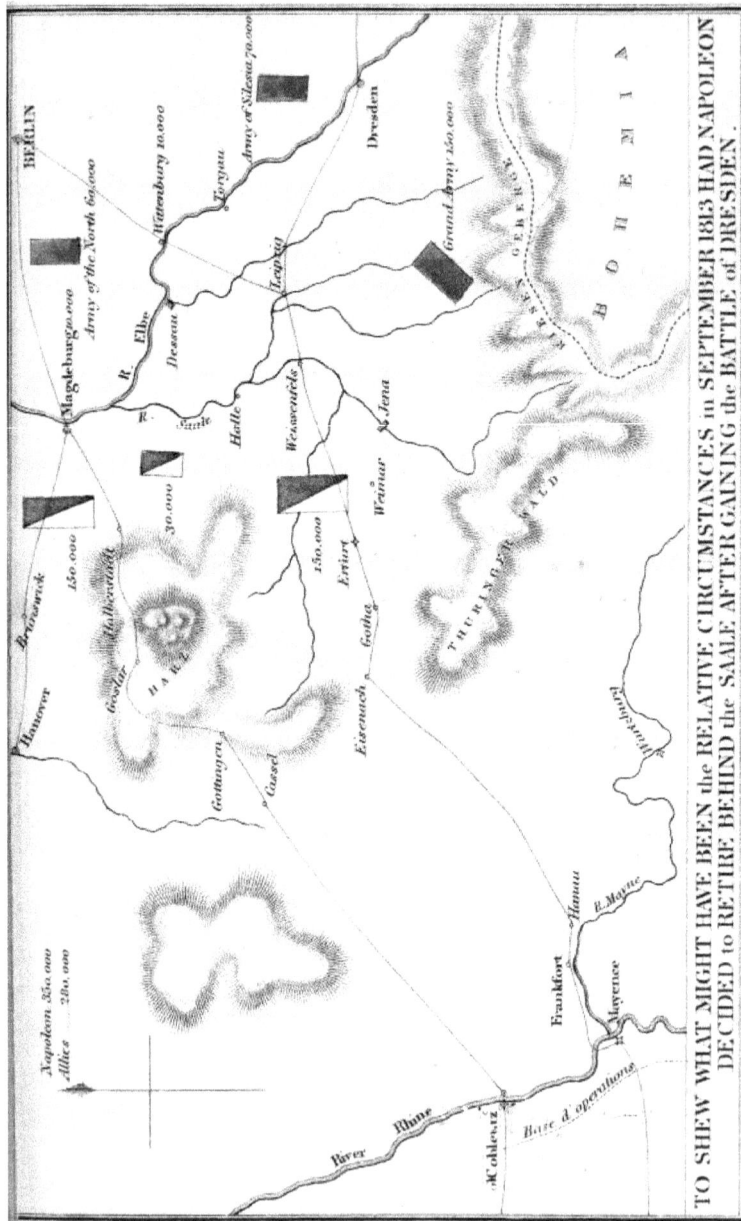

TO SHEW WHAT MIGHT HAVE BEEN the RELATIVE CIRCUMSTANCES in SEPTEMBER 1813 HAD NAPOLEON DECIDED to RETIRE BEHIND the SAALE AFTER GAINING the BATTLE of DRESDEN.

CHAPTER 16

Previous Movements Which Led to the Crisis of Leipzig

ARMY OF SILESIA.

According to the previous arrangement, General Blücher commenced the operations of the campaign of Leipzig on the 1st of October, leaving the Russian General Scherbatof at Bautzen, with a detachment of his army, consisting of 20,000 men. In conjunction with the Austrian corps of Count Bubna, amounting to 10,000, the Russian general was to cover Silesia, and to observe Dresden. Blücher marched, with expedition and secrecy, to his right, with an army of about 65,000 effective men, Russians and Prussians, divided into three corps, under the Russian generals Langeron and Sacken and the Prussian general D'York. By the morning of the 3rd of October, he had reached the village of Elster, on the right bank of the Elbe, near the confluence of the Schwartz Elster, and about ten English miles above Wittenberg.

At this point, which was favourable from the bend of the river and the nature of the ground, he proceeded to lay down the pontoons he had brought with him, and to pass his army across the Elbe. Since the defeat at Dennewiz the French forces, which were on that occasion commanded by Marshal Ney, had not been able to continue on the right bank of the Elbe. Their remains—for they had been much diminished by that disaster—were yet in possession of the bridges, and also prepared to hold the fortified towns of Wittenberg and Torgau against the attempts of the prince royal to take them.

This French Army, of the Middle Elbe, was originally formed by Napoleon of three corps, and was intended to menace Berlin, but had twice failed in that object. One corps, that of Marshal Oudinot, had suffered so severely, that Napoleon caused its small remnant to be drafted into others, and its chief was appointed to the command of a division of the Young Guard; so that the 12th corps had ceased to exist. There only remained the corps of Regnier, now reduced to 8,000, and that of Bertrand, of 14,000, with some cavalry in bad condition, exclusive of the garrisons of Wittenberg and Torgau.

Marshal Ney had already returned to his own corps. Bertrand was at Dessau, and as soon as he heard of the unexpected movement of Blücher on the village of Elster, and his preparations for crossing the Elbe, he put his corps in motion, to its right, on the morning of the 2nd, with all expedition. Although he could not arrive in time and in force to prevent the establishment of the bridges, he took up a good position near Bleddin and Wartenburg, and did his best to molest the passage and formation of the Prussians.

As soon as Blücher had sufficient force on the left bank, though little more than the corps of D'York had yet crossed, he attacked Bertrand's strong position. The Prussians carried the village of Bleddin with the alacrity of troops who had just surmounted one great obstacle, and, flushed with success, were now rushing on to a second. Although the corps of Bertrand is allowed to have done its duty nobly, it was defeated, and constrained to draw off in the direction of Wittenberg. This victory, which is called the Battle of Wartenburg, was not achieved without considerable loss, and eleven French guns remained as trophies in possession of the victors.

The Army of Silesia had not only crossed the Elbe by the 5th of October, but the heads of its columns were on the Mulde, and Blücher was preparing to cross the river at Düben, and perform his part in the general combination by marching upon Halle, in conformity with the preconcerted plan of campaign. By doing thus it will be observed, that he was about to leave the country unoccupied between the Elbe and the Mulde, but he was not, as Napoleon asserted, "*chassé*" from it.

Army of the North.

The Prince Royal of Sweden, Bernadotte, having been informed of the movement of General Blücher, and the passage of the river by his troops, caused the Army of the North to cross the Elbe on the 4th of October, at two points immediately in his front, the Russians at Acken, the Swedes at Roslau. The feeble corps of Regnier could offer no effectual resistance, and retired before Count Michel Woronzof, who commanded Winzingerode's advanced guard. During the subsequent days the Generals Bertrand and Regnier exerted their ingenuity to avoid these superior forces; but the Allied Armies of Silesia and of the North at length effected their junction on the 7th of October, in the country between the Mulde and the Saale, near Jessnitz, Radegast and Zorbig, and their combined forces now amounted to about 120,000 men.

THE ALLIED GRAND ARMY, OR ARMY OF BOHEMIA.

The Austrian corps of Count Colloredo remained at Kulm; and Beningsen and Tolstoi having arrived at Töplitz on the 4th of October, with the reserves and reinforcements from Poland, about 40,000 men, also took post in that neighbourhood, to guard the pass of Nöllendorf, or move on Dresden, or otherwise act according to circumstances. The rest of the disposable force in Bohemia, amounting to about 110,000 men, as detailed in the general statement, had already commenced their movement by corps in succession to their left, by Kommotau, and passing through the defile of Sebastiansberg, each occupied the post allotted to it on the Saxon side of the mountains, until the movement should be completed.

This preliminary operation was accomplished by the 7th of October. On the 8th the news of the Battle of Wartenburg, and of the passage of the Elbe by the prince royal, reached the Allied headquarters at Kommotau, and on this day the reserves and general headquarters crossed the mountains to Chemnitz, on the road towards Leipzig.

Ever since the retreat from Dresden, the Austrian General Klenau had been left in observation in that country, with a view to cover the defiles of Sebastiansberg, and had been frequently engaged with the corps of Victor and Poniatowski with success, though only in partial affairs. These two French corps had of late drawn off to their right in the direction of Penig, which is on the Mulde, and the corps of General Klenau now formed a sort of flanking column to the right of the main army towards Freyburg.

Wittgenstein, with whom the Prussians, under the command of General Kleist, were associated, making a united force of about 45,000 men, advanced to Altenberg. The Austrian main army with the reserves followed them, with the purpose, according to the original plan of campaign, of effecting a general reunion of the three armies somewhere in the country about Lützen, or, with reference to Napoleon's line of operations, in other words, in the country behind Leipzig, by which a regular army of about 260,000 men might have been formed in one battle array to bar the direct road to France.

"COLONNES MOBILES"

During this period small detached corps and partisans had not been idle. Prince Maurice Lichtenstein, with four light battalions and sixteen squadrons, and General Thielemann, a Saxon, who had recently come over to the side of the Allies, with a similar command, besides other separate services, had been co-operating on the Saale near Jena, and molesting Marshal Augereau in his advance with French reinforcements by Weisenfels on Leipzig. Though they took many prisoners, and had considerable success, Augereau was ably covered by General Milhaud, with some very efficient cavalry recently brought from Spain, and made good his march to Leipzig with about 20,000 men.

Platof, with about 6,000 men, chiefly Cossacks, was acting independently, and roving about the country to the eastward of Leipzig, to the great inconvenience of couriers and stragglers of all sorts.

We have now brought the three Allied Armies fairly into the field, and accounted for them up to the 7th of October, the date on which the movements of Napoleon from Dresden only commenced.

THE FRENCH ARMY.

All the sallies of Napoleon from his central point of Dresden had been frustrated, as we have seen; and at the end of the month of September, when the Allies took the field for this campaign, he found himself again in that city, with nearly all his remaining disposable force collected around it. But that force had lost six weeks of time, and one third of its strength, without having gained one real advantage, and now his communication with the Rhine was effectually cut off.

The 4th and 7th French corps have been accounted for between the Elbe and the Mulde, and their communications with Dresden were clear. The 12th corps no longer existed. The 8th corps we have described as on the lookout towards the Allied Grand Army near Penig, supported by the 2nd corps and the greater part of the remaining cavalry; but that arm had suffered severely both for want of forage and in the field, and was not in heart or condition to compete in equal force with the cavalry of the Allies. Marmont, with the 6th corps, had been sent to Leipzig, probably to keep open the communication by which Augereau was expected to arrive with about 20,000 men newly levied.

As soon as Napoleon perceived that the Allies were in motion for the opening of a general campaign, he sent the King of Naples to take the chief command of the 2nd and 8th corps, and two cavalry corps that were observing the Army of Bohemia; he also gave orders to Marmont and Augereau to consider themselves under his command.

From Napoleon's bulletins and primary direction of his columns of march, we are led to infer that Murat's instructions were to draw off these forces, and to follow a general movement which Napoleon at that time intended to make with the whole of his remaining forces towards Madgeburg, through Wittenberg, &c. The possession of all the country to the right of the Mulde by the French, and the removal of the Allied Armies of the North and of Silesia westward into the country beyond the Saale, certainly rendered this operation practicable; but whether it was expedient or not, is another question. In this case he must have made Coblentz his base, and transferred his line of communication to the north of Germany.

Of the corps that were concentrated round Dresden, the 1st and 14th were to remain in garrison; for Napoleon was unwilling to give up that city, although, by continuing to hold it, he lost the services of about 30,000 men. There remained disposable, for his intended movement, the Old Guard, the Young Guard, the cavalry of the Guard, the 5th and the 11th corps, and the 3rd corps, to the command of which Marshal Ney had returned. This force amounted to about 80,000 men; and it was not till the 6th of October that he put it in motion by the roads leading from Dresden down both banks of the Elbe to Meissen. Those on the right having crossed to the left bank by the bridge of Meissen, the whole force continued its march into the country between the Elbe and the Mulde, and, when united with the 4th and 7th corps, formed an army of certainly not less than 100,000 men.

Napoleon himself did not leave Dresden till seven o'clock in the morning of the 7th of October, when he caused the King of Saxony also, and his family, to take their departure in the direction of Meissen, under a strong escort of infantry and cavalry. On the 8th, Napoleon and his guard arrived at Wurzen, where he slept. Turning thence to the right, he quitted the Leipzig road, and proceeding to the North, accompanied by his column of guard, he descended the right bank of the Mulde, and on the 9th slept at Eilenberg. Next day, the 10th, he marched to Düben, where he halted the three following days. Meanwhile the corps of Ney had reached Dessau; Regnier had crossed the Elbe at Wittenberg, and made a demonstration on the right bank of the river; Bertrand had taken possession of Blücher's bridge, which

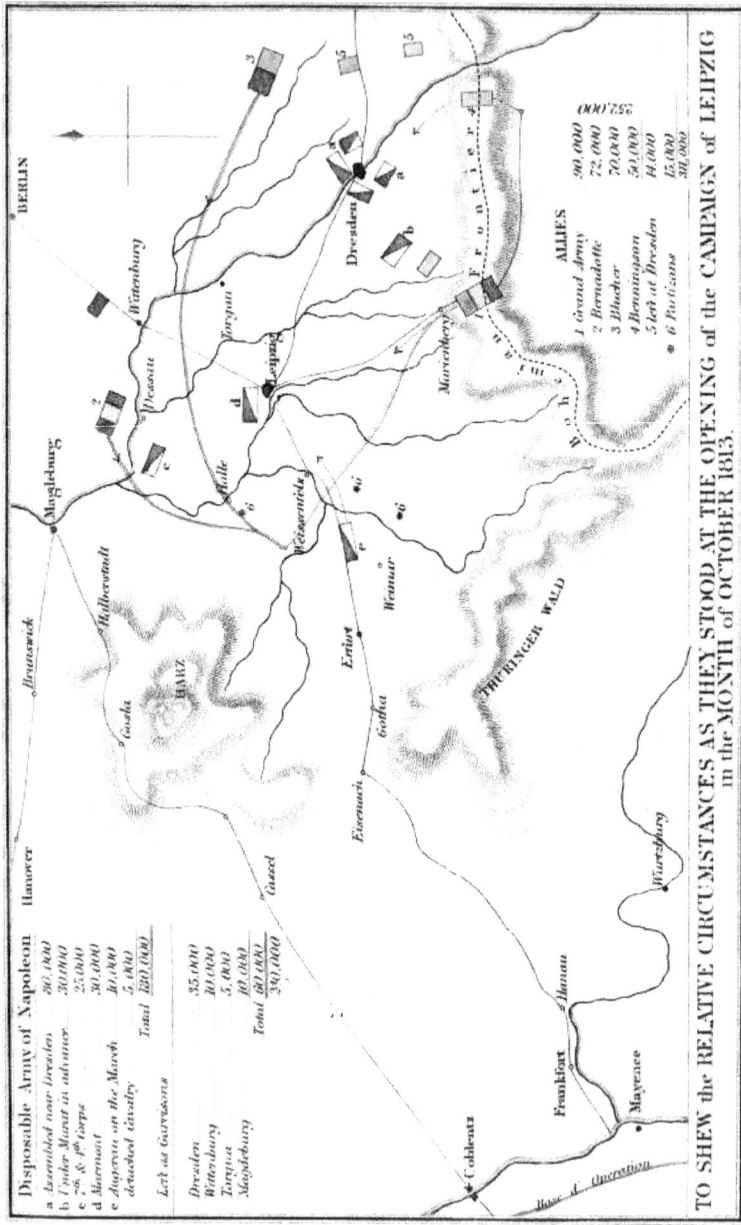

Disposable Army of Napoleon

a Assembled near Dresden	30,000
b Under Murat in advance	30,000
c 7.th & 9.th Corps	25,000
d Marmont	30,000
e Augereau on the March	10,000
detached Cavalry	5,000
	Total 130,000

Left as Garrisons

Dresden	35,000
Wittenburg	10,000
Torgna	5,000
Magdeburg	10,000
	Total 60,000
	190,000

ALLIES

1 Grand Army	90,000
2 Bernadotte	72,000
3 Blucher	70,000
4 Benningsen	50,000
5 left at Dresden	34,000
6 Partizans	15,000
	30,000
	352,000

BERLIN

Hanover

Brunswick

Magdeburg

Halberstadt

HARZ

Gotha

Wittenburg

Dessau

Torgau

Halle

Leipzig

Meissen

Dresden

Weissenfels

Weimar

Erfurt

Eisenach

THURINGER WALD

Frontiers of Bohemia

Würtzburg

Hanau

Frankfort

Mayence

Coblentz

Base d.' Operation

TO SHEW the RELATIVE CIRCUMSTANCES AS THEY STOOD AT THE OPENING of the CAMPAIGN of LEIPZIG in the MONTH of OCTOBER 1813.

had been left with only a small guard, and these corps were on the Elbe till the morning of the 14th. Marmont also manoeuvred to his right from Leipzig to Eilenberg while these operations were in progress; but on the 9th he returned to Leipzig.

It will be observed that Blücher had crossed the Mulde at Düben three days before Napoleon quitted the direct road to Leipzig, to march from Wurzen to his right on Düben. The Allied Army of the North and of Silesia continued their movement to the westward, and actually crossed the Saale, the former at Rothenburg and Bernburg, and the latter at Halle and Wettin on the 11th, the day after Napoleon's arrival at Düben.

There were sceptics who doubted if Napoleon ever seriously formed the plan of a campaign, transferring his whole force at that time to Magdeburg and the Lower Elbe (though it was afterwards avowed by himself in his fifteenth bulletin), and who asserted that this general flank movement, which actually took place, was never intended for more than a feint to put the Allies off their guard, with the hope of bringing either Blücher or the Prince Royal of Sweden to battle.

But we cannot think that such determination of purpose, as was evinced by the route of Napoleon himself, on leaving Dresden to go to Düben, and by the pointed direction of a force of 100,000 men upon Wittenberg and Dessau, is compatible with the supposition of a mere feint to facilitate a predetermined and ulterior movement on Leipzig, when every hour lost could not fail to render that movement more difficult. As to the chance of defeating the Army of the North, or that of Silesia, in detail, he could not have been ignorant that the prince royal and Blücher were no longer to be met with in that country. Be that as it may, there is no doubt that, during Napoleon's three days' halt at Düben, which he is said to have passed in evident perplexity and indecision, a new plan was formed, and orders were given for the recall of all his forces from the Middle Elbe, and for a change in the direction of them by forced marches upon Leipzig. From that time the crisis became inevitable, and the field obvious.

The sensation created by the northern demonstration was much less than might have been supposed. General Tauenzien, whose corps was at Dessau, and who had been left in observation of Wittenberg, was of course obliged to avoid the shock of forces so superior. Withdrawing all small detachments from the Elbe, he retired to place his corps in an attitude to cover Berlin. The Prince Royal of Sweden recrossed the Saale, and marched to Cöthen, detaching a force to protect his bridge at Acken; but Blücher, with the army he had led from Silesia, remained on the left bank of the Saale, and his headquarters were at Halle. On the Grand Army of the Allies this enterprise had still less influence; for it was scarcely known before its abandonment became manifest by the return of the troops that had been engaged in it.

The reason assigned by Napoleon for his sudden change of plan, and his counter-march of his army on the morning of the 14th, was the necessity of providing against the consequences of the defection of Bavaria; that event having placed two additional armies in the field against him,—the Army of Bavaria and the Austrian force that hitherto had been opposed to it; and, according to his bulletin, he first came to the knowledge of this event at Düben. The Bavarian Treaty was published at the Allied headquarters on the 12th, as soon as it was concluded; and therefore, Napoleon could not have received official notice of it sooner: but if the official notification were really his first information respecting it, he must have been ill-served by his diplomatic agents.

Another political event probably became known to Napoleon at Düben, as the news reached the Allied headquarters on the 10th. The enterprising General, Tchernicheff, conducted a partisan corps by a rapid movement, to surprise the town of Hesse Cassel, the residence of the King of Westphalia. At its approach, on the 27th of September, Jerome Buonaparte fled from his seat of government, with a portion of his garrison, but unaccompanied by a single Hessian of distinction. After pursuing for some days, Tchernicheff returned, and his adventurous little corps was not only received everywhere in a friendly manner, but the gates of Cassel were opened to him on the 1st of October, and eight hundred Hessians joined him with three pieces of artillery.

Such a manifestation of national spirit must have proved to Napoleon that the kingdom of Westphalia was virtually dissolved, and that the countries of which he had constructed that kingdom, and whose attachment to French interests had ever been doubtful, were now no longer under control, and could not be relied on as a safe medium of military communication between Magdeburg and France. This may have had its influence in convincing him that his scheme of adopting Magdeburg and the Lower Elbe as his approximate base was no longer applicable to his circumstances.

In addition to these two political causes, the progress of military events, particularly on the side of the Allied Grand Army, which had now a great numerical superiority, will show that by the 14th of October the general concentration at Leipzig had become inevitable, unless Napoleon had been prepared to remove the seat of war into the north of Germany, making the Rhine, between Cologne and Coblentz, his base, and thereby menacing Berlin, but abandoning Bavaria, Würtemberg, and in fact the whole of Germany to the southward of the Harz mountains.

The forward movements of the united corps of Russians and Prussians, that constituted the van of the Grand Army, were directed by Wittgenstein upon Altenberg, and next towards Borna, on the right bank of the Pleisse. In the first instance these were perhaps intended merely to cover the movement of the main body, yet they caused much anxiety to Murat, who, whatever his precise instructions may have been respecting Leipzig, could not fail to see the danger, if the Allied main forces, or any considerable part of them, should intervene between the small command at his immediate disposal, and the corps of Marmont and Augereau, which were also under his orders, but still at Leipzig.

Accordingly, we find it stated, in the fifteenth bulletin, that in consequence of the corps of Wittgenstein having marched upon Freyberg, and afterwards to its left on Borna, placing itself between the King of Naples and Leipzig, "the king did not hesitate respecting the manoeuvre he ought to make; he faced about, and marched upon the enemy," &c. The expression, "faced about," has reference to the previous instructions which we are told had been sent to him from Dresden on the eve of Napoleon's departure, and which had reached him on the 7th at Freyberg, " to operate on Wurzen and Wittenberg;" that is, to draw off his forces towards the north, and follow Napoleon's intended general movement on Magdeburg.

In this we have farther evidence of the reality of the intention that Napoleon avowed on leaving Dresden. It also proves that the commencement of the movement upon Leipzig had nothing to do with Bavaria, so far as Murat was concerned; for it was avowedly a departure from his instructions, and was made on his own responsibility, in consequence of Wittgenstein's advance on Borna, which is only fifteen English miles from Leipzig.

Whilst the Austrians, and the united Russian and Prussian reserves, indeed the main body of the army, continued its march towards the Elster that flows through Borna, the two flanking or covering corps of Wittgenstein and Klenau were occasionally in partial collision, as the nature of their duty required, with the corps composing Murat's command, and particularly on the 12th and 13th, when some serious cavalry skirmishes took place. On the 14th they were ordered by Prince Schwartzenberg to bring the enemy to an engagement, with a view to a reconnaissance of his force.

These instructions on the one side, and the decision of Murat to fall back on Leipzig on the other, soon brought the opposite armies in contact. A sharp but irregular engagement took place near Borna, in the open country between the Leipzig road and the Wood of the University. This affair was chiefly characterised by a mutual cannonade and several cavalry rencontres, which were of alternate success, with loss to each, and no very important result to either. Wittgenstein's cavalry was duly supported by masses of infantry in echelon, and gained the plain as far as the village of Gossa.

Later in the day Liebertwolkwitz began to be occupied by French infantry in considerable force. Wittgenstein would have wished to bring on a more decided battle, and would have endeavoured to push on by his left towards Leipzig; but Klenau, who also had followed up the movement of the King of Naples, must have co-operated by attacking Liebertwolkwitz; he considered, however, that his corps was too much fatigued, by several successive long marches, to be in a state to undertake that service, with any good effect on that evening. The commander-in-chief, Prince Schwartzenberg, who came on the ground towards night, decided with good reason that such a measure would be premature. The affair degenerated into a cannonade, till night put an end to it, and Wittgenstein retired to Espenhain.

In this reconnaissance the Allies had ascertained that Murat was in command of an assembled force had succeeded in placing himself in an attitude to cover Leipzig on the approaches from the south.

We are told, by the Baron d'Odeleben, that Napoleon having left Düben at daybreak on the 14th, halted in a field near Wurzen, on the great road from Dresden, and about fifteen miles from Leipzig, to breakfast, and to watch the movement of one of his columns. He listened with anxiety to the cannonade between Murat and Wittgenstein near Liebertwolkwitz; and the King of Saxony passed by at the same time in his carriage with his escort on the road to Leipzig. That night Napoleon slept at Reudnitz, a small village not more than two English miles from the gate of the city; it is on the Dresden road, and he probably selected this as being the most central point.

The French official statement explains the distribution of their force on the next day, the 15th of October, as follows:—

The 2nd, 5th, and 8th corps (Augereau), and the 3rd corps of cavalry (this whole force commanded by Murat,) was now in position, as we have already stated, covering the approaches to Leipzig from the south.

The 4th corps, commanded by Bertrand, was at Lindenau, covering the approach to Leipzig on the left bank of the Elster; in fact, a rear-guard to the westward.

The 6th corps, Marmont, at Lindenthal, covering the approaches from the north.

The 3rd and 7th corps, marching from Eilenberg to flank and support Marmont, or, as circumstances might require, still to the eastward.

The French Guards, infantry and cavalry, were in the neighbourhood of Probstheide, in reserve to the army of Murat, and covering the central point chosen by Napoleon as his halting place for the night.

On the 15th of October the Allied headquarters were removed from Altenberg to Pegau, which is on the Elster, and the main body of the army was between the Pleisse and the Elster. Wittgenstein continued in front of Borna, with his advanced posts stationed beyond Espenhain.

The Austrian General Klanau was, as usual, acting independently, and was some five or six miles to the right of Wittgenstein; but his corps did not amount to 10,000 men.

CHAPTER 17

Battle of Wachau

On the night of the 15th of October, Field-Marshal Prince Schwartzenberg promulgated a general order, as a prelude to the approaching battle. As it contained no instructions, and was an exhortation only, we will proceed at once to the details of the enemy's position, and to the disposition of the armies ready to attack.

Bertrand had passed through Leipzig, and was stationed by Napoleon at Lindenau as a sort of rear-guard to observe the Erfurt road; possibly also with a view to keep a sufficient space open for the formation of troops, if it should be expedient to attempt a retreat through Leipzig.

Opposed to Bertrand was Giulay and Prince Maurice Lichtenstein, their united forces scarcely amounting to 10,000 men. These were all the troops the Allies possessed on the left bank of the Elster, and though insufficient to produce any decisive effect against the well-posted corps of Bertrand, yet they were able to observe the Erfurt road, and to give assurance that there were as yet no signs of any attempt to pass troops through Leipzig, with a view to a general retreat of the French.

The probability of such an attempt, on the part of the enemy, induced Schwartzenberg to keep the main Austrian force within reach of the bridge over the Elster, and this may account for the inactive part he reserved for it in his disposition for the attack on the 16th; but there is reason to think that the order for that attack, without waiting for reinforcements, was a concession made by the commander-in-chief to the representations of the Emperor Alexander and the King of Prussia; for he certainly did not appear to anticipate success; nor, at the commencement, was he eager for its prosecution.

We have also noticed that Marmont was in position to the north of Leipzig, looking out towards Halle, and that Ney and Regnier were on their way from Eilenburg to fall in on his right.

We have now to consider the position of the remaining disposable forces of Napoleon, then assembled in the position of Wachau and Liebertwolkwitz, under the command of Murat, and opposed to the Allied Grand Army in this first general action near Leipzig.

Such descriptions as the present imply ideal lines, behind which the several corps were assembled as reserves *en masse* till they were wanted, and only certain posts were regularly occupied. In this war actual lines of troops were only formed partially, when and where they were absolutely required. The line taken up by Murat on the 14th, and viewed and approved by Napoleon on the 15th, may be said to have extended between Liebertwolkwitz and the Pleisse, at right angles to the course of that river.

The principal posts occupied, in the present instance, were Dölitz on his right, with its gardens and strong defensible ground; Wachau in the centre, a village in a hollow, with a small wood or orchard at one extremity, and, being commanded on both sides by rising ground, this was in itself a bad post for either party to hold; lastly, Liebertwolkwitz on the French left, a much better post and more considerable village, on the top of a hill which formed a regular glacis to it.

A ridge ran all the way from the shoulder of the eminence of Liebertwolkwitz to the River Pleisse, passing in rear of Wachau, and commanding it. This position could not fail to present itself to the eye of an experienced officer as the only one which that uninteresting country afforded for the purpose of covering Leipzig towards the south. The distance of the centre of this line, from the gates of Leipzig, may have been about five English miles, and its extent from right to left about three and a half. The disposition of the army which occupied it was this;—

The corps of Prince Poniatowski, the 8th, was on the extreme right, charged with the defence of Dölitz, Mark-Kleberg, and other posts on the Pleisse. On the left of Poniatowski, and covering him towards the plain, were the cavalry corps of Kellerman and Milhaud.

Victor, with his corps, the 2nd, was posted in the centre, and charged with the defence of Wachau. The corps of Lauriston, the 5th, was at Liebertwolkwitz on the left; the cavalry corps of Latour Maubourg was stationed between Victor and Lauriston.

Augereau was in second line to Poniatowski, and Victor supplied infantry supports to the cavalry of Kellerman and Milhaud.

161

Napoleon and Poniatowski at Leipzig

The corps of Macdonald, the 11th, was in echelon, though somewhat distant, to the extreme left; it had been looking out towards the east on the great road from Dresden to Leipzig by Grimma. The close presence of Platof, and possibly some intelligence of the movement of Beningsen, may have led them to expect the near approach of a formidable enemy in that direction. This corps was now at Holzhausen.

When his Guards arrived, Napoleon posted them in reserve near the village of Probstheide. The amount of the French force, thus available for the approaching battle, could not have been less than 80,000 infantry and 10,000 cavalry.

The country in front of this position is unenclosed, its surface undulating, and then consisting mostly of stubble fields or extensive sheep pastures. The River Pleisse, which closed the right flank of Napoleon's army, is there a small but deep and sluggish stream, and its banks are of course more intersected by drains and enclosures than the uplands, The disposition for the attack was as follows,—The united corps of Wittgenstein and Kleist, in their reconnaissance on the 14th, had penetrated nearly to the foot of the position now to be attacked, and had therefore become acquainted with the country. They had retired to Rötha and Espenhain, and remained there on the right of the Pleisse.

They were now charged with the attack of the position in their front, being the centre of the enemy's line, and were to be supported by the Russian and Prussian reserves. Klenau also was to pass by the farther side of the wood of the University, and attack Liebertwolkwitz on the extreme right, and Barclay de Tolly was to take the chief-command of all these forces on the right of the Pleisse.

Field-Marshal Schwartzenberg reserved to himself the duty of co-operating with his Austrians between the Pleisse and the Elster; intending in the first instance to remain in reserve near Zobigker, and to send the corps of Meerfeldt forward to endeavour to force the passage of the Pleisse near Cönnewitz, in rear of the enemy's right.

As the Russians and Prussians were thus appointed to take a principal part in the battle, a more detailed notice of their formation is necessary. Their left wing was composed of the Prussian brigade, commanded by Prince Augustus of Prussia, four battalions of Russian light infantry, and three regiments of Russian cavalry. It was assembled behind Gröbern, under the chief command of General Kleist.

In the centre was the Russian division of Prince Eugene of Wirtemberg, with a Prussian brigade in second line to it, assembled in rear of Gossa.

On the right was the division of Prince Gorczakof, with the Prussian brigade of General Pirch, in second line, assembled in rear of Störmthal.

The two divisions of Russian grenadiers, commanded by General Raeffskoi, were a support in rear of the centre, near the farm of Auenhayn.

The Russian and Prussian guards commanded by Miloradovitch, and the heavy cavalry commanded by the Grand Duke Constantine formed, as usual, the reserve, and were assembled near Magdeborn.

THE ATTACK.

About six o'clock in the morning, of the 16th of October, the troops were assembled, and about eight o'clock the attack commenced.

Kleist, advancing with the left wing, carried the village of Mark Kleberg.

Prince Eugene of Wirtemberg, with the centre, marched upon the village of Wachau, and his *tirailleurs* partially obtained possession of it, and of the little wood adjoining.

Prince Gorczakof, with the right wing, had farther to march, and directing his attention chiefly to the attack on Liebertwolkwitz, he could not afford the support and protection to the right centre that were expected from him. Klenau, who was so far off to the right as to be entirely disconnected from the corps of Wittgenstein, made, nevertheless, an animated attack on Liebertwolkwitz, and, at first, met with some success.

As soon as Napoleon observed, from the hill of Liebertwolkwitz, these movements of attack, he appears to have considered that point the key of his position, and to have directed his attention first to its security. He sent for a part of the corps of Macdonald, and one half of his Young Guard, under the command of Mortier, to support Lauriston; in the meantime, trusting the defences of the Pleisse to Poniatowski, and that of Wachau, to Victor. This force, which he directed and encouraged in person, sufficed to repulse General Klenau's attack, though not without a brave resistance on the part of the Austrians; and he ultimately gained possession of a part of the wood of the university.

Klenau was now effectually disunited from the remainder of the Allied line; Liebertwolkwitz was secured, and Napoleon turned his attention to the centre, where the Russians appeared to be gaining an advantage. To support Victor, he brought up the other two divisions

BATTLE of WACHAU NEAR LEIPZIG
16. OCTOBER 1813.

Between the Army of Prince Schwartzenberg and that of the King of Naples-Napoleon
Commanding. Movements of Attack.

a. Kleist	e. Meerveldt	i Gulay	n. Lauriston
b. Eugene of Wurtenburg	f. Russian Grenadiers	k. Poniatowsky	o. Guards
c Gorchacos'	g. Russian Reserve	L. Augerau	p. Macdonald
d. Klenau	h. Austrian Reserve	m. Victor	r Bertrand

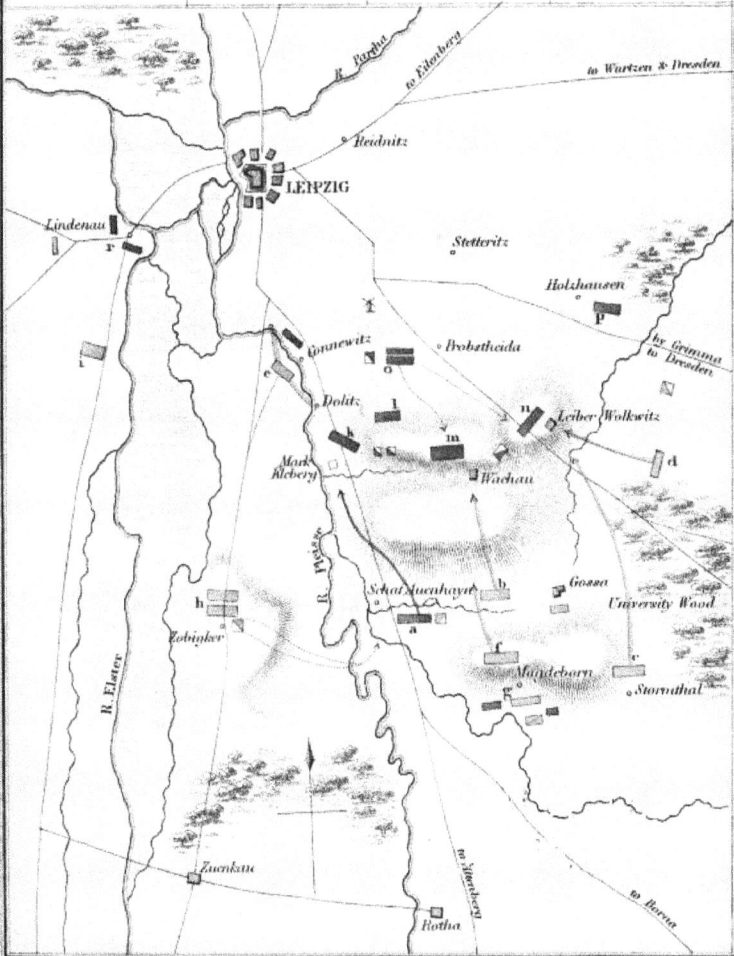

of the Guard, under the command of Oudinot, and placed his reserve artillery on the commanding ground, behind Wachau, while the cavalry of his right wing advanced, supported by squares of infantry, to attack the Russian left.

The want of force sufficient to make any impression on an enemy so powerful and so well posted, had already been felt by the Allies; and the Emperor Alexander had sent to the Field Marshal to urge him to move some Austrian troops to support the attack. Though the division of Bianchi was at length ordered to march, the distance at which the Austrian infantry was posted from the active part of the engagement, rendered it impossible for them to afford any prompt assistance; but the Austrian cavalry hastened to the scene of action, led by General Nostitz, and arrived at Goslewitz, in time to meet the enemy's cavalry, which, supported by Augereau's squares of infantry, had gained possession of the plain, and threatened to separate the Allied centre from the left wing.

In several brilliant charges the Austrian cavalry gained the advantage, and at length drove the enemy's cavalry off the field, preventing, perhaps, worse mischief than had already befallen Prince Eugene of Würtemberg, from the overwhelming force of cavalry, infantry, and artillery, that Napoleon had directed against him. As on all other occasions, Prince Eugene here shewed his usual coolness and ability; but his task had been difficult, and his means inadequate.

Now, hard-pressed by a superior enemy, he was obliged to retire across an open country, over ground that was disadvantageous to him; his left flank molested by a powerful and enterprising cavalry; his right entirely "*en l'air*,"—for the division of Prince Gorczakof had gone away towards the wood of the University, to take part in the attack on Liebertwolkwitz. It is not surprising that his division did not accomplish its retreat without losing upwards of a thousand men dead upon the field; but it maintained to the last that stern discipline, incapable of panic, which distinguishes the Russian infantry on every emergency. At length, the prince and his division, retiring slowly covered by skirmishers, reached the farm of Auenhayn, where General Raeffskoi, with the Russian grenadiers, stood in reserve, and was prepared to defend the post; to receive the attacking columns of Victor and Oudinot, and stay their further progress.

The Prussians, under the command of Kleist, in the meantime, held their ground at Mark-Kleberg; and the arrival of the Austrian cavalry having secured the connection between the left wing and the

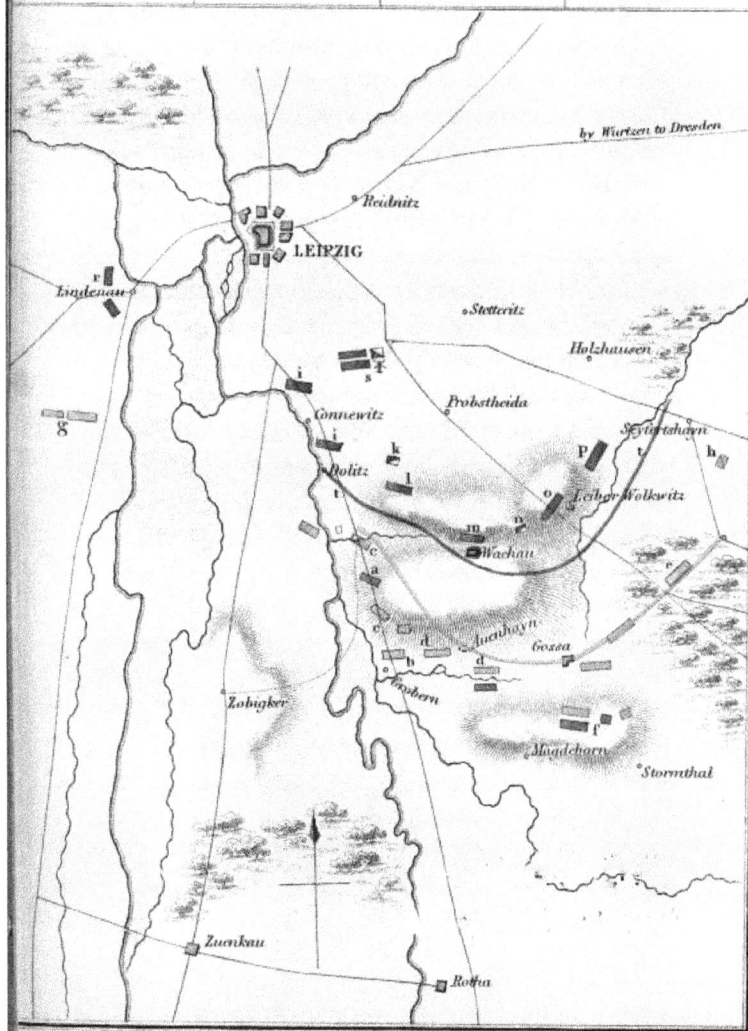

BATTLE of WACHAU.

Position of the contending armies at sunset on the 16th October and in which they remained during the 17th without fighting.

a Kleist	f Russ.n & Pruss.n reserve	l Augerau	r Bertrand
b Colloredo	g Guilay	m Victor	s Napoleons Guard & H.d Q.rs
c Austrian Reserves	h Plator	n Latour Mauboury	t French Position at Night.
d Wittgensteins Command	i Poniatowzky	o Lauriston	
e Klenau	k Kellerman	p Macdonald	

centre, the Allied line then stood with its right on Gossa, and its left wing somewhat thrown forward at an angle. The Austrian division of General Bianchi, which had followed the cavalry, at length arrived at Gröbern, and proceeded to relieve the division of Kleist, at Mark-Kleberg, which became his support. The Allied line had now gained power sufficient to resist all attacks against its left and centre.

The right of the centre, however, was not equally well protected; and, at this period of the action, which might have been about four o'clock in the afternoon, the village of Gossa did not appear to be occupied. If it were so, it could only have been by the Russian brigade of General Pirch. Excepting two regiments of light cavalry, the dragoons, and the lancers of the Russian guard, there were no troops in the plain between that village and the right of the troops occupied with the defence of Auenhayn. Murat saw this weak point, and prepared to take advantage of it. The Emperor Alexander had also turned his attention to it; and, to secure it, he had sent for the reserves, both cavalry and infantry; but these reinforcements were in rear of some broken ground, through which they had to pass towards the front, and, in the passage, the heavy cavalry became entangled with the infantry and artillery. Be this as it may, nothing arrived, and much time was lost.

At that moment the enemy's cavalry, of which we could count fifty squadrons, were standing in formidable array, on the shoulder of the hill of Liebertwolkwitz. The object of this display, probably was, in the event of the Allies having any troops, which might be concealed by the ground, in that part of the field, especially cavalry, to induce them to shew them.

A small brook or drain ran from Gossa towards the Pleisse, and in rear of the place where the two Russian regiments had taken post. Its banks happened to be swampy, and could only be passed with difficulty, and a leap across a wide drain, unless by causeways, made in two or three places by the farmers, for agricultural purposes. This obstacle was only partial, and a few hundred yards to the right, nearer Gossa, it ceased to be an impediment.

The cavalry on the hill proved to be the whole corps of Latour Maubourg, amounting to upwards of 5,000 horse; Murat had taken the command, and began to descend the hill, directing his attack upon the two Russian regiments at its foot. The French advanced, in line of contiguous columns of regiments; certainly, in one body only, that is, with no sort of second line or reserve. No doubt they expected to dispose of their first opponents easily, and then to attempt a more important attack on Wittgenstein's right. The narrowness of the front to be attacked, as well as the nature of the ground, caused this powerful force to crowd into one dense mass before it came in contact with the Russian dragoons; these were overwhelmed, and driven across the swamps, or over the causeways.

Many of the rearmost were killed; but the rest rallied as soon as they had crossed the brook. The lancers, who were in second line, retired by their left to another causeway, but did not cross it, and formed again. But the enemy themselves were unexpectedly checked by this unforeseen obstacle; their crowding and confusion increased; and at that moment the Russian regiment of hussars of the guard, which Wittenstein had sent to take part with the rest of the brigade, appeared in their rear. This caused a panic. The unwieldy mass became noisy, and attempted to retire; the Russian light cavalry instantly followed them.

The Emperor Alexander, who stood on the hill above, seized the opportunity to send off his own escort of Cossacks of the guard, amounting to several squadrons, under Count Orloff Denissof, who passed the stream at a favourable spot near Gossa, and took the retiring mass in flank. This completed the panic, which then became a flight, and the fugitives did not draw their bridles till they had regained the protection of their infantry. Latour Maubourg received a severe wound, which disabled him for life, Murat was in great danger of being taken, and six guns fell into the hands of the Cossacks.

Thus 5,000 of the French cavalry, led by Murat in person, were foiled by an insignificant obstacle. They were seized with a panic; and, for want of a second line on which to rally, and from which to take a fresh departure—a precaution without which no cavalry attack ought ever to be made—they were obliged to abandon their enterprise, and fly before a force of light cavalry, which altogether could not have amounted to 2,000 men.

More space has been given to this remarkable cavalry affair than is, perhaps, proportionate to its importance; but although it failed, there are few instances of a more determined cavalry irruption, or of one attempted under more promising auspices. If it had been fully carried into effect, its consequences, at that moment, could not have failed to be disastrous to the Allies, and its complete want of success (giving due credit to the steadiness of the Russian cavalry) is manifestly to be attributed to the greatest oversight, or fault, a cavalry officer can commit—that of engaging his whole force without a second line or reserve.

Towards evening the Russian reserves of cavalry were brought up

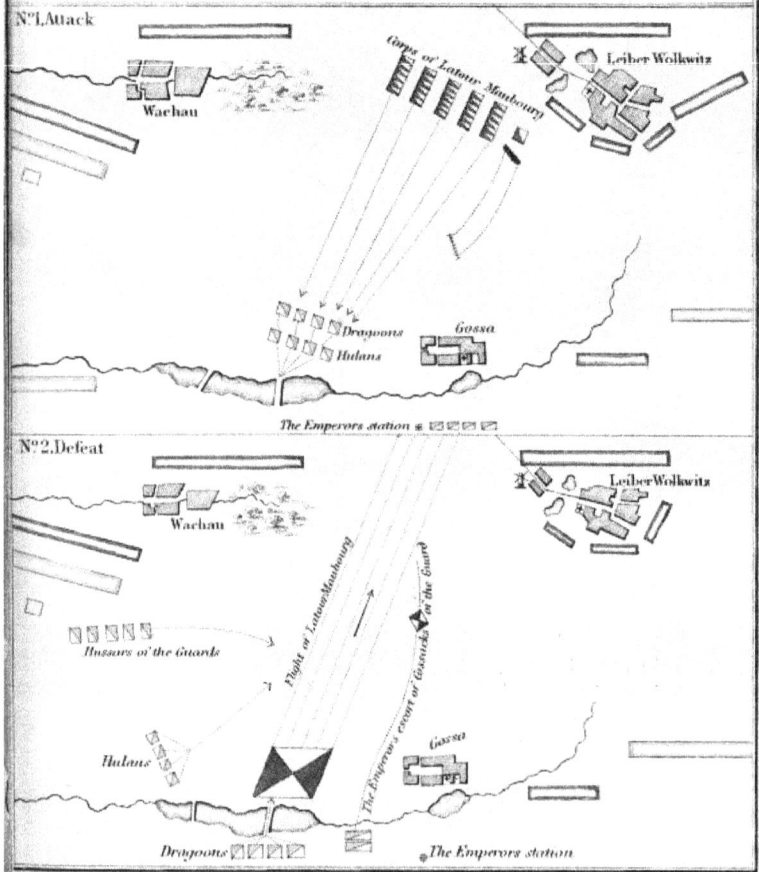

CAVALRY ATTACK
of the Corps of Latour Maubourg
Commanded by Murat in Person
in the Battle of Wachau near Leipzig
on the 16ᵗʰ October 1813.

Latour Maubourg was severely wounded &
supposed to have been killed and Murat
had a narrow escape.

Nº 1. Attack

Corps of Latour Maubourg

Leiber Wolkwitz

Wachau

Dragoons

Gossa

Hulans

The Emperors station

Nº 2. Defeat

Wachau

Leiber Wolkwitz

Flight of Latour Maubourg

The Emperor's court of Guards in the Guard

Hussars of the Guards

Hulans

Gossa

Dragoons

The Emperors station

to support the right. The light-infantry division of the Russian guards, commanded by General Yermolof, advanced to Gossa, and the enemy made a powerful and obstinate infantry attack in that quarter; but they were repulsed.

The field-marshal now appears to have considered he had sufficient force, and that it was a favourable opportunity for an advance of the whole line. The order was given; but probably it was considered too late in the day, and it was countermanded. When night put an end to the contest, the Allies stood with their right at Gossa, their centre at Auenhayn, and their left at Mark-Kleberg. The enemy retired into their original position, and of course claim this as a victory; but it was in fact a drawn battle.

In the course of the day Count Meerfeldt, in command of an Austrian corps, detached from the reserve, attempted to pass the Pleisse at Cönnewitz. It will be remembered that nearly the whole of the Austrian Army had remained on the left bank. After several failures there and at other points, all of which must have kept up an alarm, and acted as a diversion in favour of Kleist, he succeeded, it is said, in surprising a passage at some unguarded bridge, a little way below Dölitz. He crossed the river with a single battalion, to take measures for securing his advantage, till other troops could arrive; but whilst intent upon his reconnaissance, an enemy's column came suddenly upon him: his horse was shot, himself slightly wounded, and he was taken prisoner; while the battalion was forced to retire, and abandon their advantage and their general.

The Emperor Alexander with his staff, accompanied by Lord Cathcart, went to pass the night in the old plundered and forlorn *château* of Rötha. Napoleon caused his tent to be pitched not far from Probstheide, in rear of the centre of his position, and near the bivouac of his guards.

CHAPTER 18

Battle on the 16th of October

Whilst the events recorded in the foregoing chapter were taking place to the southward of Leipzig, on the north side, General Blücher, aware of the approaching crisis, and eager to take part in it, had caused his army to re-cross the Saale on the 15th, and move upon Schkeuditz, a place about fifteen miles on the direct road from Halle to Leipzig, and about half way between them. Near this spot he halted for the night.

It was the duty of Marmont, at that time, to guard the approaches to Leipzig from the north; he accordingly made Lindenthal his advanced post. About two miles in rear of this he had placed the left wing of his corps in an advantageous position, having its left on the Elster, near Möckern, and its right at Eutritzsch. He occupied both these villages, and there, in fact, his principal force was assembled. He had also placed in position, though not moveable for want of horses, about forty pieces of marine artillery that had been adapted to field service, and left in reserve at Leipzig. His right wing was detached to the right, and occupied another well-chosen position at Wetteritsch, covering the Delitch road. The cavalry of Arrighi, Duke of Padua, was with the right wing, and Ney and Regnier were destined for his support, but neither had yet joined him.

At daybreak, on the morning of the 16th of October, the day of battle at Wachau, General Blücher set his army in motion. Langeron, with his Russian corps, was directed to move across by Radefeld and Breitenfeld on the Delitzsch road, which brought him, after repulsing some advanced posts at those two places, in contact with Marmont's right wing at Wetteritsch.

General d'York, with a part of his corps, followed the line to the Elster, and drove the enemy's advanced posts and patrols from the villages on its bank with no great difficulty, till he was arrested by the village of Möckern.

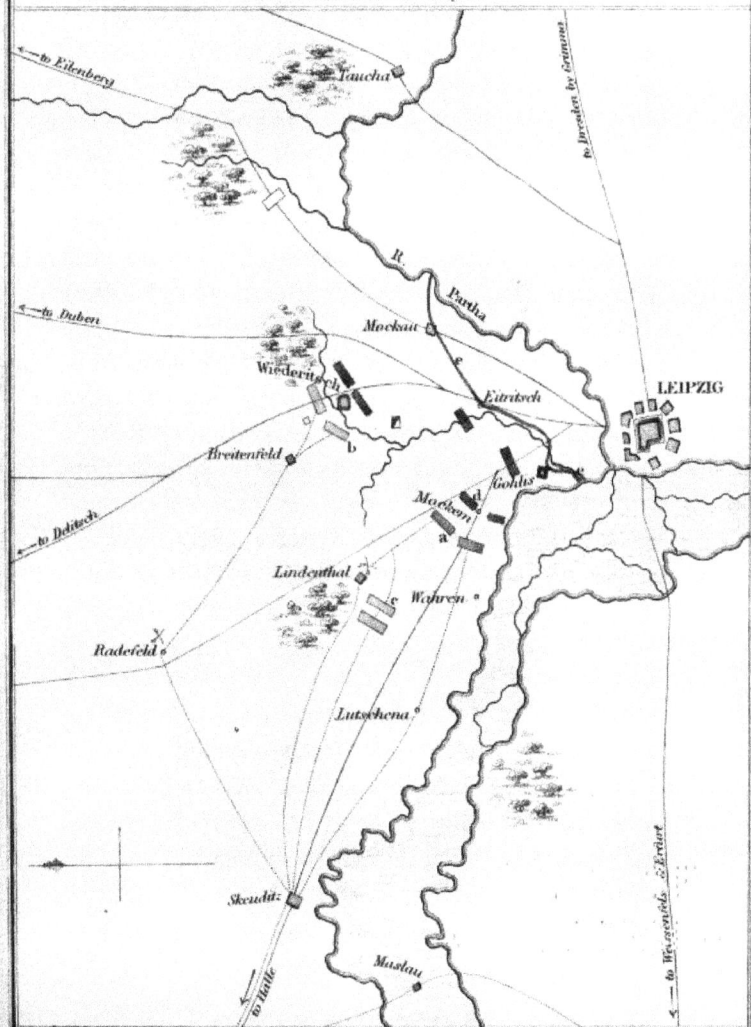

BATTLE of the 16ᵀᴴ
on the North side of
LEIPZIG.

Between the Army of Blucher and the Corps of Marmont

ARMY of SILESIA
a. D'York. b. Langeron. c. Sacken.

FRENCH
d. Marmont. e. Position at Night.

to Eilenberg

Taucha

to Duben

R. Partha

Mockau

Wiederitsch

Eitritsch

to Dresden by Grimma

LEIPZIG

Breitenfeld

Gohlis

to Dditsch

Moeken

Lindenthal

Wahren

Radefeld

Lutschena

Skeuditz

to Halle

Muslau

to Weissenfels & Erfurt

Blücher himself moved on with a central column, composed of the principal part of the corps of D'York, and supported by the Russian corps of General Sacken. He attacked Lindenthal; and that village, though occupied in some force, and favoured by the adjoining wood, being too salient a point to be supported and long maintained as part of a defensive line, the enemy were forced to abandon it. Blücher then proceeded, in concert with the column of D'York, to attack the position of Möckern and Eutritzsch, whilst Langeron attacked that of Wetteritsch. A severe contest for these villages occupied both parties for the remainder of the day with no very decisive results.

Marshal Ney, on his arrival from Düben, had placed his corps somewhere in rear of Marmont's right, in readiness to support him; but hearing the heavy firing which commenced at eight o'clock that morning in the position of Liebertwolkwitz, where the battle was raging between the army of Murat and the Grand Army of the Allies, he is said to have withdrawn his corps from the support of Marmont, and to have put it in motion towards the point where the contest seemed to require it more; for Marmont had not then been disturbed: he had not moved far before the cannon announced the unexpected approach of Blücher. Ney immediately caused his columns to countermarch, and, according to the French official account, he thus lost the day in marches, and left Marmont to contend against a superior force.

The author, not having been present, will not attempt to enter into the details of the day's work, by which Blücher and his army contributed towards the completion of the great catastrophe. The Plan, he hopes, will convey sufficient idea of the result to demonstrate its importance. The fact, that the enemy were obliged at night to retire behind the Partha, leaving 2,000 prisoners and (including all the ship-guns spiked and abandoned) 43 pieces of artillery in possession of the Allies, is sufficient to decide the claim to victory.

In justice to Marmont and his corps, we must admit that, in holding their ground till night against a force so superior, and still retaining Eutritzsch, and occupying Gohlis and Möckern as advanced posts, when they did retire, at night, behind the Partha, they have left proof that they also must have done their duty gallantly on that day.

Army of the North.

Of the apparent supineness of the Prince Royal of Sweden, and the inactivity of his army at this important period, a detailed explanation is to be found in Lord Londonderry's book concerning the war in Germany.

Lord Londonderry, at that time Sir Charles Stewart, was accredited minister to the King of Prussia; but not so to the Prince Royal of Sweden. He was, however, charged generally with the military interest of Great Britain in the north of Europe, and presented himself as a visitor at the headquarters of the prince royal. Although their presence was a stipulated article with the other sovereigns, that prince had especially deprecated having any British military officer attached to him in the field; he nevertheless received Sir Charles with civility, and allowed him to remain.

In consequence of Napoleon's demonstrations on Wittenberg, the prince royal had returned from the Saale with the Army of the North, and on the 14th of October he was at Cöthen: but Blücher, with the Army of Silesia, had not moved, and was still on the left bank of the Saale, near Halle. It may be remembered that, from the 9th to the 14th of October, Napoleon remained in force on the right bank of the Mulde: his change of plan took place on the 14th, and an officer sent with orders to Marmont was intercepted by some chance patrol of the Army of the North: from him it was first learned, at the headquarters of the prince royal, that Napoleon had decided upon a general concentration of his forces at Leipzig.

Upon this news Sir Charles Stewart was prompted by his zeal to give his advice, and urge Bernadotte to concentrate immediately on Zorbig, and advance with all celerity on Delitzch and Eilenburg; for Napoleon's columns would probably pass through Eilenburg. The prince replied, that Sir Charles was urging him to make a march with his flank to a superior enemy, which could not fail to be disastrous, and declared his intention of moving upon Halle, to place his army in second line to Blücher, whom he knew, or believed, to be about to recross the Saale, and advance directly on Leipzig.

On a repetition of Sir Charles's zealous importunity to induce the prince to move at once to his left, without reference to the Army of Silesia, it is said the prince lost his temper, and deprecating advice with some warmth, gave orders to march that night to Halle. After the troops were on the march, it appears that he changed his plan, and appointed a new disposition. His Swedes were placed on the right, between Wettin and the hill of Petersburg; General Bülow, in the centre, moved to Oppin, and Winzingerode to Zobig. Thus, the Swedes were halted on the morning of the 15th, ten English miles to the rear of Halle; but it must be remembered, that it was only on this day the army of Blücher recrossed the Saale, passing through Halle on its way to Schkeuditz, near which it was assembled that night.

In the course of the 15th, or during the ensuing night, the Army of the North made a general advance of about ten miles; and on the following day, when General Blücher was engaged in battle with Marmont, they halted on a line between Landsberg and Halle, about fifteen miles from the scene of action.

Sir Charles Stewart had been with General Blücher during the battle, and in the evening, he went to Halle in search of the Prince Royal of Sweden, to whom he had already sent several messages to urge him forward. Sir Charles did not find him at Halle, but, in the hurry of the moment, wrote him a reproachful letter, which gave great offence. Whether of his own accord, or stimulated by Sir Charles's letter, it so happened, that the prince did move his army forward that night, and arrived, with the Russian and Prussian corps of Winzingerode and Bülow, at Breitenau about noon on the 17th. The cavalry of Winzingerode moved on towards the Partha, and some Cossacks even reached Taucha. The Swedes having been on the right were now necessarily a day's march in the rear.

There is no doubt that, with a little exertion, the Army of the North might have been in this attitude twenty-four hours earlier; it was now four-and-twenty hours too late to be of any use. Yet it is fair to consider that the intentions of Napoleon and the circumstances of the Grand Army could not be fully known; and if a great superiority of force had been directed against the Army of Silesia, the Army of the north would not have been ill placed, as a support in second line to it, with its right on the Saale. In the event of a forced passage of the French Army through Leipzig, with a view to retreat on Erfurt, which was no doubt to have been expected, the Army of the North would have been well placed for crossing the Saale, and hindering that operation.

The remarkable manner in which the Swedish contingent happened to find itself placed, out of the reach of harm, on this and on all other occasions during the war, certainly bears more the appearance of design than of chance. Under this impression, many motives have been assigned for the apparent chariness of the prince royal with regard to the lives of his newly-adopted countrymen; among these, a reluctance to weaken or harass a force which he might need to secure the ultimate possession of his own expected sovereignty; a fear of compromising his popularity in Sweden by sending home a dismal list of killed and wounded; or, perhaps, a reluctance to break off all chance of reconciliation with the French soldiery, and render his name odious to them, by allowing his own national contingent to come to actual blows with them, are the most plausible. But it is useless to investigate political motives, where military facts speak for themselves, as far as these commentaries profess to be concerned.

THE ALLIED GRAND ARMY.

The 17th was a day of comparative repose; the Allies and the enemy occupied much the same ground on which they had stood at the close of the battle on the day preceding. Their respective lines of sentries were in most places within musket-shot of each other.

A renewal of the fight was of course to be expected, and that morning the two Allied sovereigns and the field-marshal were upon the ground soon after day-break. The enemy showed some large masses of infantry on the high ground between Liebertwolkwitz and Wachau, and the cavalry of Latour Manbourg was displayed in one extended line, as it had been the day before; but they appeared to stand on the defensive, disinclined to commence the attack.

The field-marshal, wishing to await the arrival of Beningsen and Colloredo, who had been sent for, and were marching up from the neighbourhood of Dresden, and were now close at hand, did not of course take any steps to provoke a battle: but a curious and important occurrence which happened on this day must not be omitted here. When the Emperor Alexander came upon the ground that morning, he was met by General Count Meerfeldt, who had been taken prisoner the preceding evening in attempting to pass the Pleisse, near Dölitz.

Napoleon, in his critical position, did not neglect to avail himself of the chance that had placed an Austrian officer in his power, equally experienced in military and diplomatic affairs, and, after a personal interview with him that night in his tent, Napoleon sent him back next morning, under parole, with a flag of truce, charged with certain peaceable overtures,—no doubt in the anxious hope of retrieving by negotiation some of the military advantages which, as he must have been conscious, he had lost to his army through false movements and delay; and probably too much reliance on that chance may have induced him to waste the night of the 16th, and day of the 17th, in standing fast to keep a good countenance during his negotiation, instead of filing through Leipzig, and gaining the country behind the Saale with his army: this, at all events, would have been more easily accomplished at that time, than it actually was two days later with a defeated army, and less perilous also than to risk a battle against an overwhelming and increasing superiority of numbers, in a bad position, and with a river in his rear traversed by only one line of retreat.

We will not here stop to consider the particulars of Meerfeldt's interview, or the diplomatic proposals of Napoleon, as similar proposals formed, in fact, the basis of subsequent negotiations, but on this occasion were unheeded. The point of military interest was Napoleon's offer, that if the Allies would entertain his proposals, and agree to an armistice, by which the Russians and Prussians should retire behind the Elbe, and the Austrians into Bohemia, he himself would retire behind the Saale, and, he added, that if they thought he should retire behind the Rhine, he must be forced to it by lost battle; this, he said, might happen, but as yet it had not.

These overtures were also communicated to Lord Cathcart on the field that morning, as His Britannic Majesty's ambassador, by Count Meerfeldt, at Napoleon's express desire, and they were received for the consideration of all the Allied powers: but such proposals could not be entertained, and no suspension of hostilities was granted.

In the afternoon, Prince Schwartzenberg held a council of war in the village of Lestowitz, and after ascertaining that Beningsen could not reach Naunhof till night, that Colloredo had not yet arrived, and nothing certain being known respecting the Army of the North, it was determined to postpone the attack till the following day. Colloredo joined the army about four in the afternoon, and took his station at Gröburn. Beningsen arrived at Naunhof that night, and before morning it was known that some of Winzingerode's cavalry, the advanced guard of the Army of the North, had reached Taucha.

In the direction of the Army of Silesia, some firing had been heard early in the morning of this day of repose with the Grand Army. Blücher was reported to be driving in the enemy's advanced posts across the Partha, and it turned out that in this service General Wasiltschikof, with four regiments of Russian cavalry, and some Cossacks, distinguished themselves by defeating the cavalry of the Duke of Padua.

Blücher, not hearing any cannonade in the direction of the Grand Army, did not continue his operations that day farther than the banks of the Partha. In the evening he had an interview with the Prince Royal of Sweden, and concerted measures for their co-operation on the ensuing day. Nothing farther of importance occurred on the 17th, and the Emperor of Russia, accompanied by Lord Cathcart and the rest of his suite, returned as before to the *château* of Rötha for the night.

CHAPTER 19

General Battle on the 18th Around Leipzig

Murat still retained the command of that portion of the French Army which was opposed to the Grand Army of the Allies, though Napoleon himself was present; while to Ney was assigned the chief command of the three corps opposed to the armies of Silesia and of the north.

The forces under Murat's command remained stationary during the whole of the 17th, and no material alteration of their position or circumstances took place during the day; but towards night the bivouac fires of Bensingsen's corps were to be seen at Naunhof, opposite Murat's left flank, somewhat to the rear of its principal *appui* of Liebertwolkwitz, and only about four English miles distant. A part of Winzingerode's cavalry arrived at Taucha; and being known, of course, to be the advanced guard of the Army of the North, they indicated plainly the near approach and intended mode of co-operation of that army.

These two facts were sufficient to convince Napoleon that it was now time for him to draw in his forces (which had hitherto been posted in two separate and extended arrays, one facing towards the north, and the other towards the south), with a view to act on the offensive. He now proceeded to unite them round Leipzig in a position more concentrated, and more exclusively of a defensive character.

Accordingly, after an interview with Murat and Ney, he gave orders to throw back their respective exposed flanks. The new defensive position was now a semi-circle, having Leipzig for a centre, and a radius of about two English miles. The Partha and the Pleisse were the base or diameter, and secured each flank. Murat's command might now be considered as the right wing of this general semi-circular line, and Ney's as the left wing. To maintain this position during the approaching day was indispensably necessary at all events; for a retreat through the defile of Leipzig in open day, and in presence of a superior enemy's force, would have been impossible.

The principal points occupied by the French were Cönnewitz on the extreme right, and the village of Probstheide, while the left of Murat's army was to rest on the village of Stötteritz. The villages of Paunsdorf and Shönefeld, and the north suburbs of Leipzig itself, near the confluence of the Partha and the Elster, were of no less importance to the force under the chief command of Ney. The circumstances of these two forces were nearly similar, with this exception,—that, from the greater remoteness of the Allied Army of the North, the necessity for immediate change of position was less pressing upon Ney than upon Murat, who was threatened by the actual arrival of Beningsen at Naunhof, with an increase of force to the Allied Army of at least 25,000 men, threatening the rear of his left flank.

Accordingly Ney's own corps stood fast; but of Murat's command, the corps of Macdonald, Lauriston, and Victor were put in motion that night, to fall back on Holzhausen, and ultimately to occupy the two villages of Stötteritz and Probstheide, and the intervening space, in force sufficient to defend them; retaining strong concentrated reserves in the rear for their support,—it being of paramount necessity to defend those two villages to the last.

As to Napoleon himself, we learn from the Baron d'Odeleben, that after passing a very anxious and disturbed night, he left his tent about two o'clock in the morning of the 18th; and travelling in the dark, sometimes in a carriage and sometimes on horseback, he visited Ney, whom he awoke out of his sleep in his quarters at Reudnitz, and conferred with him for an hour. He then passed by the suburbs, round Leipzig, and across the bridge of Lindenau, to the Weisenfels road, where he saw General Bertrand, and personally gave him orders to march to Weisenfels, and, with a view to retreat, to secure that passage of the Saale.

After having made a careful reconnaissance of the bridges and other important objects immediately in rear of Leipzig, he returned through the town, and arrived at eight o'clock in the morning, before the action commenced, at an old windmill which stood on an eminence about an English mile behind Probstheide; near this his Guards had bivouacked; and on the previous evening his tent had been pitched near this spot, which had proved, and was still about to prove, the well-chosen position for his valuable reserve. Here, we are told, Napoleon took up his station, and here he remained nearly all the rest of that memorable day.

The Emperor Alexander, attended by the British Ambassador and his usual staff and suite, was on horseback before daybreak, and proceeded to the plains of Gossa, where he was joined by the King of Prussia. The Field-Marshal, Prince Schwartzenberg, as soon as he had ascertained in what manner the enemy's forces had been drawn in, made his disposition, and issued orders to follow them up without delay, with a view to a general attack, in which he hoped to be seconded by the Army of the North, in conjunction with the Army of Silesia.

In the general plan of the attack to be made by the Grand Army of the Allies, that army was to be considered as forming three great columns,—

First, General Beningsen, who, with his own corps and the division of Bubna, had already advanced well on to Seyfartshayn that morning, received orders to take command of the right column, composed of his own corps, with the Austrian division of General Bubna, and the corps of General Klenau, then at Grosse Pössna, to which the Prussian division of Ziethen was also attached for that day. With this force of about 35,000 men, he had it in charge to advance on Holzhausen, and operate according to circumstances on Murat's left—a duty in which it was expected that he would be joined by the Army of the North.

Secondly, the central column was placed under the chief command of Barclay de Tolly, and ordered to assemble near Gossa. It was to be composed of the Prussian corps of Kleist, from which, however, the division of Ziethen had been detached, the corps of Wittgenstein and the Russian reserves, both infantry and cavalry. After making due allowance for the severe duty the troops that composed this column had performed on the 16th, we may still estimate their number at about 45,000 effective men, who were ordered to advance on Wachau.

Thirdly, the left column, chiefly Austrians, was to be placed under the command of the hereditary Prince of Hesse Homburg, and to consist of the Austrian divisions under Generals Bianchi, Prince Alois, Lichtenstein, and Wissenwolf, supported by their reserve cavalry under Count Nostitz, and the corps of Colloredo. This column could not have amounted to much more than 25,000 men. It was to advance along the right bank of the Pleisse, upon Dösen and Dölitz, whilst the division of General Lederer, formerly Meerfeldt's corps, continued to act on the left bank, and was to advance on Cönnewitz, on that side

GENERAL BATTLE ROUND LEIPZIG 18TH OCTOBER.

FRENCH

a. Poniatowski
b. Napoleon & Guards
c. Victor
d. Lauriston
e. Macdonald
f. Ney
g. Marmont
h. Reignier & Saxons

ALLIED ARMIES

i. Austrian Army
j. 3 Prussian Brigades
k. Wagenstein
l. Russian Cavalry
m. Russian reserve
n. Allied Sovereigns

o. Zieten
p. Klenau
q. Beningson
r. Bubna
s. Woronzof
t. Army of the North

v. Vintzingerode
w. Saken
x. Langeron
z. D'York.

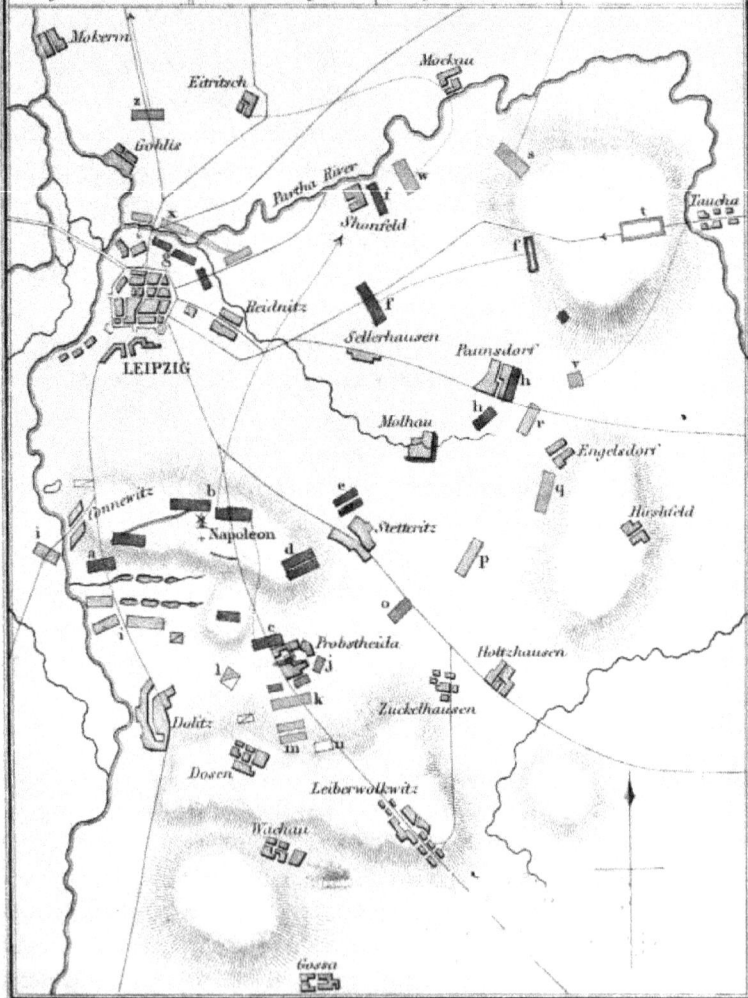

Mokern
Eitritsch
Mockau
Golilis
Partha River
Shonfeld
Reidnitz
Sellerhausen
Paunsdorf
LEIPZIG
Molhau
Engelsdorf
Connewitz
Hirshfeld
Napoleon
Stetteritz
Probstheida
Holtzhausen
Dolitz
Zuckelhausen
Dosen
Leiberwolkwitz
Wachau
Taucha
Gossa

of the river.

General Giulay and Prince Maurice Lichtenstein's light division, were still in the neighbourhood of Lützen, and were intended to observe the Weisenfels road.

All these arrangements were effected before nine o'clock in the morning, and the several columns were in motion before that time to act upon their instructions.

Beningsen found little to oppose the advance of his main column on Hobzhausen; for Macdonald, who had halted there, finding that post too much in advance, had retired to Stötteritz, leaving only some small outposts to cover his movements. But Ney had been in no hurry to throw back his right, and withdraw his advanced posts into the intended defensive position, because the Army of the North had not yet appeared in any force on the Partha, or attempted to pass that river; therefore, Beningsen could not continue his movements to his front on Stötteritz, but was obliged to make a flank movement with his own corps to his right, and place it on some rising ground near Engelsdorf. From this village he drove the enemy's advanced posts, and was obliged to remain in position, until the arrival of the prince royal's army should give sufficient occupation to Ney, and thereby set him at liberty to direct all his force against Stötteritz. Regnier still occupied the village of Mölkau, against which Bubna was directed.

The Prussian General Ziethen advanced on Zuckelhausen, which his division attacked and carried with its usual spirit, taking some guns as the French attempted to retreat; and Klenau attacked Holzhausen with similar success, driving from it Macdonald's rear-guard.

The central column, under the command of Barclay de Tolly, had assembled near Gossa, and advanced on Wachau; the three Prussian brigades of the corps of Kleist (which were that commanded by Prince Augustus of Prussia, that of General Pirch, and that of General Klux,) leading and clearing its front. They found Wachau unoccupied; and, as the country over which they had to pass was unenclosed, they met with little to impede them, till they came in front of Probstheide, a large circular village, with a space in the centre, which (from its villas and walled gardens, then fully occupied by the corps of Victor) was a formidable and well-guarded post.

Although it stands isolated in the plain it was well flanked by the corps of Lauriston and the cross fire from the village of Stötteritz on its left, and amply supported by Napoleon's guard on the Windmill Hill behind it, and not above a mile distant, as a last resource if required. Thus, the force immediately available for the defence of this essential post, which was not above a mile in extent, and strong in itself, could not be less than 80,000 men.

On arriving in front of Probstheide the leading brigades were halted, to give time for the columns of Wittgenstein, which had followed closely, to come into their place, and form as a support, as well as for the Russian guard and grenadiers, who constituted the reserve to take post near a brick-field which was on the road, and about half way between Liebertwolkwitz and Probstheide, directly in front of the latter place, and not above an English mile from it. The reserved cavalry formed in the plain to the left of the infantry.

We may here remark, that in this brick-field Napoleon had pitched his tent on the two preceding nights. The Emperor of Russia and King of Prussia, who had advanced with the central column, took their station about noon on a small eminence in front of it, which commands an admirable panoramic view of the whole plain, and towards evening they were joined at that spot by the Emperor of Austria.

The third or Austrian column also commenced its movement about nine o'clock in the morning along the right bank of the Pleisse, led by Bianchi in first line, and Weissenwolf in second to him, the rest in reserve. They got possession of Dösen and Dölitz, though not without having to overcome the most strenuous resistance on the part of the brave survivors of Poniatowski's corps, now much diminished by constant hard fighting, but still commanded by their gallant chief. At Dösen the Hereditary Prince of Hesse Homburg received a wound, which obliged him to relinquish the chief command to General Bianchi; and a vigorous effort on the part of the Poles (supported by Augereau and the cavalry of Kellerman) to retard the progress of the Austrians, was not without success; but Colloredo coming into action with his corps recovered the advantage; and the Austrian column ultimately reached Cönnewitz, and obtained possession of that place.

But the French availed themselves of some strong ground near Cappelle flanked by the Pleisse, and were now rendered confident by the close proximity of Napoleon's guard, a division of which, under Oudinot, was sent from the Windmill Hill to their support. They were not to be forced any farther by the power opposed to them, and, with the exception of some profitless skirmishing and a continued cannonade, nothing worth recording occurred in that quarter during the rest of the day.

Let us now return to the central column, which we left as it arrived and formed in the plain in front of Probstheide, and preparing to attack that important post.

Napoleon well knew the importance of Stötteritz and Probstheide, in every respect similar posts; and the distance between them being less than an English mile, they mutually flanked each other. These two villages he knew to be the only security for the centre of his line, short of the immediate suburbs of Leipzig, and he therefore directed his chief attention to their defence. In this he was admirably seconded by the active and energetic Murat, who, entrusting the defence of Probstheide to Victor, and that of Stötteritz to Macdonald, took post between the two with the corps of Lauriston to support both, while Napoleon himself, with the greater part of his guard, stood on the Windmill Hill, determined, cost what it might, to secure Probstheide, which was the more salient, and therefore the more vulnerable, point of the two.

The supports and reserves of the Allies having arrived, and formed on their appointed ground, and a sufficient power of artillery having come into action, the order for the attack was given to the three Prussian brigades in front. This order was instantly obeyed with so much alacrity and spirit, that, under cover of a powerful and concentrated fire of artillery, Probstheide was entered on the first assault, and possession of the half of it was gained by the brigades of Prince Augustus and General Pirch. This happened about two o'clock in the afternoon, and we learn, from the Baron d'Odeleben, that Napoleon, who beheld the key of his position thus in jeopardy, at that moment rode down from the Windmill Hill, leading his Old Guard into Probstheide, and by that reinforcement, and the encouragement of his presence, recovered possession of the village.

The Prussians being driven out, rallied on their supports in the plain; and soon after a body of the enemy's infantry, supported by cavalry, was seen to appear to their right of the village, threatening to take the Prussian line of skirmishers and their supports in flank. This menacing force, which did not advance into the plain far enough to be charged, was held in check by a movement of the Russian cavalry under the Grand Duke Constantino, supported by a sufficient force of infantry.

The attack on the village was several times renewed, and some of Wittgenstein's infantry took part in the assault; but the exertions of Murat (in supplying it constantly with fresh and ample reinforcements, to recruit the waste of life occasioned by the continued and concentrated fire of the Allied artillery) rendered the contest interminable, though desperate. The formidable flanking fire, maintained by the artillery of Victor, Lauriston, and Macdonald, would have made any serious attempt to force the enemy's line at this point too expensive of life, and too uncertain of success to have been justifiable, whilst the non-arrival of the Army of the North suspended the co-operation of General Beningsen, who was expected to attack Stötteritz with his whole force. The village of Probstheide had long been in flames; but the cannonade continued with unabated violence on both sides till night; and up to that time the enemy still lined all the garden walls and other defensible places with their infantry.

During this severe contest for Probstheide, Ziethen, supported by Klenau, whose corps were all that Beningsen could detach for the purpose, moved to attack Stötteritz; but that village being somewhat more retired, with reference to Napoleon's general line, than the salient angle which Probstheide formed, it was too well flanked and supported to be easily approached, and was too strongly guarded by Macdonald to be in any danger from the inadequate force directed against it: for, as the Army of the North did not arrive on the high ground, in front of Taucha, till about three o'clock in the afternoon, Beningsen continued to be held in check by the corps of Regnier and Ney on his right, and could take no part in that attack.

 It therefore never amounted to more than an ineffectual skirmish and a continual cannonade of shot and shells, maintained by Klenau and Ziethen, which soon set the village on fire, and harassed the troops that occupied it till long after dark. Nothing farther occurred to the armies worth recording; and neither of these contending forces had to boast of any decided advantage on this day. It is fair to observe, that although there appears to be a great superiority on the side of the Allies, on comparing the whole of their forces with those of Napoleon; yet, as regards the army of Murat and Napoleon's guard, they will be found to amount to somewhere about 96,800 men; whilst, if we deduct the 25,000 men of Beningsen and Bubna, who were held in check, and neutralized by Ney, in consequence of the non-arrival of the Army of the North, the army of Schwartzenberg, immediately opposed to Murat's command, amounted to no more than 104,000, a superiority of only 8,000 men.

Having now followed out the struggle between these two contending armies, on the southward of Leipzig, to an advanced period in this eventful day, we proceed to the attacks simultaneously directed against the troops under the command of Marshal Ney, who was expecting the arrival of the army of the prince royal towards the east.

It was arranged in the morning between the two co-operating chiefs, Blücher and Bernadotte, that the Russian corps of Langeron, which properly belonged to the Army of Silesia, should for that day act with the Prince Royal's Army, and be considered part of it. This corps accordingly passed the Partha, near Molkau, and Woronzof, who commanded Winzingerode's advanced guard, crossed somewhere higher up the river, early in the afternoon, perhaps an hour before the rest of the Army of the North appeared on the high grounds in front of Taucha, and began to communicate with Beningsen.

Upon these demonstrations, Ney was at length constrained to draw in his forces, and he took up a defensive position, causing his own corps, and a part of Marmont's, to form between Schönefeld and Sellerhausen. Regnier still continued to occupy ground somewhat in advance near Mockau, in which he had been long engaged by Bubna; and although he had hitherto been well able to maintain it, he was now held in check by Platoff, with his Cossacks, who hung on his left flank.

Unless Ney had made some movement to bring him off, it is probable that he could not have retired with safety if he had wished it; but at this moment eleven Saxon battalions, with three squadrons of cavalry and three batteries of artillery (altogether a considerable part of Regnier's small corps) deserted in a body, and marched over to Bubna, declaring themselves ready to take part against the French, and proving their sincerity by turning the fire of their artillery against their former comrades.

By this time the cavalry of Winzingerode had come up on Beningsen's right; and, at the request of Sir Charles Stewart to the prince royal, the English rocket brigade, that had been sent out as an experiment, and attached to the Army of the North, was brought into action in aid of the attack made by Bubna upon Regnier. Its commanding officer, Captain Bogue, was killed by a musket shot; but it did some execution under the command of Lieutenant Strangways, who succeeded to the command, and is said to have produced a sensation by its novelty in the part of the field in which it was employed.

Napoleon, hearing of the desertion of the Saxons, and aware of the exposed situation of Regnier, sent what troops he could find at hand, with a large force of cavalry, to make a forward movement by Molkau to relieve him, and inflict some retaliation, if possible, upon the leading columns of the Army of the North: but the close neighbourhood of

Bubna and Beningsen, the formidable attitude assumed by them, and the presence of the cavalry of Winzingerode and Platoff, prevented this force from effecting anything beyond the relief of the remains of Regnier's corps.

Later in the evening the corps of Bülow, of the Army of the North, came into action, and was directed by the prince royal against Paunsdorf. After a contest this village was abandoned by the enemy, and occupied by the Army of the North.

Langeron had crossed the Partha much earlier, although he had waited to give time for the circuitous movement of the Army of the North by Taucha; and, on gaining the left bank of the river, he immediately directed his corps to the attack of Schönefeld. At first, having to contend singly against Ney, his corps several times nearly carried the village, but was as often repulsed. However, when Bülow attacked Paunsdorf, Langeron carried Schönefeld, and Ney retired upon his position towards Reudnitz. This is all that can be said of the Army of the North on that day. The Swedes had not arrived, but the prince royal made Paunsdorf his headquarters that night.

Since Blücher had placed the corps of Langeron, which constituted one third of his army, under the orders of the prince royal, his own means were small on the 18th. With these, however, he attacked the northern suburb of Leipzig, which the Partha, and numerous houses and gardens, enabled Marmont to defend with great pertinacity. In this severe duty, Blücher employed the Russian corps of Sacken only; for the corps of D'York, which had been constantly engaged on the two preceding days, was in reserve, and not in action on this day.

After driving the French back into the suburbs, and making many fruitless attempts to force the passage of the Partha, which is fordable in some places, Blücher at length succeeded in crossing the river, and actually got possession of Reudnitz, which may almost be considered as part of the suburbs of Leipzig. Napoleon saw the danger, and collecting what troops he was able, he repaired to the spot, and succeeded, as he had done at Probstheide, by his personal exertion and encouragement, in leading his soldiers to recover the village. Still Blücher held his ground that night on the left bank of the Partha.

Ney and Regnier fell back on Reudnitz, and the alarming inroad of Sacken's corps had perhaps as much influence in compelling Ney to retreat, as the attacks of Langeron and Blücher in his front.

The cannonade and skirmishing of advanced posts in all quarters, did not cease till after dark; and, at the time the emperor left the ground, thirteen conflagrations of villages or large farms, marked the field of battle. Along this line, from Cönnewitz to Schönefeld, which formed a semicircle of more than one German mile, perhaps six English miles, the three great Armies of the Allies were, for the first time, united and placed in juxtaposition with each other, as well as in contact with the enemy, along their whole front. Now, also, the Allied chiefs first became confident that a complete and signal defeat of the enemy must, on the following day, reward their exertions, and decide the final issue of the campaign in their favour.

Blücher, convinced that a general pursuit would become the order for the next day, caused the corps of D'York to commence its march on Halle and Merseburg. The whole army bivouacked for the night; the prince royal made Paunsdorf his headquarters, and the Emperor of Russia and King of Prussia retired to sleep at Rötha.

CHAPTER 20

The City of Leipzig Stormed

When the Russians and Prussians of the Allied Grand Army commenced the series of battles that took place near Leipzig, by the attack on Murat's position at Wachau and Liebertwolkwitz, the old desolate *château* of Rötha was well chosen for the emperor's headquarters; for the route by that place and Zwenkau, is the nearest regular road by which troops can cross the Pleisse and Elster, to the southward of Leipzig. If Napoleon had decided to move off, by the road to Erfurt, without risking a general action in front of Leipzig, the Russians and Prussians, then united under the chief command of Barclay de Tolly, could best have traversed the intervening, swampy, and intersected country, by the road through Rötha and Zwenkau; and having thus turned Leipzig might have placed themselves on the flank of the enemy's line of retreat.

To avoid encumbrance on this important route, all the baggage of headquarters (the emperor's not excepted,) had remained at Borna, ten miles still further to the rear; and during the whole time that public events continued undecided and uncertain, with the exception of the emperor, who enjoyed the luxury of a camp bed, all those assembled at headquarters slept in their clothes, and were satisfied with such scanty provisions as their servants and orderlies could obtain for them. From the advance of the armies, the distance to Rötha had now become more than ten English miles from the front, and the reason for going all the way back to Rötha, on the night of the 18th, was chiefly for the purpose of meeting the baggage which had been ordered up to that place;—a precaution which had become really necessary for procuring more sufficient food and raiment than time or opportunity had afforded during the three preceding days and nights. The King of Prussia, who had hitherto made Borna his headquarters, also slept at Rötha on the 18th.

The previous fatigues rendered it perhaps a little later than usual, on the morning of the 19th, before the two sovereigns, and their "*cortége*" were (soon after daylight,) on horseback; and, by about nine o'clock, they were again, after a ten miles' ride, in front of Probstheide. On their arrival they were informed that, at daybreak, it had been discovered that the enemy had withdrawn their forces from Cönnewitz, Probstheide, and Stötteritz, and from all other advanced posts during the night, which had been unusually dark, close into the town and suburbs of Leipzig, leaving only the slightest possible line of picquets to mask their movements, and keeping up bivouac fires to deceive their opponents, as is usual on such occasions.

It was further ascertained, that they had been busily employed all night, filing off in succession through Leipzig onwards, by the Erfurt road. On the side of the Allies, detachments of their three great armies, well supported, were already seen driving in the enemy's picquets, and the main columns advancing to make a general attack on the city.

Field Marshal Schwartzenberg had intended that the Austrians, who composed the left column of the Allied Grand Army on the preceding day, should march that morning on Zwenkau, with orders to cross the Elster, join General Giulay, in the country of Lützen, and use all diligence to fall in with and molest Napoleon's retreating columns; but the transmission of the orders was delayed, or failed, and that force still advanced on Leipzig. Yet hopes were entertained that the corps of D'York, which Blücher, in obedience to an express command of the King of Prussia, had despatched in good time, on the evening of the 18th, in the direction of Merseburg, might be able to effect a passage of the Saale and Luppe, and the intervening morass near that place, or, at all events, to turn those obstacles at Halle, and to be in time to take in flank those leading columns of the enemy which might have passed through Weisenfels, and placed themselves behind the Saale.

Leaving the Allied columns on their march to the assault of Leipzig, we will now avail ourselves of the Baron d'Odeleben's interesting account, as well as of the admissions contained in Napoleon's own bulletin, to trace what had passed in the enemy's camp.

We learn that after the final repulse of Blücher's attack on Reudnitz, towards the close of the day on the 19th, (when Napoleon had exerted himself personally, at the head of a division of his guards,) he was at length convinced, not only from his own observation, but from the reports of Ney and Regnier, whom he met in that quarter, that since the arrival of the Allied Army of the North, the force opposed to his left flank had become so overwhelming, that it would be impossible to withstand it on the following day; and therefore he decided upon a general retreat, to be effected under cover of night, through Leipzig.

After some conversation with Murat, whom he found at his post, between Stötteritz and Probstheide, when he probably communicated his intentions to him, Napoleon returned to his station near the old windmill. It was about six o'clock in the evening, and consequently dark. The battle was over for the night, and nothing but a partial cannonade disturbed the repose of the hostile posts, as they prepared to lie down in their respective positions, and pass the night under arms, in expectation of another day's fighting, as soon as morning should dawn.

Napoleon caused a bivouac fire to be lighted for himself, and gave orders to Berthier for the general retreat. While that able and experienced chief of the staff was engaged in making the arrangements for the execution of this difficult movement in all its details, with the requisite expedition, and dictating and despatching his orders, Napoleon threw himself upon a stretcher that had been brought out of a neighbouring cottage, and fell asleep, exhausted by the cares and fatigues of the day. In little more than a quarter of an hour he awoke, and was further convinced of the perilous situation of his army, and the necessity of an immediate retreat, by the report of the chief of the artillery—that in five days the army had expended 220,000 cannon balls—that only 16,000 remained, including the reserve—and that no fresh supplies could be obtained, unless from Magdeburg or Erfurt.

About eight o'clock in the evening, he called for his horse, rode to Leipzig, and took up his quarters at the Hôtel de Prusse, in the suburbs; there he remained all night, engaged sometimes with Berthier, Caulincourt, or the Duc de Bassano; and sometimes watching the long columns of troops which, towards morning, began to pass under his window, in full retreat. At daybreak, his horses were saddled and ready; but it was not till eight in the morning of the 19th, when the guns of the Allies announced their approach to attack the town, that Napoleon mounted his horse, and proceeded first to make a hasty reconnaissance towards the assailants. On that occasion, the bulletin states, he was on the point of ordering the suburbs to be set on fire, which might have afforded a temporary advantage to the defenders; but, from regard to the king, he mercifully forbore to do so.

Leaving the chief conduct of the defence and the farther passage of the troops to Marshal Macdonald, at half-past nine he rode into the town to take leave of the unhappy sovereign, who was about to become the victim of his steady adherence to an unrighteous cause, from which, however, it must in justice be admitted, he never before possessed the power or opportunity to disengage himself, without certain and immediate ruin to his people and kingdom. At this interview Napoleon, who really appears to have had a personal regard for the Royal Family of Saxony, left the king at liberty to do as he pleased—to quit Leipzig, and trust to his protection, or remain there at the mercy of the Allies.

Upon the king's adhering to the latter alternative, he gave him full sanction to make what terms he best could for himself and his subjects, but recommended the wounded to his especial care. Napoleon then caused a Saxon battalion, which had been attached to the Imperial Guard, to take post in front of their king's abode; there to remain and serve as a guard and protection against "*les premiers mouvements*" of the assailants, justly to be dreaded when a town is about to be entered sword in hand. After taking his final leave of the king, queen, and princess, in their awful situation of suspense, as well as of real and imminent danger, he left them to their fate, and about ten o'clock began to make his way towards Lindenau.

After several unsuccessful attempts to force a passage through the crowd of men, and confusion of guns and baggage that blocked up the gates of the town, towards the rear, he at length succeeded in effecting his escape through a garden; and as he crossed the Elster, he ordered the bridge to be mined, in readiness to be blown up as soon as the rear-guard should have retired over it.

At least 30,000 men and 100 guns, including all the artillery of the Young Guard, and some hundreds of waggons, still remained in Leipzig at that time, besides the professed rear-guard of 6,000 men, with sixty pieces of cannon. The retreat of this body might be considered as cut off; for it could only be effected slowly, by the men in single files, through the motionless mass of carriages and guns in the defile. Under these circumstances, the premature explosion at the bridge took place, and there is no reason to doubt that this catastrophe was occasioned, or at least hastened, by a panic that seized the artillerymen, who were charged with the duty, and that Napoleon was, as he declared himself to be, innocent of a premeditated and unnecessary sacrifice of the numerous troops and distinguished officers, including no less than four chiefs of corps, whom he knew to be still in Leipzig, conducting or covering the retreat.

The bridge over the Elster is close to the gate of the city, and the panic which seized the artillery-men is easily explained by the fact that Blücher by that time had passed some light infantry of Sacken's corps over a branch of the Elster into the Rosenthal, which is a sort of island separated only from the line of retreat by another of the numerous ramifications of that river. The Russian skirmishers, therefore, although in fact the river intervened, must have appeared to have turned the artillery-men's post already, and to threaten the causeway in their rear.

Napoleon did not remain long at Lindenau, but hastened to Mark-Ranstedt, anxious, no doubt, to restore order among the troops that remained to him. About 80,000 men, including his guard, are believed to have effected their retreat; but not without confusion of corps, and even dispersion of regiments, amounting almost to entire disorganisation.

About the time when Napoleon was aroused by the first guns of the Allies, announcing their approach to attack the town, and mounted his horse, the Emperor of Russia and King of Prussia arrived in front of Probstheide. It would be difficult to describe the state in which we found that village, as we rode through it; the heaps of dead and dying in the streets and lanes, were evidence of a gallant and obstinate defence, and the burnt carcasses of men and horses, occasioned by the general conflagration, from which their wounds had probably prevented their escape, formed, indeed, a lamentable picture of the horrors of war.

The sovereigns did not remain long to contemplate so unpleasant a scene; but riding onwards, the emperor arrived at the Windmill Hill, that had been Napoleon's station on the previous day, and he halted there some time, as it was not above a mile from the suburbs about to be attacked, and afforded a panoramic view of the whole combined operation. Although the emperor and king made excursions to watch, or superintend more nearly, the steady progress of the attacking columns, in which they were severally interested, yet this commanding station seemed to be made their concerted rendezvous during the rest of the morning. The disposition for the attack was thus:—

The Grand Army, that is Schwartzenberg's command, moved on to the attack of the southern portion of the suburbs, precisely in the order of the preceding day—the Austrians, next to the river on the Cönnewitz road—the corps of Wittgenstein, preceded by Kleist, and supported by the reserve, to the left of the Probstheide road.

Under the direction of General Blücher, on the extreme right, the

Russian corps of Sacken attacked the gate of Halle, and was supported by the Russian corps of Langeron. That northern quarter of the town was close to the only bridge over the Elster that afforded the means of retreat, and had therefore been rendered as strong as possible by temporary outworks. The defence of these was entrusted to the corps of Regnier.

In the centre, on the Reudnitz or main approach, the Army of the North advanced to the attack. In this the Prince Royal of Sweden gave it in charge to General Bülow, to storm the "*Hinter-thor*" and "*Kohlgartner-thor,*" with the Prussian brigade of Prince Ernest of Hesse-Homburgh, supported by that of General Borstell; and being anxious to give to his own peculiar contingent a conspicuous participation in the glorious termination that might reasonably be expected, he had, by forced marches, brought forward six Swedish battalions on the right of the Prussians, supporting them with five battalions of Russian *chasseurs*, under the command of Count Michael Woronzof.

Leipzig was once a walled town; but its old defences had long been neglected, and were in themselves of little value; indeed, they have probably been suffered to remain with their gates and barriers only as enclosures to secure the collection of customs and municipal dues. A circular walk and avenue of trees, which surrounded the town and separated it from the suburbs, had taken the place of whatever outworks or glacis it may have had; but the space kept open by this circular walk still facilitated, in a remarkable manner, those temporary means of defence which, with proper management and a sufficient force, may render even an open town of small dimensions no easy conquest to an army far superior in number to the defenders.

Stockades and barriers had been constructed. Projecting buildings of the town and suburbs, capable of affording a cross or reserve fire, had been loopholed, and were strongly occupied. At certain angles, redoubts, to serve as bastions, had been thrown up for a flanking fire, and all the direct approaches through the suburbs were duly enfiladed with cannon. Only three sides of the town, if we consider it as contained in a square, were liable to be attacked; for the fourth was secured by the river; and, consequently, the whole front to be defended, from the Partha to the Pleisse, did not exceed two English miles in length.

According to the French bulletin only 6,000 men are stated to have been left for the defence under the command of the Marshals Macdonald and Poniatowski; but it is certain that the corps of Regnier, much reduced it is true by the desertion of the Saxons, was engaged

THE TAKING of LEIPZIG
19 OCTOBER 1813.

1 The Austrian Column
2 The Column of Barclay de Tolly.
3 The Column of Benningson.
4 The Prussians Attacking Column
   of the Army of the North.
5 The Swedish Dr supported
   by Wormzoff
6 Langeron.
7 Sacken.
8 The Army of the North
9 The Old Mill
10 Reignier
11 Macdonald
12 Poniatowsky
13 Troops Cut off
14 Bridge Blown up
15 Oudinot as rear Guard.

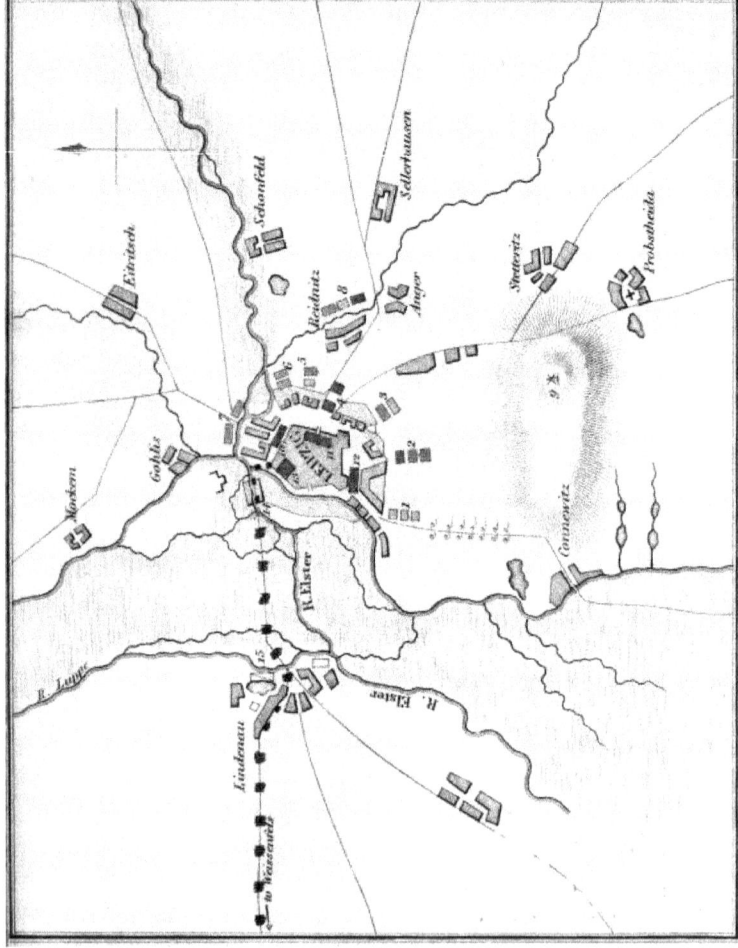

with Sacken in the north suburb, and when the bridge was blown up at least 30,000 effective men remained in Leipzig; the greater part of whom, being commanded by four of the most distinguished chiefs of corps in the French Army, were available for the defence, and were no doubt employed in it while awaiting their turn to file off regularly in succession; until they were panic-struck and disheartened by the premature blowing up of the bridge in their rear, which cut off all possibility of retreat, and rendered them incapable of farther resistance.

About eleven o'clock in the morning, when the actual attack on the town had commenced on all sides, the Emperor Alexander was on horseback, near the old windmill, surrounded by his suite, and anxiously watching the progress of the troops, at that moment a flag of truce was brought to him, with a message from the King of Saxony, the purport of which was, a proposal to treat of a capitulation. The emperor chose to receive the message publicly, and to answer it at once, in the hearing of all around him. It may be supposed that he was not inclined to give the enemy so favourable an opportunity to complete their escape, as a suspension of the attack, for the purpose of negotiating, would have afforded them: he said, with a distinct delivery, and in very good German, as the Germans that were present admitted:—

A victorious army in pursuit of a flying enemy was not to be arrested in its progress by any consideration for the preservation of the town. If the gates were immediately opened, the most strict discipline would be observed; but if not, he must continue his fire upon the town.

He added:—

As for your king, tell him he has broken his solemn engagement with me within these few months; I can therefore no longer respect or place confidence in him; but for every German who will join his countrymen in the liberation of Germany, he shall be received as a brother.

The emperor sent General Toll, one of his *aides-de-camp*, who was himself a German by birth, to re-conduct the flag of truce, and make sure of the correct delivery of this answer to the king. While General Toll was executing his commission, and still in the king's apartment at Leipzig, he heard a brisk fire of musketry gaining ground on the town. He ran downstairs, and found some Prussians in possession of the end of the street, and skirmishing with part of the king's guard. He instantly ordered the guard to lay down their arms, and took measures with the Prussian commanding officer for the security of the king's person. Having ascertained that the town had been entered by force at several points, and was securely in possession of the Allies, he hastened to communicate the intelligence to the emperor, whom he found yet on the Windmill Hill.

Sacken, Bülow, and the Swedes, and Beningsen's advance guard had forced an entrance into the town at various points, nearly at the same moment, though not without having to contend for some time against a strenuous resistance. Sacken and Langeron had been gallantly opposed by Regnier, and with difficulty had entered the gate of Halle, and the northern side of the town. In the attack on the eastern side the Prince of Hesse Homburg was wounded, and his brigade failed in its first attempt to force an entrance for the Army of the North: he was succeeded in the command by General Borstell, who gained a lodgement, but was still strenuously opposed.

Beningsen also had gained the suburbs in his front, and was proceeding to the assault, when the panic of the French paralysed all their power of farther defence, or even inclination to resist, except in some few remote parts of the town and suburbs towards the river, where a desultory but animated skirmish was still kept up.

No sooner had General Toll made his report, than the Emperor of Russia and King of Prussia rode down the hill, and placing themselves at the head of their guards, who were already at the gates, they entered the town about noon, and were no less anxious, by their presence and the good discipline of their reserve, to prevent those excesses that almost invariably follow the capture of a town by assault, than eager to ascertain and to secure the prize that had fallen into their hands. At the entrance of the town the emperor and the king had to force their way through streets that were crowded with the dejected and disarmed prisoners, the wounded, and the inhabitants, who (some in consternation and to propitiate the victors; others in honest exultation at their happy deliverance) came out into the streets, and rent the air with their cheers and shouts of "*Vivat Alexander!*" "*Vivat der König von Preussen!*"

As we passed the house in which the King of Saxony had taken up his abode, the Saxon Guard was still there, formed on its post, with arms reversed. The king, with the few members of his court that were with him, had come down to the street, and was standing on the steps of his house; but the emperor passed by him without notice, and rode on through the market place, to the gate of Mark-Ranstedt. Finding that exit completely impassable, and learning that every possibility of the farther retreat of the French had been effectually cut off, he returned, and took up his station in the centre of the great market-place. A battalion of the Russian guard was placed for the protection and custody of the royal prisoners; and the proper officers of the several departments were charged, under the emperor's immediate superintendence, who sat there on horseback, to secure all arms and military stores, to re-establish order, and to prevent plunder or excess of any kind.

The victorious troops of various nations, who had entered the town first, and who, from their natural excitement, might have been less manageable, were ordered, by virtue of the supreme authority which on that occasion he did not hesitate to assume, to withdraw, and a regular Russian garrison and commandant were immediately appointed to relieve them. The promptitude, good order, and complete success with which these arrangements were made and carried into effect, exceed perhaps any triumph of discipline recorded in history, when towns have been taken by assault, and do equal credit to the heads and to the hearts of the sovereigns and the commanders of armies, by whom an event, which must always be most critical and perilous, was accomplished, and brought to so happy an issue.

In the grand market-place of Leipzig the interest of that remarkable scene was raised to the highest degree. The sovereigns were joined there by the Prince Royal of Sweden, by Schwartzenberg, Blücher, Beningsen, and many others of the most distinguished generals of the Allied Armies, each mounted and with his staff; and though all had co-operated, many of them had not met since the commencement of the campaign.

There, amidst the clamorous cheers of the crowd, the sound of skirmishing, which, though hopeless, was not yet extinguished in remote streets towards the river, and the occasional shot and shells of heavy calibre, from the other side, which continued to be thrown wantonly and at random into the town, the cry of "*Platz!*" "*Platz!*" from time to time, excited new and intense expectation and interest, as some fresh prisoner of note was brought through the crowd to be presented to the emperor.

Among these the most distinguished were Generals Regnier and Lauriston, chief of corps. Marshal Macdonald had escaped with difficulty, by plunging into the river, and it is said his horse was drowned, and that he himself narrowly escaped, by seizing hold of the branches of a tree. Poniatowski, less fortunate, was drowned in making a similar attempt. Upwards of two hundred pieces of cannon had been taken, and trophies, carts, carriages, and prisoners without number. Thus, the amount of the prize, and the consequences of the victory, seemed gradually to develop themselves at that place and at that moment, as in the last scene of a drama realized.

The Emperor of Russia was courteous to all his prisoners, and particularly gracious to Lauriston, who was in the full uniform of his rank, with epaulettes and decorations; but, in the hope of avoiding notice till he could effect his escape in the general confusion, he had wrapped himself up in an old, rough, drab great-coat. In this garb, and on horseback, he was taken and brought before the emperor, by whom he was much esteemed, being well known to him in consequence of having been recently ambassador at the court of St. Petersburg.

This scene lasted perhaps an hour, after which the emperor went to a residence that had been prepared for him in the town, and the King of Prussia to another in the suburbs. The Emperor of Austria arrived an hour or two later, and proceeded to the quarters reserved for him. In the afternoon Lord Cathcart accompanied the Emperor Alexander to review the contingent of the Prince Royal of Sweden, at the particular desire of that prince. All was then as tranquil as if nothing unusual had occurred. We found the Swedish Army formed in line to the number of about 20,000 men, seemingly in good order, and certainly not much the worse for the military service they had endured. The emperor also inspected the English rocket-brigade attached to that army, and under the command of Lieutenant Strangways. In the evening we returned to Leipzig for the night.

CHAPTER 21

Retreat of Napoleon to Erfurt

The number of prisoners taken at Leipzig, and in the battles fought in its neighbourhood, amounted to about 52,000, of whom 30,000 are said to have been fit for duty, and 22,000 sick or wounded. The loss in killed on both sides must have been great, but is not easily ascertained; 250 guns, 900 ammunition and other waggons, besides valuable military stores and magazines, remained in possession of the Allies. Notwithstanding his severe losses, it has been estimated that Napoleon may have found collected around him at Mark-Ranstedt, on the night of the 19th of October, a force of about 80,000 men, who had made good their retreat, or rather their escape, through Leipzig. Besides these he had the corps of Bertrand at Weisenfels, amounting perhaps to 10,000 or 15,000 more.

Though this may still appear a respectable force on paper, it must be considered that the troops, which were hurried through Leipzig on the night of the 18th and before daylight on the 19th, had entered the town in several columns, and by different gates, whilst there was only one outlet for them, and that on an encumbered defile, an elevated causeway across a swamp three English miles in length, in which there were no less than five bridges in succession, over as many unfordable streams, but which must be crossed.

This process was an unavoidable necessity; but if it had been in-tended for the confusion of corps and the wreck of an army, it could not have been better designed, and it completed the demoralisation which usually follows lost battles and precipitate retreats. To restore or-der, and renew a right spirit in such a case, is a work of difficulty, not to be accomplished in the discouragement and hurry of a forced retreat.

On military grounds alone, therefore, it was no longer possible for Napoleon to make a stand at Erfurt, or to attempt, by skilful manoeu-vre in the favourable country behind the Saale, to divert or even delay his immediate expulsion from Germany. Besides this, he could not fail to recognise the spirit of independence renewed throughout all Germany as the political consequence of his lost time on the Elbe, and lost battle on the Elster, nor to perceive that the Bavarian and Saxon defections were only coruscations from a vast smouldering volcano, ready to burst forth into a general eruption, as soon as the tidings of his disaster should spread, and carry assurance of the strength of the Allies to protect their confederates in liberating their native land.

Under these circumstances Napoleon left Mark-Ranstedt, in his *caleche*, at three in the morning of the 20th of October, escorted at a foot's pace by his Old Guard, to follow the line of march of his discomfited and crestfallen host; and without doubt he had made up his mind to a retreat across the Rhine, with as much expedition and as little farther loss as possible. At daybreak he arrived at Lützen, and became fully aware of the helpless condition of his army; for the defile occasioned by the town had checked the stream, and this of course proved a severe test of discipline. It was not till Murat, who had accompanied him so far in his carriage, mounted his horse, and used his personal exertions and authority, that sufficient order could be restored to enable Napoleon to proceed through the town, a little beyond which he halted.

On this occasion he appears to have experienced no small anxiety, lest his disheartened and surly soldiers, many without arms, and all without ammunition, should be attacked by some cavalry force of the Allies, as they continued their route across the plains of Lützen, before some degree of order could be restored to render them capable of resistance. Whilst Murat and the other chiefs, with their staffs, were busily employed, like shepherds or drovers in the confusion of some great cattle fair, in endeavouring to disentangle their respective flocks and herds, Napoleon strove to renovate the spirits of his troops as they passed onwards in better order than he had witnessed on the other side of the defile, and did not fail to administer the sort of cordial best suited to French vanity on such occasions.

He ordered bands to play and drums and trumpets to be as clamorous as possible, while he caused 4,000 Austrian prisoners to be displayed at the road side, and produced numerous colours taken long ago at the Battle of Dresden; thus, performing the farce of a review after the tragedy of a disastrous battle. This display happened to take place at the spot where Marshal Bessières was killed on the eve of the Battle of Lützen, about six months previous, which was the first event in his renewal of hostilities in 1813.

As to immediate danger from direct pursuit, none was to be apprehended; for all the bridges on the Lindenau causeway had been destroyed by Oudinot, who remained on the left bank of the last stream, the Luppe, with his division of the Young Guard, to dispute the passage; and the mere manual operation of repairing the road and the bridges, so as to render them passable, even if unopposed, would require not less than one whole day's work.

The arrival, however, of a hostile cavalry force, despatched by some circuitous route, on the evening of the 18th, when all was secure, or even an attack by Giulay and Maurice Lichtenstein, might have been reasonably expected at that moment, and might have been inconvenient to the French; but no cavalry had been despatched in time; and those two Austrian generals, whose corps together did not amount to more than 10,000 men, either kept aloof, on account of their weakness, or were decoyed away towards Naumburg, by the movement of Bertrand, and these were the only troops of the Allies previously on that side of the river, and now within reach of the enemy.

Napoleon, therefore, meeting with no impediment, marched on to Weisenfels, and in the course of the evening of the 20th, or before daylight on the following morning, he succeeded in passing his whole force across the Saale at that place, in two columns, one by the regular bridge, and the other by a temporary one of rafts, which had been prepared by order of Bertrand.

In crossing the Saale at Weisenfels, which implies a departure from the great road instead of ascending its right bank, Napoleon's object was probably to place the river between his army and the enemy as soon as possible, and at the same time to avoid a dangerous and inconvenient defile at Kösen, occasioned by a commanding ridge that bounds the valley of the Saale. Here the regular causeway towards Erfurt, after ascending the course of the river along the right bank from Weisenfels and through Naumburg, is made to cross the river; and the prudence of his decision in this respect was vindicated by the severe molestation which Giulay was able to inflict, from the heights of Kösen, upon the corps of Bertrand, who, after having built the second bridge at Weisenfels, moved on to secure that of Kösen, and guard the passage of the Saale at that point.

By crossing the Saale at Weisenfels, Napoleon subjected his army to a difficult march along bad roads, through a hilly country, intersected by vineyards, and occupying an angle formed by the confluence of the River Unstruth with the Saale, which exposed them also to the necessity of crossing two rivers instead of one.

General d'York, who had been sent off from Leipzig on the eve-ning of the 18th, having gone round by Halle, could not arrive in time to disturb the passage of the French over the Saale at Weisenfels; but he lost no time in falling upon the rear of enemy's columns, as they crossed the Unstruth at Freiburg. On this occasion, after a sharp skirmish, in which Napoleon remained with his rear guard to the last, General d'York took some prisoners, forty guns, and many waggons, besides liberating the 4,000 Austrians, the same unfortunate prisoners that Napoleon had recently paraded near Lützen, and who continued to be dragged after him probably to give some colour of plausibility to his claim of victory at Leipzig, in which he still persevered, through blind infatuation or politic effrontery. The seventeenth bulletin says:—

> The French Army, though victorious, is arriving at Erfurt as a defeated army would have arrived.

And he attributes this entirely to the premature explosion of the bridge over the Pleisse, by a corporal of sappers.

After crossing the Unstruth, Napoleon continued his retreat by Eckardsberge; his proper right flank was covered by Bertrand, who still held the bridge at Kösen, and after regaining the great road near Buttelstedt, he arrived, without farther inconvenience, at Erfurt on the 23rd of October.

We now return to the Allied Army assembled at Leipzig on the 19th, and trace the general arrangements made for the pursuit.

Napoleon, when forced to retire, had been severely punished for his imprudence in risking a general action, with not only a river but a conflux of five unfordable streams, immediately in rear of his position, by the loss of one half of his army, and the hopeless discomfiture of the remainder. Yet the same remarkable and complicated barrier now befriended him, by effectually covering his retreat, and giving to those of his troops, who had been fortunate enough to pass it, a start of four-and-twenty-hours before their pursuers.

The Allies did not wait in tranquillity for the re-establishment of the only direct communication; but immediately after the surrender of Leipzig, they concerted, and acted upon the following disposition for the pursuit, by the least circuitous routes that remained open to them:—

First, the Grand Army, under the chief command of Prince Schwartzenberg, and accompanied by the Emperor Alexander and the King of Prussia, was to march to its left, through Zeitz and Jena on Wiemar.

Secondly, Blücher, with the corps of Langeron, was to follow the route taken by General d'York. In marching to his right, he descended the right bank of the Elster; but hearing of a practicable route across the swamp between the Elster and the Luppe, not far from Schkeuditz, the two corps effected their passage in the course of the 20th, slowly and with difficulty, across the Merseburger Aue. This extensive morass occupies the space between the rivers, from the neighbourhood of Leipzig till those two deep and sluggish streams terminate their parallel courses in the Saale below Meresburg.

Blücher, having left this difficulty behind him, marched upon Lützen as soon as possible; but, owing to the delay occasioned by the morass, he could not arrive there till Napoleon had escaped him. Seizing some stragglers and much baggage, he continued his pursuit by Weisenfels and Freiburg on Langensalza.

Thirdly, the prince royal, with the Army of the North and the corps of Beningsen, was to follow, as soon as the road could be opened, through Leipzig, Lützen, and Merseburg.

These arrangements brought the whole of the survivors of the Allied Army which had fought at Leipzig within reach of concentration, in the course of the 24th and 25th of October, for another battle, had it been required, in the neighbourhood of Erfurt.

Napoleon was then at Erfurt, with a strong rearguard in position towards Wiemar. The Emperor of Russia, who had halted at Jena on the 23rd, traversing the fatal field of 1806 in his route, took up his quarters at Wiemar on the 24th. As it appeared that Napoleon declined another battle, the King of Prussia now left the army to make a hasty visit to his dominions.

By this time news must have reached Napoleon that the Bavarian General Wrede, with his combined force amounting to about 35,000 men, had arrived on the Maine, and commenced the bombardment of Würzburg on the 22nd. At the same time, he was aware that the Allied Grand Army had reassembled in the neighbourhood of Wiemar, while the army of Blücher was already on Napoleon's flank, moving to turn Erfurt by Langensalza; and the Army of the North was also advancing, and not far distant. Resistance on the part of the French Army was out of the question. They had not a moment to lose.

A continued and precipitate retreat was their only chance of escape. In the one day's halt on the 24th, which Napoleon allowed himself at Erfurt, no time was lost by him; for while his columns closed up, and renewed their march in better order, he caused supplies of arms and ammunition, rations, and other things needful for his troops, to be distributed to them, as far as time and the stores of that depot would allow. Leaving a garrison in the town of Erfurt and citadel of St. Petersberg, he withdrew his rear-guard in the morning of the 25th, and, covered from direct pursuit in some measure by the fortress, he resumed his retreat.

At Gotha and Eisenach his rear-guard was roughly handled by General d'York and Rudzewicz, part of the army of Blücher, who reached Langensalza with the remainder on the 25th. Thence Napoleon hastened to throw himself, with his harassed army, into the wild forest country of the Thuringer Wald, through which the great road by Salzungen and Hanau passes towards Frankfort and Mayence.

These forest districts afforded shelter to stragglers, and facilities for desertion to the Germans, who had yet remained in his ranks; but though the nature of the country tended greatly to diminish his force by desertion as well as starvation, it was favourable to the protecting services of his rear-guard, and though occasionally incommoded by the partisan corps of Platoff, Tchernicheff, and Illowaisky, his army was no longer seriously molested by its pursuers. But he was soon to encounter a new and formidable enemy, though recently his friend and ally, whom he knew to be moving with rapid strides to cross his path, and intercept his return to the frontier of France.

When it was known, at the Allied general headquarters at Wiemar, that the enemy had continued his retreat from Erfurt, the following disposition was adopted for the ulterior pursuit:—

First, Blücher, although his advanced corps commanded by D'York had overtaken the corps of Bertrand near Eisenach and done it considerable mischief, was now directed to move by the road to Giessen and Wetzlar, and leave the great road, by which the enemy had retired, open for the main Austrian column of the Grand Army. That column was on its march through the Thuringer Wald by Schmalkalden, but unfortunately could not arrive in time to be of the same use in the direct pursuit that D'York might have been, if he had not been thus diverted from it. However, the precise circumstances of D'York on the 26th could not have been anticipated at headquarters on the 25th when the order was issued, and the object of Blücher's new route was to cut off the possibility of a retreat of the French upon Coblentz.

The retreat to Erfurt

Secondly, the Allied Grand Army, the Austrians, and the reserve, moved through the forest to Schmalkalden and Meiningen. Wittgenstein and Kleist were charged with the blockade or reduction of Erfurt, and made Gotha their headquarters.

Thirdly, the prince royal, with the Army of the North, did not continue the pursuit farther than Salzungen, but marched by Cassel and Hanover round the mountainous country of the Harzback to the Lower Elbe, to watch Davoust and the Danes, and the other forces of the enemy that remained in our rear, and which, though disconnected and scattered along the Elbe from Dresden to Hamburg, and many of them sick and wounded, amounted, including the Danes, to not less than 80,000 men. Beningsen, who was in future to be attached to the Army of the North, was also sent back by the direct route on that service, and particularly charged, in the first instance, with the observation of Magdeburg.

The news of the Battle of Hanau, the details of which are reserved for another chapter, reached the headquarters of the grand array at Meiningen. At this court the duchess dowager, the duke, then a minor, and the Princess Adelaide, since the universally beloved and lamented Queen of William IV. of England, entertained the Emperor Alexander and his suite, the field marshal, and various other princes and chiefs who halted there one day, with cordiality and hospitality, which evinced the joy with which they, in common with all true and loyal Germans, appreciated the exertions, and gloried in the triumphs, of their liberators.

CHAPTER 22

Battle of Hanau and Retreat of Napoleon

From Eisenach, the great road (by which Napoleon retreated, after passing through the extremity of the Thuringer Wald) proceeds by Fulda and Schluchtern; and thence, having attained the summit level, descends by the course of the River Kinzig, along its left bank, by Gelnhausen to the town of Hanau, through which the route passes on to Frankfort and Mayence. This line is the great post-road and military communication. There is indeed another road through Hersfeld and Friedberg; but that route is too circuitous and difficult to have suited the purpose of the retreating army.

Hanau, a large town, with old dismantled fortifications, then for the most part converted into gardens, is seated in the angle formed by the confluence of the little River Kinzig, with the broad and navigable Maine, and is little more than ten English miles from Frankfort.

Napoleon, aware of Wrede's arrival at Hanau, decided upon turning the town by an old road through the woody country on the right bank of the Kinzig, and made his arrangements for forcing his way past his antagonist by that route. As he was not pressed by his pursuers this operation was neither difficult nor hazardous, even if resistance should be offered; for his numbers were at least double those of his opponent.

As soon as Wrede was aware of Napoleon's intention he crossed the Kinzig, and gallantly but rashly prepared to bar the road against the homeward bound and desperate French Army, which even now could not have amounted to fewer than 60,000 men (by this time, if not veterans, at least inured to war), while the Allied force at Wrede's disposal was little more than 30,000; and a large proportion of these were recruits or soldiers who had never been in action. With this intent the Bavarian general took up a position about a mile from the town, facing towards the north-east, and occupied it in the following manner:—

The right of his line rested upon the Kinzig near the bridge of Neuhof. The village of Neuhof was also occupied, and the left of his line of infantry extended to the old road from Gelnhausen, near the spot where it emerges from the wood through which Napoleon was expected to advance. In the plain beyond the left of the line, and a little retired, the Austrian and Bavarian cavalry were placed in echelon, and with them a large proportion of light artillery. Some marshy ground, with woodland beyond it, closed the extreme left.

On a convenient eminence, near the left centre, a powerful battery of heavy artillery was concentrated, for the purpose of commanding, by its cross fire, the point where the road issues from the wood, and of preventing the enemy's columns from forming in the plain. Tchernicheff, with his Cossacks, had passed by the right flank of the enemy's columns, and joined the Bavarians; he was posted in rear of the left, towards the marsh, and in observation of the road from Friedberg. The Austro-Bavarian line was formed at a little distance from the skirts of the extensive woodlands of Pappenwald and Lambois through which Napoleon's route lay, and light infantry in the wood was extended along the whole front.

At about noon on the 30th of October, Napoleon's *tirailleurs* drove in some advanced posts that were stationed farther in the forest, and then engaged the skirmishers along the skirts of the wood; but the difficulty of bringing up sufficient support, and the efforts of the Allies to prevent any formation in the plain, for a long time kept the enemy at bay. At length, Napoleon reconnoitred the position, and observed that the left flank was its most assailable point; he then brought his Old Guard forward on the Gelnhausen road, and by a spirited attack cleared space enough for the formation of his cavalry.

General Nansouty, with the cavalry of the Guard, and that of Sebastiani, said to have been a force of eighty squadrons, then succeeded, notwithstanding the heavy cannonade of the Allies, in forming three lines which simultaneously attacked the Austro-Bavarian cavalry, and the left of the line of infantry. This overwhelming cavalry attack being duly supported, ultimately prevailed; and a powerful artillery force having by great exertions been brought forward by General Druot, to oppose the heavy battery of the Allies, and support the attack, while a large column of infantry debouched near the same point, and proceeded to form upon the Allied left flank, the advantage gained by Nansouty's cavalry attack was rendered permanent.

General Wrede now made his arrangements for a retreat of his whole army to his right, across the Kinzig. This was a difficult operation in presence of the enemy, as the whole of the infantry and artillery had to move off in succession from the left, and retire in rear of the line by the bridge of Neuhof. The Allied cavalry were driven back to Hanau, which they entered by the bridge, on the Frankfort road, and retired through it under the protection of an Austrian infantry brigade, which had been left in charge of the town.

As the battle was decided by the successful employment of a great superiority in cavalry, it was not long in suspense; and the retreat commenced before the enemy could bring any large infantry force into action on their left. This circumstance, and the narrowness of the ground in his rear, for he now had the wood on his right and the town on his left, enabled Wrede to conduct his movement in a masterly manner, and without confusion or disaster, though not without severe loss in killed and wounded. The loss of the enemy was also severe, and was chiefly occasioned while forming for the first attack, by the well-posted and well served artillery of the Allies.

Wrede did not attempt to hold the town of Hanau, though perhaps he might have done so with safety and effect, if he had occupied it in force as an entrenched position, from which to sally forth as soon as the enemy should resume his retreat, and leave opposed to him only so much force as he could follow and attack with prospect of advantage. Napoleon appears to have supposed that he would do so, for he did not attempt the town that day. The Austrian brigade remained in it till night; but Wrede retired by the Aschaffenburg road, and took up a position across it with his left to the Maine, his centre at the farm of Lehrhof, and his right towards an extensive wood. The reason he assigned for not occupying the town was his reluctance to expose it to a bombardment.

Next morning at eight o'clock Napoleon took possession of Hanau, the Austrian brigade retiring from it; and having caused the corps of Bertrand, Ney, and Marmont to cross the Kinzig, he commenced an attack upon Wrede's new and very indifferent position. Although this was not a very serious attack, the Allies were obliged about midday to throw back their right, and stand in line with the Aschaffenburg road, their backs to the Maine, and the cavalry on their left *"en potence"* towards the town.

The object of this second day's fighting, on the part of Napoleon, was to gain time for some artillery and baggage, as well as the Young Guard commanded by Oudinot, which were arriving by the Gel-

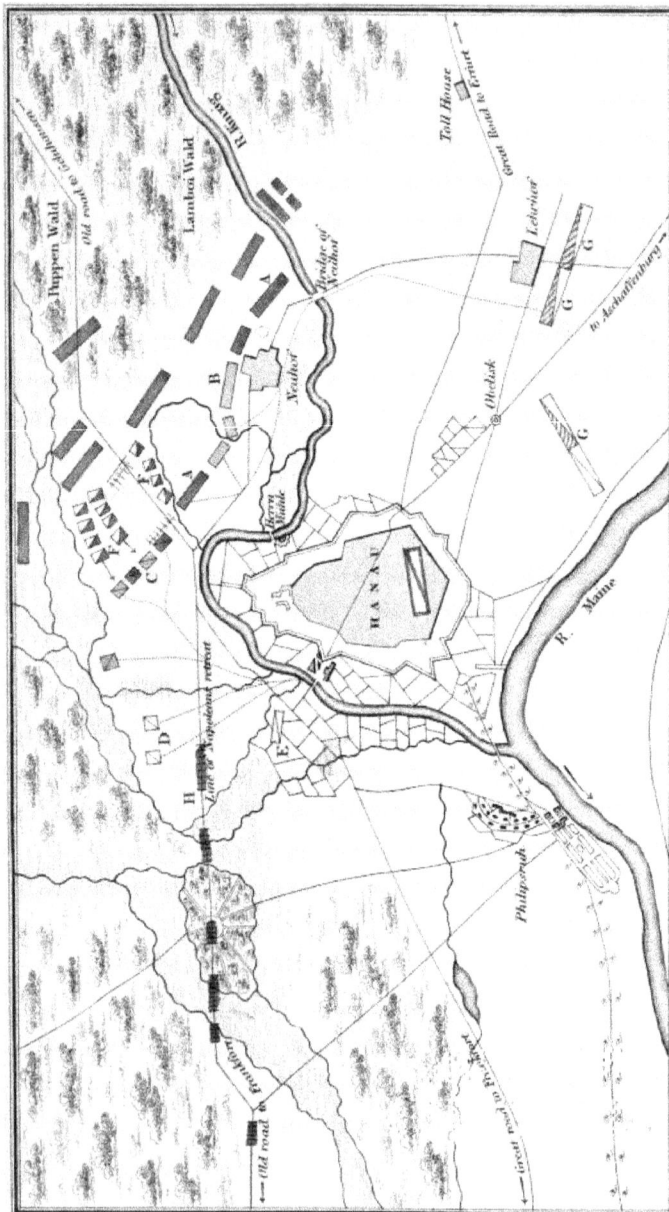

BATTLE of HANAU

A Bavarian Infantry
B Austrian Infantry
C Austrian & Bavarian Cavalry
D Thorwacht
E Austrian Brigade of Infantry
F Cavalry attack at Manzouly
G Several position of the Austro Bavarian Army
H Line of March of the French Army on Frankfort

nhausen road, to come up and pass by in safety. When this object was accomplished the several corps engaged withdrew in succession as gradually and imperceptibly as they could, and recrossing the Kinzig, partly by the bridge of Neuhof, and partly through the town, they continued their march on Frankfort. As soon as Wrede became aware of the enemy's retrograde movement, he gave the order for a general attack; but before he could come up with them, nearly the whole French Army had succeeded in working round its opponents, and was in full retreat upon the Frankfort roads.

Of the corps of Bertrand, which was appointed to cover the retreat, there remained only two battalions in the town, and a small rear-guard at the bridge of Neuhof. The Bavarians and Austrians lost no time in attacking those two strong posts, and carried them at the point of the bayonet. It was in advancing to the assault of the bridge on the Frankfort road, by which the enemy had retired from the town, and which their rear-guard obstinately held, that General Wrede, who had personally conducted the Bavarian attack, received a shot through the body, which, though it did not prove mortal, was believed to be so at the time. The command devolved upon the Austrian General Fresnelle.

After quitting Hanau, Napoleon retreated to Frankfort, where he halted one day, while his columns continued their march towards the Rhine. On the 2nd he went to Mayence, and his rear-guard retired from Frankfort; on the same day it was occupied by the Austro-Bavarian Army.

When the news of the battle at Hanau reached the Imperial Headquarters at Meiningen, it appeared to give a fresh stimulus to the pursuit. The Austrian column arrived at Frankfort on the 4th, and the Emperor Alexander, by forced marches (but by the circuitous route appointed for the reserve by Schweinfurth, Würzburg, and Aschaffenburg, to the southward of the Rhon Geberge), reached Frankfort on the 5th, and made his entry about noon at the head of some 10,000 Russian cavalry. The infantry of the reserve could not arrive till several days later. The Austro-Bavarian Army moved to Hesse Darmstadt.

On the 5th Schwartzenberg, with his Austrian column, proceeded from Frankfort to follow the enemy in their retreat to Mayence. Although Napoleon, with the principal part of his force, had crossed the Rhine two or three days before, he had left General Bertrand, with 5,000 men, on the right bank at Hochheim, to improve its defences, and entrench himself there as an advanced post to the fortress of Cassel, which, being situated on the right bank of the Rhine, is the *tête du*

BATTLE OF HANAU

pont to the flying bridge which crosses the river at Mayence.

This gave the Austrians the opportunity of winning the last laurels of the campaign without the participation of any of their Allies. Accordingly, on the 9th of November, the field-marshal commanding in person directed the corps of Giulay, Bubna, and Alois Lichtenstein, to attack Bertrand's post at Hochheim. There had not been time to complete the defences; the place was immediately carried by assault, and the Austrian standard planted upon its ramparts.

Bertrand, when forced to abandon it, availed himself of some intervening woods, and succeeded in withdrawing the garrison with little loss and without hurry into Cassel. The loss of the Austrians, also, was inconsiderable. This affair terminated the campaign of 1813, so far as the Grand Armies of the contending powers were concerned; and the liberation of Germany from Napoleon's yoke, which it had been compelled to endure in abject submission for the preceding seven years, may be considered to have been then accomplished.

The Emperor of Austria reached Frankfort on the 6th, and the King of Prussia, who had found time since the battle of Leipzig to visit Berlin and attend personally to the internal affairs of his country, joined the two Imperial sovereigns soon after.

Napoleon sent Macdonald to Cologne to assume the command, and organise an army, with all diligence, for the defence of the Lower Rhine, and gave to Marmont and Victor similar commissions, the one at Mayence, and the other at Strasburg, for the defence of the Upper and the Middle Rhine; and having farther charged Kellerman with the formation of a reserve at Metz, he went to Paris, and arrived at his palace of St. Cloud on the 9th of November.

The temporary cessation of hostilities which succeeded, like the calm after a storm, was not the consequence of any armistice, but arose from the necessity, common to all the contending armies, of repose sufficient to recruit their energies, and to enable them to prepare for another contest.

Germany had indeed been liberated; but it was evident that the tranquillity of Europe could not be established upon a safe and permanent basis, until the disturber of the peace of nations, who had been hunted up to his stronghold, but not subdued, should be brought by force of arms, or by negotiations, carried on at the head of formidable armies, to submit to restrictions much more binding than any he had yet been disposed to endure. But although the work of retribution was not yet completed, the necessity of restoring the ranks (after the losses incidental to the severe contest at Leipzig, and the continual forced marches which had followed, as well as the precaution, no less indispensable, of providing supplies and means of support for a winter campaign in an enemy's country,) placed it out of the power of the Allies to pursue their advantage any farther in that campaign. For two months they allowed themselves an interval of repose, intending to take the field again in the month of January 1814, to cross the Rhine at the head of armies amounting to more than 200,000 men, and with renewed vigour to carry the war into the enemy's country.

CHAPTER 23

Conclusion

Although it was the purpose of the author to confine himself as much as possible to the proceedings of the Grand Army with which he was present, yet to render the history of the War of Liberation in Germany complete, it may be satisfactory to take a view of the affairs of the Danes, and of the other hostile forces that remained in arms against the Allies, and were in their rear when they advanced to the Rhine; as well as of the progress made by a part of the Army of the North in the liberation of Holland.

After remaining some time in Hanover, the prince royal, with his Swedes, resumed active operations against the Danes, with as much of the Army of the North as he could devote to a service in which he was personally most interested. He proceeded, on the 4th of December, to march against Marshal Davoust and the Danes, who were together in the country of Holstein, and on crossing the Stekenitz he learned that Davoust had abandoned his Allies to their fate, and, notwithstanding, the exertions of Woronzof and others to intercept him, had succeeded in throwing himself, with his French *corps d'armée*, into Hamburg.

Prince Frederick of Hesse, who commanded the Danes, retreated, and was ultimately forced back by Walmoden, Dornberg, and others, to Rendsburg. After some farther unavailing resistance, the King of Denmark was obliged to sue for peace on such terms as the Allies should think fit to dictate. By this treaty, which was concluded on the 14th of January, 1814, the King of Denmark agreed to receive Swedish Pomerania, in lieu of Norway, which was to be annexed to Sweden; he also agreed, not only to join the Alliance, but (for a subsidy of 400,000*l.*, to be paid by Great Britain) to furnish a contingent of 40,000 men.

In Holland, it was expected that the arrival of part of the victorious army would produce political effects destructive of French influence, and favourable to the cause of the Allies. Generals Winzingerode and Bülow, of the Army of the North, were accordingly detached for the purpose of marching thither; and performed the duty assigned to them successfully. By the 12th of November Winzingerode had crossed the Issel; and having advanced and taken possession of Amersfort on the 18th, Generals Arrighi, Le Brun, and the other French authorities found it full time to leave Amsterdam. The population of the town rose with one consent, and declaring themselves independent of France, they proclaimed the Prince of Orange as *Stadtholder*.

On the 2nd of December the prince arrived from England, and was received with every demonstration of loyalty and joy. On the 6th the first division of the British expedition arrived under the command of Sir Thomas Graham, and disembarked at Amsterdam.

Dantzig on the Vistula was defended by the French under General Rapp, and after a protracted siege it was surrendered to Prince Alexander of Würtemberg, brother to the empress-mother, and uncle to the Emperor of Russia. The garrison consisted of 9,000 men, who became prisoners of war, and on the 30th of November they were marched into Russia.

Stettin on the Oder surrendered on the 21st of November, with a garrison of 7,600 men.

Torgau on the Elbe surrendered to General Tauenzien on the 26th of December, with its garrison of 10,000 men.

Erfurt capitulated on the 20th of December; but the governor and garrison retired into the strong fortress of St. Petersberg. Upon this General Wittgenstein and General Kleist, leaving a sufficient blockading force, proceeded to join the army on the Rhine.

Davoust retained possession of Hamburg on the Elbe till after the restoration of the Bourbons. In the meantime, he gave employment to a blockading force of 35,000 men, commanded by General Beningsen; but the town was spared the disastrous consequence, of a siege or bombardment. The garrison may have amounted to 20,000 men; but after their long confinement the troops were in a very unhealthy state.

At the close of 1813, Wittenburg on the Elbe still remained in possession of the enemy; but as soon as Torgau surrendered, General Tauenzien transferred his forces to press the siege of Wittenburg, and ultimately succeeded in taking this fortress. Magdeburg on the Elbe also remained in a state of blockade at the end of 1813.

The active and brilliant services of Generals Walmoden, Tettenborn, and Dornberg, had prepared the north of Germany, including Hanover, for its final liberation. This was accomplished when the Army of the North passed through the Hessian and Hanoverian territories, after Napoleon had been driven from Erfurt; and on the 19th of December the Duke of Cambridge arrived to take possession of Hanover.

At Dresden, General St. Cyr, after a vain attempt to elude or repulse his blockading enemies, in the hope of effecting a junction with some of the other forces on the Elbe, was induced to capitulate to General Klenau, who had been sent back from Leipzig to reinforce General Tolstoi's corps and the other forces of the Allies that were left in observation. By this capitulation General St. Cyr and Mouton, Comte de Löbau, were actually suffered, without waiting for its ratification, to march out with the 1st and 14th corps, the whole effective force of the garrison, without arms, but not as prisoners—the terms only requiring their peaceable return to France, and that they should not serve again till exchanged.

These terms were not ratified, and the French generals, with their unarmed followers, had reached Altenberg when they were halted, and the option was given them, either to return to Dresden, with the promise that everything should be restored to them in the same state as when the capitulation was accepted, or else to surrender at discretion. St. Cyr yielded to the "*droit du plus fort*," and decided on choosing the latter alternative: 1,759 officers, including the two chiefs, and many other distinguished generals, and 33,744 rank and file, was the amount of the garrison of Dresden. Of these, about 6,000 were left sick in the city, and these, as well as their comrades, who had marched unarmed into Bohemia, were ultimately made prisoners of war.

LEONAUR

ALSO FROM LEONAUR
AVAILABLE IN SOFTCOVER OR HARDCOVER WITH DUST JACKET

AFGHANISTAN: THE BELEAGUERED BRIGADE *by G. R. Gleig*—An Account of Sale's Brigade During the First Afghan War.

IN THE RANKS OF THE C. I. V *by Erskine Childers*—With the City Imperial Volunteer Battery (Honourable Artillery Company) in the Second Boer War.

THE BENGAL NATIVE ARMY *by F. G. Cardew*—An Invaluable Reference Resource.

THE 7TH (QUEEN'S OWN) HUSSARS: Volume 4—1688-1914 *by C. R. B. Barrett*—Uniforms, Equipment, Weapons, Traditions, the Services of Notable Officers and Men & the Appendices to All Volumes—Volume 4: 1688-1914.

THE SWORD OF THE CROWN *by Eric W. Sheppard*—A History of the British Army to 1914.

THE 7TH (QUEEN'S OWN) HUSSARS: Volume 3—1818-1914 *by C. R. B. Barrett*—On Campaign During the Canadian Rebellion, the Indian Mutiny, the Sudan, Matabeleland, Mashonaland and the Boer War Volume 3: 1818-1914.

THE KHARTOUM CAMPAIGN *by Bennet Burleigh*—A Special Correspondent's View of the Reconquest of the Sudan by British and Egyptian Forces under Kitchener—1898.

EL PUCHERO *by Richard McSherry*—The Letters of a Surgeon of Volunteers During Scott's Campaign of the American-Mexican War 1847-1848.

RIFLEMAN SAHIB *by E. Maude*—The Recollections of an Officer of the Bombay Rifles During the Southern Mahratta Campaign, Second Sikh War, Persian Campaign and Indian Mutiny.

THE KING'S HUSSAR *by Edwin Mole*—The Recollections of a 14th (King's) Hussar During the Victorian Era.

JOHN COMPANY'S CAVALRYMAN *by William Johnson*—The Experiences of a British Soldier in the Crimea, the Persian Campaign and the Indian Mutiny.

COLENSO & DURNFORD'S ZULU WAR *by Frances E. Colenso & Edward Durnford*—The first and possibly the most important history of the Zulu War.

U. S. DRAGOON *by Samuel E. Chamberlain*—Experiences in the Mexican War 1846-48 and on the South Western Frontier.

LEONAUR

ALSO FROM LEONAUR
AVAILABLE IN SOFTCOVER OR HARDCOVER WITH DUST JACKET

OFFICERS & GENTLEMEN *by Peter Hawker & William Graham*—Two Accounts of British Officers During the Peninsula War: Officer of Light Dragoons by Peter Hawker & Campaign in Portugal and Spain by William Graham .

THE WALCHEREN EXPEDITION *by Anonymous*—The Experiences of a British Officer of the 81st Regt. During the Campaign in the Low Countries of 1809.

LADIES OF WATERLOO *by Charlotte A. Eaton, Magdalene de Lancey & Juana Smith*—The Experiences of Three Women During the Campaign of 1815: Waterloo Days by Charlotte A. Eaton, A Week at Waterloo by Magdalene de Lancey & Juana's Story by Juana Smith.

JOURNAL OF AN OFFICER IN THE KING'S GERMAN LEGION *by John Frederick Hering*—Recollections of Campaigning During the Napoleonic Wars.

JOURNAL OF AN ARMY SURGEON IN THE PENINSULAR WAR *by Charles Boutflower*—The Recollections of a British Army Medical Man on Campaign During the Napoleonic Wars.

ON CAMPAIGN WITH MOORE AND WELLINGTON *by Anthony Hamilton*—The Experiences of a Soldier of the 43rd Regiment During the Peninsular War.

THE ROAD TO AUSTERLITZ *by R. G. Burton*—Napoleon's Campaign of 1805.

SOLDIERS OF NAPOLEON *by A. J. Doisy De Villargennes & Arthur Chuquet*—The Experiences of the Men of the French First Empire: Under the Eagles by A. J. Doisy De Villargennes & Voices of 1812 by Arthur Chuquet .

INVASION OF FRANCE, 1814 *by F. W. O. Maycock*—The Final Battles of the Napoleonic First Empire.

LEIPZIG—A CONFLICT OF TITANS *by Frederic Shoberl*—A Personal Experience of the 'Battle of the Nations' During the Napoleonic Wars, October 14th-19th, 1813.

SLASHERS *by Charles Cadell*—The Campaigns of the 28th Regiment of Foot During the Napoleonic Wars by a Serving Officer.

BATTLE IMPERIAL *by Charles William Vane*—The Campaigns in Germany & France for the Defeat of Napoleon 1813-1814.

SWIFT & BOLD *by Gibbes Rigaud*—The 60th Rifles During the Peninsula War.

www.ingramcontent.com/pod-product-compliance
Lightning Source LLC
Chambersburg PA
CBHW032053080426
42733CB00006B/259